JOHN BROOKES

GARDEN AND LANDSCAPE DESIGNER

JOHN BROOKES
GARDEN AND LANDSCAPE DESIGNER

Barbara Simms

conran
OCTOPUS

In whatever part of the world, and in whatever period of history, the garden has always adapted itself to the needs of the owner, whether providing a shelter from nature, or a retreat from the heat; a place for entertaining, for household use or, latterly, a place for parking the car. Plants are important, of course, but the first consideration should be the fitness of the garden for family use. ˮ[1]

Published in 2007 by
Conran Octopus Limited
a part of Octopus Publishing Group
2–4 Heron Quays, London E14 4JP
www.conran-octopus.co.uk

British Library Cataloguing-in-Publication Data. A catalogue record for this book is available from the British Library.

Publishing Director Lorraine Dickey
Editor Robert Yarham
Art Director Jonathan Christie
Book Design The Bridgewater Book Company
Production Manager Angela Young

ISBN-13: 978-1-84091-448-1
Printed in China

Contents

Preface

I first heard of John Brookes when I was studying architecture. His book, *Room Outside*, was required reading on the course, and it had a profound impact on my career. It was a book which opened eyes and minds to the potential of external spaces and their importance to modern architecture. Although I was brought up to enjoy gardens, reading *Room Outside* was the first time I saw gardening in the context of contemporary design, for Brookes made the connection between architecture, plants and art. Later, as I developed my own work in landscape design I would have the good fortune to meet John on many occasions – at conferences, on committees, at presentations and socially – and I came to appreciate the extent of his influence and his generosity with ideas.

For British designers, John Brookes has been the shining light as modern design emerged in the latter part of the 20th century. He has been the pioneer for a new approach which demonstrated the impact new design could make on people's lives. In the modernist tradition he has always sought out new movements, travelling extensively so that, through his books and his teaching, he has kept us informed about what was happening on the international scene. He has brought a new sense of optimism; through his influence gardens are now light and accessible, places to be used and enjoyed. New materials, lighting, sculpture, textures and architectural planting have been used to create a new style for outdoor living. Now that vibrant outside spaces are central to our lives it is difficult to remember that it was not always so.

It is no accident that he has made such a huge impact. He gravitated towards the best people, to work for, to collaborate with and to learn from. Sylvia Crowe and Thomas Church were huge influences in the landscape arena but similar high-level contacts were made in the circles of art, architecture, horticulture and history. His research was thorough and included specialist studies, for example on Persian gardens, so that he was well equipped to articulate his philosophy for design. Always enquiring, open to new ideas and well informed he has raised the profile of garden design in the minds of other professionals. A great communicator through his books, of course, but also through other writing, teaching and lecturing, and his own remarkable garden at Denmans, he has been a superb catalyst for a new profession. I can so easily call to mind that distinctive voice of his challenging and persuading, always encouraging us to find better ways to make gardens and landscapes.

His has been the clear voice for contemporary design in British gardens and it is wonderful that, through this book, we now have the chance to learn more about John Brookes himself. We have been lucky indeed to have John in our ranks, to challenge and to champion garden design and particularly to remind us of the importance of gardens in our culture and the importance of culture in our gardens.

Christopher Bradley-Hole

Foreword

(right) John Brookes at Clock House, his home and studio since 1980.

Having to read a synopsis of one's life, and then having one's work analyzed as well, is an alarming event. I suppose that having led a self-employed existence one is necessarily more concerned with today and tomorrow rather than yesteryear. And here I was presented with a retrospective to face all the twists and turns of my past career. It was a strange feeling – all so far away now; though happily nothing regretted.

Having said all that, I am all too aware of basing much of my so-called forward thinking on inspiration from the past; people in history have always fascinated me, particularly those in garden history. I suppose that what I am being forced to realize is that each of us is only a stepping stone along the way – my experience is based upon that of my predecessors – and one is increasingly aware that current experience is based upon my own generation. Not only experience affects us but time, of course, and social change. And there has certainly been change through my life span!

It is interesting that the concept of the garden as a retreat has not really changed, however, although it's now a retreat into nature, not a retreat into fantasy or theatre. It is probably sad that fewer and fewer people achieve this concept for themselves with such invasive urbanization, but it remains an aspiration. Increasingly this link with nature I think is important – and the realization that we are part of it too. Global warming and 'eco' concerns have to impinge upon the future garden – after fighting against the use of too many exotics, they may have to become the norm. What becomes increasingly important is that we retain a sense of place; that we recognize the specialness of an area, cultural as well as horticultural, and learn to work with it. This shouldn't inhibit design progress – rather condition it, for I have always found that the tighter the brief the more rewarding the result.

I would like to congratulate and thank Barbara Simms for all her work, and to thank all friends, colleagues and clients who have been so forthcoming in their help to her.

John Brookes MBE, DU (Essex), FSGD

Exhibition Garden

Chelsea
Flower
Show, 1962

JOHN BROOKES

GARDEN AND LANDSCAPE DESIGNER

John Brookes changed the way people think about their gardens, transforming them from a place to display plants to a stylish, outdoor room to be used by the whole family. As a young landscape designer in the early 1960s, he challenged the traditional concept of the private garden – 'We're still wallowing in rusticity (Figure 1) and crazy paving'[2] – as well as the limited vision of architects who gave little consideration to the spaces between and around buildings. Relatively new in his chosen field, nonetheless Brookes's avant-garde views and design potential were noted by rising young architects Theo Crosby[3] and Michael Manser,[4] as well as the established landscape architect Geoffrey Jellicoe, who encouraged his interest in modern art and design.[5] Well versed in the history of garden and landscape design, Brookes's own modernist-inspired designs for courtyard gardens at the Manser House (1961), the Chelsea Flower Show (1962) (Figures 2 and 3) and Penguin Books (1964) brought him to public attention. By the end of the decade, with the publication of his first book *Room Outside*, he was acknowledged as *the* designer for the 'modern' garden.

Since those early years, Brookes has published 26 books, established and taught at schools of design worldwide and produced nearly 1,300 designs for town and country gardens, ranging from 'rooms outside' to landscape gardens of 18th-century magnitude. A vigorous and outspoken campaigner for the recognition and development of garden design as a profession, Brookes supported first the Institute of Landscape Architects (ILA) and then the Society of Garden Designers (SGD), serving as its chair from 1996–99. Still at work today, he has remained at the forefront of design by creating distinctive gardens and landscapes based on the current awareness of ecological principles and the necessity to design in harmony with nature and the local vernacular – without losing sight of his belief that 'a garden is fundamentally a place for use by people'.[6] Brookes's achievements have been recognized by many awards including the Award of Distinction for his 'unique and exceptional contribution to the profession of landscape design' by the American Association of Professional Landscape Designers (2004), an MBE 'for services to horticulture in the UK and overseas' (2004) and an honorary doctorate from the University of Essex 'for services to the horticultural industry and specifically garden design' (2006).

This book explores the development of John Brookes's philosophy and design principles, and assesses his contribution to the history of garden and landscape design through his drawings, writings and teaching over a period of more than 50 years. Analysis of key designs in England, mainland Europe, Japan, Australia, the USA and South America demonstrates Brookes's working methods and records, often in his own words, how his ideas take form to become stunning, contemporary gardens with a sense of purpose and place.

Figure 1 (top) John Brookes as photographed for *House and Garden* March 1966.

Figure 2 (above) The soft curves of concrete Ali Baba jars and hour-glass-shaped containers contrast with the strict geometry of the Exhibition garden's design.

Figure 3 (opposite) Cover of the brochure for the Institute of Landscape Architects Exhibition Garden designed by John Brookes for the Chelsea Flower Show 1962.

EARLY INFLUENCES

John Andrew Brookes was born in Durham City, County Durham, on 11 October 1933. He was the second son of (Edward) Percy, a civil engineer, and Margaret Alexandra (known as Poppy), the daughter of the architect Edward Reid, a descendant of the family of silversmiths who moved from Edinburgh to Newcastle in the late 18th century. Percy and Poppy married in Sunderland in 1924, their first son Michael being born the following year. By the time John was born, Percy Brookes was working as a civil engineer, following in the footsteps of his own father, who had been county surveyor for Durham (Figure 4). In the early years of World War Two, John, then aged eight years, transferred from Bow Preparatory School to Durham School, developing an interest in the arts and the countryside, rather than traditional academic subjects or sports. He won an art prize, played the violin in the school orchestra and enjoyed camping on the moors to the west of Durham (Figure 5). Brookes also enjoyed working in the family garden where his mother was responsible for cultivating flowers and his father for providing vegetables (Figure 6).[7]

Although Percy Brookes had a car for work purposes, petrol rationing (and Percy's disinclination for such trips) meant that family outings to visit a pantomime, ballet or a play were rare. When aged 12 and old enough to travel alone, however, John began visiting his aunt, a painter and musician, at her house near Amersham, in the Chiltern Hills, Buckinghamshire.[8] Walks in the beech woods with views to the rolling agricultural landscape of Shardeloes (once parkland designed by landscape gardener Humphry Repton in 1794), a contrast to rugged Northumbria, gave him an early understanding of regional landscape variations. These visits, and regular trips to the cinema in Durham, gave him tempting glimpses of life outside the north of England. Later, unenthusiastically

working for his school certificate, Brookes sought to broaden his education by frequent use of the public library in Durham City, where he recalls finding a copy of Dorothy Stroud's appraisal of Lancelot 'Capability' Brown's 18th-century landscape gardens.[9] His passionate interest in the arts was disregarded, however, when it came to a choice of career and his father discouraged him from attending art school. Notwithstanding, Brookes's enduring love of the countryside and his fascination with the patterns of the landscape drew him to a career where he could be 'close to the land'. Agriculture or farming was his second choice of career, but his father again advised against an employment he saw as insecure – and buying a farm was expensive.[10] Unaware of the range of career opportunities then opening in post-war landscape design, his early interest in gardening eventually led Brookes to apply for a course in commercial horticulture.[11]

By the time he began his National Service (Royal Artillery) in 1951, Brookes was more conversant with contemporary trends in the fields of architecture and landscape (Figure 7). In particular, he had been excited by discovering Christopher Tunnard's seminal book, *Gardens in the Modern Landscape*, in a junkshop.[12] Stationed at Lark Hill near Stonehenge on Salisbury Plain, Brookes explored the ancient landscape while spending his weekend leave either with his aunt in Amersham seeking out modernist houses, such as High and Over (shown in Tunnard's book),[13] or visiting gardens in Surrey with the plantsman and garden designer Geoffrey Chadbund and his wife.[14] At the age of 20 years, when Brookes finally enrolled for a horticulture course at the Durham County School of Agriculture, Houghall, his interest in garden design was already well developed.

The Houghall course provided Brookes with a basic plant knowledge that he absorbed with interest and ease, achieving top of his year and being offered a scholarship to read for a BSc degree

Figure 4 (opposite left) Percy and Poppy Brookes in the Teesdale countryside (early 1950s).

Figure 5 (opposite centre) John Brookes on holiday in Teesdale (early 1950s).

Figure 6 (this page left) Percy Brookes working in his Durham vegetable garden.

Figure 7 (this page right) Brookes during his National Service (1951–1953).

in Horticulture at Reading University.[15] He recalls that he tried to persuade the University to allow him to transfer to the landscape course run by Frank Clark (then one of the few landscape courses in the country), but when this failed he accepted instead the offer of a three-year apprenticeship with Nottingham Corporation Parks Department, a premier parks department at the time.[16] His apprenticeship (from 1954) provided a sound, practical training in amenity horticulture, but it was the last six months in the parks design department that gave him the additional skills and confidence to consider a change of direction in his career. During that period he worked with a Dutch landscape architect, Harry Blom, who not only taught him how to draw to scale and in ink, but also introduced him to the scope of a landscape architect's work and the techniques of office management. While apprenticed, Brookes also pursued his earlier interest in garden design by following a correspondence course. He was determined that his future lay in landscape design.

From the early decades of the 20th century, a re-evaluation of the theoretical basis of landscape design had engaged the minds of many practitioners, who believed that designers should be inspired by the age in which they lived, rather than constrained by the past. In Britain, the ILA provided a focus for both this and the promotion of landscape architecture as a profession. Two of the Institute's most active members were Brenda Colvin and Sylvia Crowe.[17] Sharing an office in central London, Colvin and Crowe were involved in major post-war planning projects and were both authors of books that became standard texts for the profession.[18] Colvin's publication *Land and Landscape* gave the discipline of landscape planning a philosophy and a methodology, and inspired Brookes to send her samples of his own drawings. In 1957, Colvin invited him to work as a junior assistant in her office, 182 Gloucester Place, London W1.[19]

Figure 8 (above left) A small town garden in London's Hampstead by Brenda Colvin 'in which curves have been used to counteract the rectangles of the site and give a sense of space'.

Figure 9 (above right) Geoffrey Jellicoe's design for the back garden of a terraced house on the Lansbury estate, in London's East End, England, as part of the Festival of Britain (1951). The garden is paved with concrete slabs and includes space for growing vegetables and flowers, hanging out the washing and coal sheds.

Although a significant contributor to the new, broader conception of landscape architecture, Brenda Colvin nonetheless remained committed to the small domestic garden as a significant part of people's lives. Articles and photographs of her garden designs in popular magazines during the inter-war and immediate post-war period documented her increasing conviction that 'A garden can be thought of as an extension of the house... a place to live in and should be designed primarily for that purpose' (Figure 8).[20] The concept of the garden as an outside room was not new in 1950s Britain and had, indeed, been promoted to the general public as part of the 1951 Festival of Britain (Figure 9), but it had yet to loosen the stranglehold of the nostalgically romantic Arts and Crafts-style garden, popular since the late 19th century. Although more traditional in her own work, Colvin would have been familiar with the earlier, well-publicized modernist designs of Christopher Tunnard in England (Figure 10). Furthermore, through her international contacts and publications, she would also have been well informed about modern gardens in mainland Europe, such as those by Otto Valentien in Germany, Franz Singer in Austria and Jean Canneel Claes in Belgium.

Of particular interest to all contemporary designers was the innovative work of the landscape architect Thomas Church, who was revolutionizing the 'backyards' of the wealthy residents of San Francisco Bay, northern California, by creating 'indoor-outdoor living' spaces (Figures 11 and 12). The concept of the outside room was integral to Church's Californian style of modernism, and prompted designs that merged the inside and the outside, with the garden deck, increased use of paving for easier upkeep, planting beds with an architectural feel and swimming pools that took their shapes from the lines of the landscape. Church's ideas had a profound influence on American gardens and his 1955 book, *Gardens are for People*, promoted the concept internationally.[21] Also of note, further south in Brazil, Roberto Burle Marx, the flamboyant artist-gardener, was using native

Figure 10 (above left) A section of the courtyard garden at St Ann's Hill, Chertsey (1935), England, designed by Christopher Tunnard to complement a modernist house by Raymond McGrath. The fountain is a stone sculpture by Willi Soukoup.

Figure 11 (above right) A San Francisco garden designed by Thomas Church as an indoor-outdoor living space.

plants on the roof tops and promenades of Rio de Janeiro, creating broad organic sweeps inspired by abstract art (Figure 13).[22]

Brookes's three years as Colvin's assistant changed his life, taking him into a world vibrating to the lively debate on the future of landscape design; a world in which the roles of landscape architect, garden designer and artist were interwoven. Sylvia Crowe had just been elected president of the ILA when Brookes joined the staff to work alongside her assistants Michael Laurie[23] and Anthony du Gard Pasley.[24] She had also just completed her book *Garden Design*. Setting garden and landscape design in an historic context, Crowe proposed that a promising model for the modern garden was an informal space closely related to the house with a strong feeling of design, ground contouring, planting groups with contrasting pattern and texture and sculpture to give a focal point. She supported Colvin's view on the relationship between house and garden, stating that it 'has progressively increased until in some modern houses the garden forms an outdoor room which is almost one with the glass-fronted living room, itself so lavishly set with plants that it is hard to see where the house ends and the garden begins'.[25] On taking on the ILA presidency in 1957 she also confirmed her commitment to garden design: 'the discipline of designing small gardens, the problems of compact yet free planning, the sensitivity of detail and the close relationship with architecture and the outer landscape is perhaps the finest of all trainings for every other branch of landscape design'.[26]

Even before Brookes joined Colvin's office, he was aware of these contemporary trends in design, in particular the work of Thomas Church, and was keen to adapt the idea of the outside room to the needs of the British homeowner.[27] One of his earliest designs (1956), for a small London roof

Figure 12 Church incorporated existing trees into his iconic design for the swimming pool area of a garden in Sonoma, California, in the USA (1948).

Figure 13 The roof garden of the Resurgeros Insurance Building, Rio de Janeiro, Brazil, by Roberto Burle Marx (1938), shows his characteristic use of native plants to create ground patterns.

Figures 14 and 15 (above left and right) John Brookes's 1956 sketches for a London roof garden indicate an early interest in the concept of designing the garden as an extension of the house: (left) view from the living room to the garden; (right) view looking back to the house.

garden (Chesham Street, SW1) 'designed for sitting on, entertaining and to provide some culinary herbs' (lemon balm, rosemary, fennel, thyme and mint), features a pergola, blue colour-washed walls and container plants with 'variation in size of leaf, height... form... colour'. These included *Rhus*, ferns, *Kniphofia* (red hot poker), *Potentilla*, *Salvia*, *Acanthus*, *Brachyglottis greyii*, *Cytisus multiflorus*, *Cistus* x *hybridus* (rock rose), *Caryopteris* and *Iris*, with *Parthenocissus henryana*, ivy and white honeysuckle as climbers. Brookes's pencil sketches confirm his interest in linking the inside and the outside space to create a 'room outside' (Figures 14 and 15). In the same year at Langland Gardens, London NW3, he experimented with ground contouring along one side of a serpentine-shaped lawn, timber decking and a pergola constructed from white, softwood horizontals on black scaffolding poles, a signature feature of his early designs.

From the early years of her practice (established 1920), Brenda Colvin was a noted plantswoman and, as her assistant, Brookes prepared planting plans for her private garden designs, as well as drawing up her designs.[28] Colvin's tenet that the setting and grouping of plants 'is of far greater consequence than the individual beauty of any single plant or flower'[29] confirmed Brookes's own belief that trees, shrubs and flowers should be planted to create a definite composition. Colvin believed that in the modern garden plants should be chosen for their 'beauty of form and texture', replacing the traditional 'flat two-dimensional pattern' and 'horticultural confusion' of earlier years.[30] In the larger garden, other features she recommended were woodland with native planting, 'mown grass paths running through orchard trees with rough grass on either side', and informal sculpture groups amongst trees. This restrained and elegant planting style is also seen in Brookes's 1959 scheme for Colvin's alterations to the Sussex

Figure 16 (top) *Composition* (1955) by Willem de Kooning.

Figure 17 (above) *Green, Red, Blue* (1955) by Mark Rothko.

garden of Donald Gomme, the furniture maker who coined the name G-Plan in 1953, developing it to become a style icon of the 1960s.[31]

Close association with Colvin and Crowe in the period 1957-60 not only increased Brookes's awareness of topical landscape issues, but also provided the opportunity to meet some of the key personalities involved. Chief among these was Geoffrey Jellicoe, who was then exploring his late appreciation of modernism and modern art, and his growing interest in the concept of the unconscious in his designs.[32] Jellicoe encouraged Brookes's interest in modernism by taking him to the garden at St Ann's Hill, Chertsey (1935), designed by Tunnard, and introducing him to modern art through his own collection at 19 Grove Terrace, his Hampstead house.[33] This inspired visits to art galleries with colleague Michael Laurie, and was the beginning of Brookes's own appreciation of the works of abstract expressionist artists such as Willem de Kooning and Mark Rothko (Figures 16 and 17).[34] Jellicoe's belief that it was a sense of (albeit unconscious) abstract design that linked form (the allocation of space) and content (planting) when planning a garden, underpinned his design philosophy. In particular, he considered strong design to be an essential quality of 'the small and physically confined space of modern gardens', the function of which was to create a refuge, 'a personal environment to provide the security and reassurance of a cabin'.[35] Brookes's evolving design principles were embedded in a familiarity with these ideas, the writings and designs of Colvin, Crowe and Jellicoe and, most importantly, the opportunity to discuss ideas and work with them.[36]

By 1960 Colvin was spending more time at her Gloucestershire home (Filkins, near Lechlade) providing Brookes with the opportunity to work with Sylvia Crowe on a number of new town and landscape projects. These included housing projects at Harlow and Basildon, Trawsfynydd nuclear power station and the courtyard at Imperial College, London, later to inform his design for the Penguin Books Courtyard, Harmondsworth.[37] Brookes also contributed drawings to her books *Landscape for Roads* and *Landscape for Power*.[38] Believing that his future lay in the emerging field of landscape architecture, Brookes attended the evening part-time landscape design programme, while in the Colvin-Crowe office, under landscape architect Peter Youngman at University College, London (UCL), being awarded his certificate in March 1960.[39] In September 1957 Brookes had became a probationer member of the ILA and an active participant in its activities. He served first on the Entertainments Committee (with Anthony du Gard Pasley) and then the Exhibition Sub-Committee responsible for the selection and presentation of the Design Section of the 1959 Chelsea Flower Show.[40] He contributed letters and articles to the Institute's

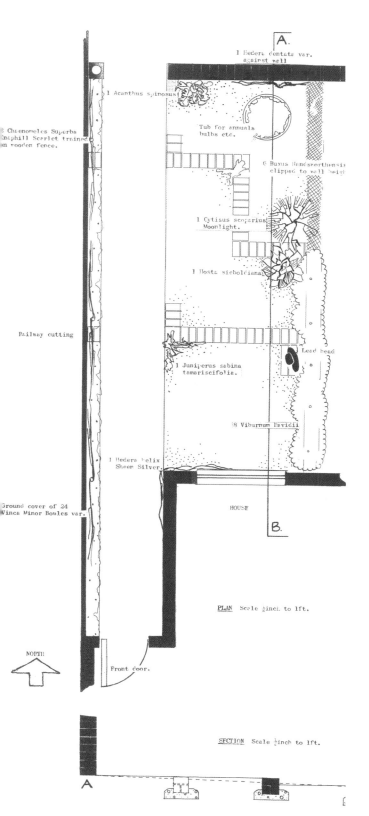

Figure 18 Layout for a small north London garden exhibited by John Brookes in the Design Section of the Chelsea Flower Show, undated but pre-1962.

Journal,[41] took part in debates,[42] sat on the Journal Committee from August 1960 (eventually being responsible for the Journal's format and layout),[43] and exhibited design drawings at the Chelsea Flower Show, along with Anthony du Gard Pasley, Brenda Colvin, Sylvia Crowe and others.[44] Brookes's rationale for his design exhibit of a small north London garden, emphasizing a strong ground pattern, integration of house and garden, and planting in gravel, is indicative of the direction of his future work (Figure 18).[45]

Despite his active involvement in the ILA, Brookes was also outspoken in his criticism of its poor representation of garden designers and lack of practical support for student members. Keen to promote the Institute as an organization for garden as well as landscape design to Chelsea visitors, he suggested in a letter to the Journal that at future Chelsea Flower Shows 'a small garden... constructed on the barest allowance' would be 'a pointer for them [the public] to see in practise the theories we hand out of form, texture and ease of maintenance'.[46] Brookes also proposed a partnership between contractor, designer and the ILA to finance a Chelsea garden (a suggestion implemented in the ILA exhibit for the 1962 show).[47]

In October 1960, following completion of the UCL course, Brookes was elected a student member of the Institute.[48] However, later that year, despite exemption from the intermediate examination (as he held the Certificate in Landscape Design) and his working experience with Sylvia Crowe, he failed the design set piece examination (a necessary qualification for associate membership).[49] At the time he was 'frankly miffed', but, perhaps, more importantly, it forced him to seriously consider his career options.[50] Observing the difficulties experienced by Crowe in her campaign to preserve the visual quality of the British landscape, while also providing the infrastructure needed, and the frustrations of new town work – 'endless tedious plantings, later ripped out' – Brookes had become increasingly disheartened by the bureaucracy of public-sector landscape architecture: 'I was of the era of Thomas Church – where could I work like that? I wanted private work and that meant gardens'.

Encouraged by Geoffrey and Susan Jellicoe, towards the end of 1960 Brookes accepted an editorial post in the London office of *Architectural Design* under editors Monica Pidgeon and Theo Crosby. The office hours of midday to 8pm allowed him the flexibility to develop a garden design practice, while also gaining an insight into new aspects of architecture and design.

NEW THINKING IN GARDEN DESIGN

Brookes's work in the small editorial department of *Architectural Design* and visits to international exhibitions in Switzerland and Germany kept him up-to-date on developments in art, architecture and landscape. The International Union of Architects Conference, held on London's Festival of Britain site on the south bank of the Thames in 1961, also gave him an opportunity to become more actively involved in exhibition work. Entitled *New techniques and materials – their impact on architecture*, the conference promoted a more rigorous integration of art and architecture. Theo Crosby's 'uncompromising constructivist design' for the long, low conference buildings enclosed a courtyard laid out by Brookes, with an Anthony Caro bolted iron sculpture as its centrepiece. The interiors of the buildings featured murals and sculptures by modern artists, such as John Ernest, Mary Martin, Anthony Hill and William Turnbull. It was considered 'an aesthetic breakthrough' (Figure 19).[51]

Stimulated by this success, in the months following the exhibition, Crosby prepared to actively promote the integration of the arts in *Architectural Design*. John Brookes, with his ready appreciation of modern art and realization that most architects gave little serious consideration to the spaces between and around buildings, was the perfect partner for the project. From the October 1961 issue, Crosby began a regular column simply entitled 'Art', which dealt with current art exhibitions, 'the London art scene', but, as explained by Crosby, the column 'will be not so much about paintings or sculptures as such, but about how painters and sculptors might be brought into a more meaningful relation to architecture'. Adjoining Crosby's column, Brookes's contribution, 'Landscape Design', dealt with the importance of designing a building and landscape as an entity in harmony with their surroundings, using as an example Bentley Wood, East Sussex (1935), designed by the Russian architect Serge Chermayeff as his family home, with advice on landscape design by Christopher Tunnard. Henry Moore was commissioned to provide a sculpture (*Recumbent Figure*, 1938) to be sited on a plinth at the far end of the terrace.

This was the beginning of Brookes's career as a writer and, for a young, relatively inexperienced designer (he was 28 years old and not yet established in private practice), his articles demonstrated a wealth of practical knowledge and confidence.[52] Later issues in his column, intended to 'educate' architects, included the use of plants in design – 'plants can be regarded as an artist would his oils, to be used after he has prepared his outline sketch and worked out his proportions';[53] the aesthetics and practicalities of ground shaping;[54] the creative use of textures and surfaces – 'The continuation of a building line from the vertical into the horizontal, done if possible in the same material, stabilises the building and links it into its surround';[55] and the creation of an 'intimate' outside place, 'which can be used with pleasure throughout the year'.[56]

Figure 19 The temporary buildings for the International Union of Architects Conference 1961 were constructed at cost by Taylor-Woodrow Construction Company from components given or lent by the building industry to a design by Theo Crosby. The courtyard was laid out by John Brookes.

Brookes was able to both promote the concept of the outside room and achieve publicity for his growing practice when his 1961 design for the garden of a new house by Michael Manser featured in *Architectural Design* (Figures 20 and 21).[57] Although Brookes had also advised on the garden around Manser's single-storey house, Golden Grove in Leatherhead (Surrey), it was the enclosed courtyard that attracted attention. With glass walls on three sides and sliding doors from the living room, the architectural design of the courtyard was complemented by Brookes's strictly geometric ground patterning of brick infilled in part with grass and planting. The subsequent working relationship with Manser, an architect inspired by the Modern Movement, was an important one for Brookes in the early 1960s, helping him to establish a reputation as a designer of 'modern' gardens. During this period they worked together on a further six houses and gardens, providing the opportunity for Brookes to develop both his planting and design repertoire.[58]

Although still at an experimental stage in his career, Brookes's method of designing the garden in proportion to features of the building provided what Jellicoe had called a unifying 'sense of abstract design', and became the foundation on which Brookes's future work was built.[59] This was illustrated by his assured design for a small town garden as the ILA exhibit for the Chelsea Flower Show 1962.[60] Won by competition, and the first Chelsea show garden by a designer rather than a nursery, it was designed 'to show the way in which new creations in cement, concrete and asbestos can all be put to harmonious use' in the modern garden. The 23 x 10-m exhibition garden contained different levels, textured coloured paving, an innovative Buky Schwartz sculpture, massed foliage planting, an L-shaped pool, concrete pergola and pavilion with translucent roof, unified by an underlying design of interlocking squares.[61]

Using a limited palette of shrubs, groundcover plants and bulbs, Brookes used the exhibition as an opportunity to emphasize the proper place of plants in the modern garden: 'Planting has been considered as an integral part of the design, though not an end in itself; thus plant masses are important while individual plants making up the masses are not'.[62] The garden was awarded the Flora silver medal by the Royal Horticultural Society (RHS). This ambitious (and controversial) entry confirmed Brookes's modernist approach to design – the desire 'to get away from the usual box-like appearance of the gardens of terrace houses', to use new materials and to create a functional, low-maintenance outdoor space where the 'house and garden blend'.[63]

The publicity generated by the Chelsea Show garden led to an increase in the number of Brookes's commissions during 1962 and 1963, over three-quarters being for London gardens. The majority of clients had houses or apartments in fashionable areas such as Chelsea, Kensington and St John's Wood, where land values were high and gardens small – often no more than a courtyard or, in some cases, a roof garden. As in most urban centres, London gardens are often surrounded by tall buildings, creating not only a lack of privacy, but limited light and considerable

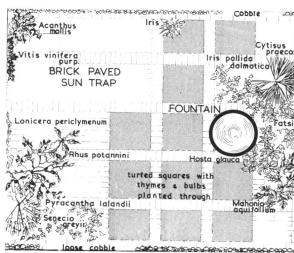

Figure 20 (top) The Manser House, Leatherhead, Surrey, view from the courtyard to the house.

Figure 21 (above) Plan for the Manser House courtyard.

 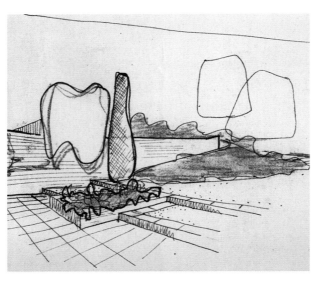 

Figure 22 (above left) Brookes used white gravel chippings, white trelliswork and colour-washed walls to create light in the basement garden at Montpelier Street, London SW7 (1962).

Figure 23 (above centre) Sketch proposals for alterations to Airlie House, London W8 (1962). Planting plans for the bank recommended flowering and evergreen shrubs, such as *Buddleija davidii* 'White Cloud', *Hydrangea paniculata* and *Ceanothus* 'Gloire de Versailles' with lavender, rosemary and *Dianthus*.

Figure 24 (above right) Brookes's own garden in Montagu Mews, London W1 (1964) featured his signature pergola with black scaffolding poles and white softwood horizontals.

shade. Brenda Colvin was of the opinion that 'no miracles can be worked in London gardens',[64] but Brookes employed imaginative techniques to create tranquil oases in these inward-looking spaces. Although demonstrating an ability to adapt to the characteristics of each individual site and the needs of its owners, a number of standard features appeared in his early designs. These included the use of overlapping squares in the underlying abstract design to create a zigzag movement (much favoured by Thomas Church), dark blue-grey paving, white gravel chippings, white trelliswork and light colour-washed walls. These features were used in numerous small, enclosed basement gardens, for example in Montpelier Street SW7 (1962), to create light in dark areas (Figure 22).

Lack of space and light also limited the range of plants that could be grown in town gardens and Brookes's selection often included evergreen architectural plants, such as *Yucca recurvifolia*, *Rhus typhina* and *Fatsia japonica*, with climbing roses and ivy on the walls and bulbs as underplanting, or in pots. Larger gardens allowed more scope for experimentation with the underlying abstract design to create curving lawns bordered by evergreen and flowering shrubs, as in a garden at St John's Wood (1962). At Airlie House, in W8 (1962), Brookes's sketch proposals document a further early attempt at ground shaping (Figure 23) and plans include Brenda Colvin's favourite combination of flowering trees set in rough grass with bulbs. During the early 1960s, Brookes also worked with the landscape architect John St Bodfan Gruffyd (ILA president 1969–71), providing planting plans for a design for the Australian owners of Fiddlers Copse, Sussex. A report on the garden comments that 'Some risks were taken with planting to accentuate the illusion of the warm south round the sitting area... This introduced grey foliage so red foliage accompanies it out of compliment, with blue and red flowers. Shrubs with yellow and white flowers have been grouped separately to provide a complementary colour design theme in the garden'.[65]

Brookes favoured a pergola to create a formal outdoor space adjoining the house and, by 1964,

he had abandoned the traditional wooden or masonry verticals for a versatile, light structure of scaffolding poles (often painted black) with narrow, white softwood horizontals, well suited to the small town garden and used in his own London garden in Montagu Mews, W1 (Figure 24). It became a hallmark feature of his 1960s town gardens, attracting the attention of *House and Garden* magazine, which published an article on the Kensington garden of Madame Jean Gimpel of the celebrated Gimpel Fils Art Gallery.[66] Here, Brookes used the pergola (together with white chippings, blue-grey concrete slabs, ochre-painted walls and white latticework) to create an integrated living room and garden, extending the living space both physically and visually (Figure 25). It was an adaptable feature and Brookes also regularly used a pergola in country gardens to divide the space (Figure 26). The Gimpel commission had come in January 1964, together with another important request to design gardens for the west London offices of Penguin Books. By this time Brookes was finding it increasingly difficult to develop his private practice on a part-time basis and, in early 1964, he left *Architectural Design* to establish a full-time design practice.

During the 1950s and 1960s expenditure on private gardens was far less than in the pre-war years, but Brookes's design practice slowly began to expand. Commissions were often through personal recommendation or because clients with town houses also had houses in the country and, sometimes, abroad.[67] Repeat commissions from members of the Gimpel family and, after he had designed and planted her garden at Pelham Cottage SW7 (1965) (Figure 27), from Annabel Birley (later Annabel Goldsmith), were crucial at this time and facilitated the development of a client base. Now that he could devote more time to design work, Brookes's drawings more frequently included sketches, as well as designs and sections, clearly and attractively presenting ideas to his clients (Figures 28 and 29). A recommendation from Annabel Birley to her brother Lord Londonderry also provided Brookes with his first commission to work on an historic garden and landscape at 19th-century Wynyard

Figure 25 (above left) John Brookes at Drayton Gardens, London SW10, designed for Madame Jean Gimpel (1964).

Figure 26 (above right) White softwood horizontal beams are combined with brick piers to create a pergola walk in a country garden in Berkshire (1964).

Figure 27 (below) Pen and ink drawing for Pelham Cottage, London SW7, dated 10 May 1964.

Park, County Durham (1964). To assist with major earth moving and estate road construction, Brookes drew on his father's civil engineering experience (Figure 30). Many of Brookes's gardens of this period were built by Victor Shanley of Clifton Nurseries. More experienced than Brookes, Shanley was also able to advise him on structural details and, Brookes recalls, 'bailed me out quite a lot'.[68]

Early in 1964 Brookes began designs for the Penguin Books offices, the main garden being the canteen courtyard. On published plan, the courtyard is comprised of geometrical shapes of water, planting, paving, grass and white chippings, the blocks divided by concrete paving slabs (Figure 31). The use of an underlying abstract theme, considered to be reminiscent of a Piet Mondrian painting, attracted public attention and was seen as a symbol of modernity – it matched the clean, simple lines of swinging sixties style.[69] The project also brought Brookes wider professional acclaim – and selection for inclusion in Geoffrey Jellicoe's book of 42 modern gardens.[70] This was recognition indeed for a young designer, as the other gardens selected were by iconic figures such as Sylvia Crowe, Brenda Colvin, Thomas Church, Roberto Burle Marx and Russell Page, designers whose work and writings had influenced Brookes's design philosophy.

While establishing his practice, Brookes also taught landscape design at the Institute of Park Administration at Pangbourne, near Reading, and at Regent Street Polytechnic, London W1. The need to communicate his ideas to students prompted him to examine his philosophy and to provide a rationale and methodology for his design and planting techniques, his conclusions informing the content of *Room Outside* several years later.[71] He also continued to play an active part in the ILA, suggesting the creation of a travelling garden exhibition (sponsored by a commercial firm) to

Figure 28 (top) Pencil, pen and ink drawing for the terrace area of Gildown, Leatherhead, Surrey. Dated 1 January 1965.

Figure 29 (above) Pencil, pen and ink drawing for a roof garden in Eaton Place, London SW1. Dated 12 December 1964.

Figure 30 (right) Alterations at Wynyard Park, County Durham, England (1964), required major earth shaping to set the mansion in its landscape.

promote the Institute's work,[72] and remained on the Journal Committee until 1967, during which time he oversaw the transformation of the publication into a larger and more professional-looking format.[73] However, Brookes's dissatisfaction with the landscape architect's attitude to the garden designer remained strong and he took every opportunity to express his views, as in his review of Susan and Geoffrey Jellicoe's book on modern gardens:

" *Garden design contains the essence of most other forms of landscape design, albeit reduced in scale, but magnified in the precise detailing and use analysis necessary. If it fails to work for its owner, no matter how beautiful, the design is no good... Designers tend to alienate themselves because it is beneath them 'to do' a garden, which in many cases has more varied and harder wear than the comparative area of a town centre. "* [74]

He used a subsequent review of a book on Isamu Noguchi's sculpture to criticize the training of landscape architects for its concentration on 'technical knowledge and administrative ability' at the expense of 'an awareness of forms, of shapes and spaces, and of his [the landscape architect's] basic material – earth'.[75] His thesis was that design training should ensure that the landscape architect, like Noguchi, was a sculptor 'moulding an environment for use by everyday people'.

Brookes also worked with several home and garden magazines on which, by the mid-1960s, a number of contacts from his *Architectural Design* days had prominent positions. David Papworth, then art editor at *Ideal Home*, proposed a monthly feature on garden design, and Beverley Hilton, when she became editor of *House Beautiful* in 1967, appointed Brookes as landscape consultant.[76] His main role was to contribute to a new information service 'Help!', which offered room planning (£1), legal advice (10s.), architecture planning (10s.), home finding (free) and garden design (£1 or 10s.): 'Whether you've just acquired a desert or a jungle, landscape designer John Brookes will provide an easy-to-follow scheme. For written advice only, enclose 10s. For a fully drawn up plan enclose £1'. The first issue to offer this service in November 1967 also contained the first in a series of articles following Brookes's design and construction of the 'real-life' garden of a new house in Crawley owned by *House Beautiful* assistant editor, Michael Hill.[77]

Providing 'designs by post', answering readers' letters and writing articles provided a regular income in Brookes's early years in private practice. When he left *House Beautiful* in 1968 he continued to design for *Good Housekeeping* under editor Laurie Purden, completing more than 500 plans for town and country gardens nationwide.[78] Examination of these early drawings illustrates their value in providing Brookes with the opportunity to experiment with combinations of shapes (primarily squares and circles), garden features (rough grass with bulbs, fruit trees, vegetable plots, pergolas, views out and planted gravel areas) and presentation styles. Most of these '65-shilling designs' lack the elegance of his later drawings, particularly those for large country gardens, but a few echo the sophistication of previous commissions. Of particular interest is Miss Lemon's town garden (location unknown), which features Brookes's signature scaffolding pergola and an early example of a planted gravel bed (Figure 32).

Commercial and private client work during the late 1960s confirmed Brookes's stylistic versatility, and his willingness and ability to design a functional space according to his client's needs and existing features. This was emphasized in a 1966 *House and Garden* article, in which he featured as one of five 'eminent' garden designers along with Lanning Roper, Russell Page, Mary Lees and Ian Mylles, who became a close colleague before returning to Australia. Asked what he aimed at when designing a garden, Brookes's down-to-earth reply was: 'I do not try to superimpose my own ideas upon a client, but try to deduce what they really want, what they can afford, what they must have for practical reasons, and translate these ideas into a working design to suit the site and its position in town or country'. [79]

Figure 32 (below) Miss Lemon's town garden, a 65-shilling design by post through *Good Housekeeping*. Date unknown (late 1960s).

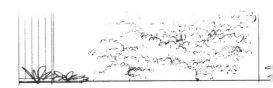

Section A-A

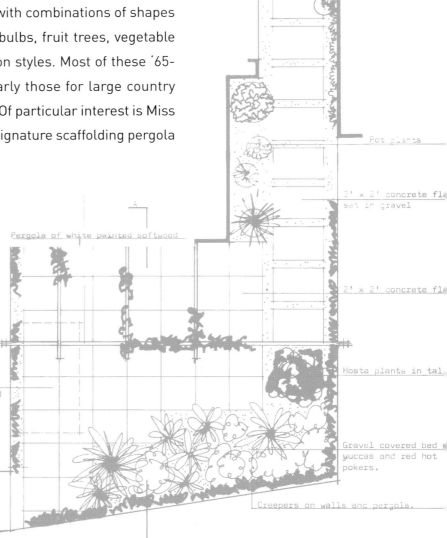

Pergola of white painted softwood

Ex. bed, concreted and paved over

Pot plants

2' x 2' concrete fla set in gravel

2' x 2' concrete fla

Hosta plants in tal

Gravel covered bed yuccas and red hot pokers.

Creepers on walls and pergola.

Brookes's designs during this period included a series of gardens for south-east London show houses by Wren Properties (1965) (Figure 33),[80] a communal garden in Bryanston Square, W1 (1966), the extensive gardens around two Leonard Manasseh houses on the London fringes at Petersham, Surrey (1966) (Figure 34), Heals and Harrods in-store displays (1968), and gardens for Imperial Chemical Industries (ICI) at Syon Park, Isleworth, Middlesex (1968). Nonetheless, his work continued to include elegant 'rooms outside', as at the home of the Gaspar family in Ladbroke Grove, London W11 (1968) (Figure 35). Several of his designs also featured in the ILA Journal as examples to show 'that the art of garden design on an intimate scale is still an important activity within the landscape profession'.[81] Brookes's diverse and increasing workload at this time justified taking on part-time assistance, one of the first being the writer Nan Fairbrother, who had just completed *The House in the Country* (1965) and was seeking working experience.[82]

In the summer of 1969 John Brookes published his first book, *Room Outside – A New Approach to Garden Design* (Figure 36). The publication not only offered practical advice on design, hard landscape features and planting, but also promoted the concept of the garden as an extension of the house – a room outside. Brookes's thesis was that, historically, gardens had met the needs of their users in this way 'whether consciously designed to do so or not', but that by the mid-20th century they had become 'a time-consuming chore, offering no pleasure, privacy or shelter, and a constant burden which restricts other activities'.[83] By the launch of the book, he had designed over 250 gardens, increasingly outside central London and, occasionally, abroad. By the beginning of the 1970s, stimulated by television gardening programmes, DIY books, show gardens, easy access to garden centres (new in the 1960s), increased leisure time and disposable income, and affordable package holidays, an increasing number of people had acquired a taste for Mediterranean-style open-air living. John Brookes's timely publication provided amateur gardeners, as well as professional designers, with the inspiration and practical knowledge to create their own 'room outside'.[84]

Figure 33 (bottom left) Garden for a Wren Properties show house, London (1965).

Figure 34 (bottom centre) Two houses in Petersham, Surrey, by the architect Leonard Manasseh, shared an extensive country-style garden designed by John Brookes (1966).

Figure 35 (bottom right) The London garden of the Gaspar family – an outdoor room with Brookes's signature pergola (1968).

Figure 36 (below) The cover of *Room Outside* (1969), depicting the elegant, yet functional, garden space promoted by the book.

FROM GARDEN TO LANDSCAPE

In autumn 1969 Brookes left London, having bought a thatched cottage in the picturesque village of Great Haseley, Oxfordshire. His brother Michael and his family lived nearby in Great Milton. Brookes modernized the cottage and made plans for redesigning the garden, the 35 x 25-m plot providing scope for experimentation with his favourite features, which he also continued to recommend to readers of home and garden magazines who wished to revitalize 'an unpromising back yard', an 'uninspired front garden of an Edwardian house', 'a rambling old garden without sacrificing its best features' or 'a cat-infested back yard'.[85] His own garden included a gravel area, zigzag-edged terrace with water feature, pergola-covered sitting area and a small orchard in rough grass, enclosed on the eastern boundary by a beech hedge (Figures 37 and 38). On a higher level, accessed by steps from the terrace, a mature walnut dominated the lawn, which was separated from a vegetable plot by a deep shrub border (Figure 39). The massed planting of a few varieties of shrubs and herbaceous plants, with plenty of evergreens to provide year-round structure, was emphasized in both Brookes's own garden and his articles. The most commonly recommended plants were laurel, *Fatsia japonica*, *Cotoneaster atropurpureus* 'Variegatus', *Hydrangea*, pampas grass, *Yucca flaccida*, *Bergenia purpurascens*, Japanese anemones, *Iris foetidissima*, lavender, evergreen honeysuckle and *Catalpa bignonoides* 'Aurea'.

The success of *Room Outside* brought Brookes new publishing opportunities. He was first commissioned to write three more books – inexpensive paperbacks with black-and-white illustrations.[86] These largely reiterated the rationale for

Figure 37 (bottom left) In 1969 Brookes relocated to Great Haseley, Oxfordshire, where he started to redesign the garden. The new pergola-covered sitting area on the north garden boundary.

Figure 38 (bottom centre) The completed ornamental pool on the terrace near the house.

Figure 39 (below) The garden plan for Great Haseley, undated.

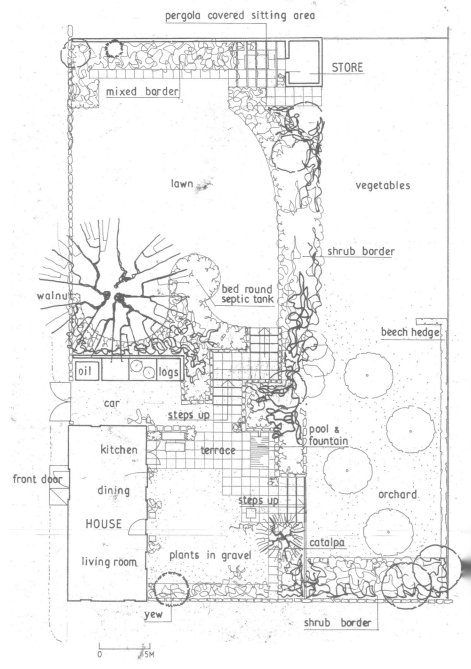

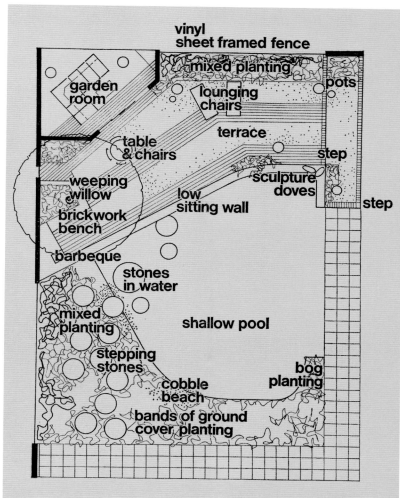

planning and planting a small garden of the earlier publication – to create 'a unified, restful layout which all the family can enjoy' instead of 'the usual rag-bag garden layout'[87] – but allowed a wider dissemination of his ideas to the burgeoning garden centre market. From a different mould was his 26-page contribution on designing and furnishing a garden in Terence Conran's *The House Book* (1974). Initially an in-house training manual for Habitat staff, the popular, large-format book with full-colour photographs brought modern interior design and the concept of the room outside to a wider, younger audience.

Brookes's growing reputation also brought him to the attention of the *Financial Times*, whose chairman the Earl of Drogheda had decided that a garden at the Chelsea Flower Show 'would be a helpful promotional exercise for demonstrating... that the *Financial Times* was not simply interested in money and business'.[88] Brookes's design for a Town Garden in 1971 was the first of three for the *Financial Times*, all of which were awarded RHS gold medals (Figure 40). The 1972 Suburban Garden exhibit, 'a modern terrace-garden, imagined as part of a wider setting planted for form as much as flowers and dominated by a mirror of water', demonstrated a loosening of the geometric rigidity seen in many of his town garden designs. Furthermore, although influenced by Japanese gardens in its simplicity, the design

Figure 40 (top left) The *Financial Times* Town Garden, designed by Brookes for the Chelsea Flower Show 1971.

Figure 41 (above) The garden plan for the 1972 *Financial Times* Suburban Garden from the Chelsea Flower Show leaflet.

Figure 42 (right) The 1972 *Financial Times* Suburban Garden. The view from the cobble beach across the informally planted pool to the garden room.

reflected his continuing concern for the environment and wildlife. A shallow pool with bog planting and a cobble beach was planted with bold architectural plants, including *Gunnera, Rodgersia, Petiphyllum, Acanthus* and *Yucca*, combined with 'a wide range of May flowering plants, many of them specially suited to the waterside' (Figures 41 and 42).[89] Following the 1973 Country Garden, Brookes collaborated with horticultural correspondents Robin Lane-Fox and Arthur Hellyer on *The Financial Times Book of Garden Design* (1975). Taking the three gardens as 'touch-stones', Brookes's contribution discussed how the thinking behind them could be applied to any site whatever the location, and provides an insight into his inspiration for, and implementation of, the three show gardens.

As well as confirming his reputation as a garden writer and a Chelsea Flower Show medallist, the five-year period after the publication of *Room Outside* was also Brookes's most prolific in terms of commissions, which numbered nearly 200 by the end of 1974. It was also the period when his work in the wider landscape began to expand, with 20 per cent of commissions being for commercial, civic or educational institutions. By the early 1970s, through his contacts at Syon Park, where he designed the landscape around the garden centre, lake and restaurant, as well as many demonstration gardens, Brookes was working on a number of sites for ICI and for Charles Notcutt. Charles had become managing director of Notcutt's Nursery in 1964 and, by the 1970s, the firm was in the forefront of the new garden centre business. Brookes landscaped the grounds around a number of its centres, including St Albans (Hertfordshire), Sydenham (Kent) and Birmingham (Figure 43). Through a contact from the Nottingham Parks Department, a commission also came for the landscaping around a sport's centre at Sutton in Ashfield (1971).

Other public and private sector work during the early 1970s included: landscaping at St Peter's College, Oxford (1971), later opened by Harold Macmillan, where Brookes created an elegant triangular-shaped area with ground patterning reminiscent of the abstract design for the Penguin Books courtyard (Figure 44); the communal gardens and play area of Stantonbury, a housing development in the iconic new town of Milton Keynes (1974); and the first of six projects for Portakabin Ltd (1974–6), three of which were in mainland Europe (Germany, Netherlands, France). In the late 1970s, the number of non-domestic commissions was less, but Brookes remained

Figure 43 (top) Demonstration area designed by Brookes for the Notcutt Garden Centre, Birmingham.

Figure 44 (above) Ground patterning divides up the space in the Besse area, St Peter's College, Oxford (1971).

Figure 45 (right) Proposed garden alterations at Horsenden Manor, Princes Risborough, Buckinghamshire, 1974.

Figure 46 (below right) A view across the canal at Horsenden Manor towards a modern sculpture, framed by the parkland in the distance.

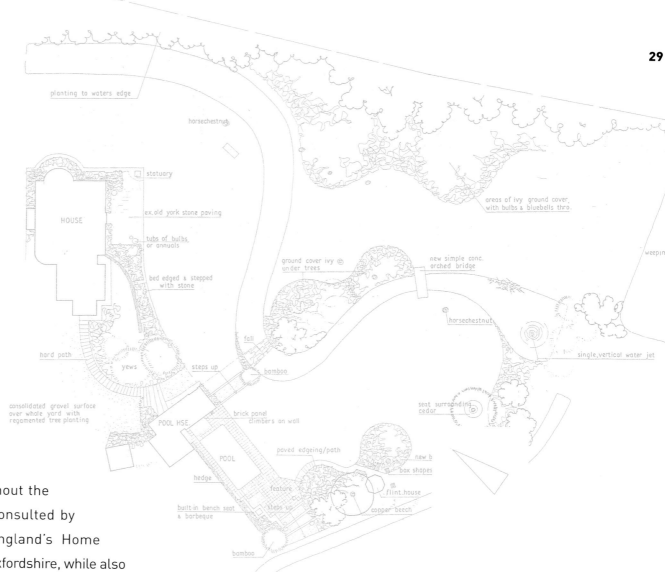

the designer of choice to landscape the settings for garden centres. He also worked with Geoffrey Jellicoe on the redesign of London's Fitzroy Square (1976), one of the city's best-preserved Georgian squares.

In the domestic sector, throughout the 1970s, Brookes was increasingly consulted by those with country gardens in England's Home Counties, particularly in Surrey and Oxfordshire, while also maintaining a high volume of London and town garden commissions, including a number of roof gardens. Two major country estate projects, however, were in Buckinghamshire – at Fairview House, Beaconsfield (1972), and at Horsenden Manor, near Princes Risborough (1974). These extensive gardens, both with large bodies of water, provided the opportunity for Brookes to design grounds truly in harmony with their surroundings. At Fairview House, an organic-shaped pool was the central feature on the main garden front. Its natural curves and bog planting were juxtaposed with the angularity of brick terraces and a wooden deck extending over the water. The removal of a hedge and the creation of a ha-ha not only opened the views to the countryside but also allowed the owner to keep Highland cattle in his parkland. Horsenden Manor is a medieval site, whose mansion, park and garden have been remodelled by many owners through time. Its unique feature is a lake and serpentine canal snaking through the garden. Brookes's task was to create a setting for the house, uniting the house, garden and surrounding landscape (Figures 45 and 46). His alterations retained views across the canal towards

the lake, inserting a single, vertical water jet at the head of the canal to be visible from the house. New planting areas were proposed near the house and swimming pool, and the existing boundary planting on the far side of the water was extended with ivy ground cover and bulbs to mimic the curves of the canal. The landscape was linked to the house by broad steps up to the pool area and a new concrete bridge arched across the canal.

Beginning in 1968, Brookes also took the opportunity to design a number of gardens in the Channel Islands, where the largely frost-free climate allowed the use of a wider range of plants than in England. Through Arthur Hellyer, he had developed a friendship with the writer, plantswoman and camellia enthusiast Violet Lort-Phillips and her husband, who in 1958 had bought a home in Gorey, Jersey, on the east side of the island. Brookes was a regular visitor to their house, La Colline, with its steeply sloping garden and advised on the creation of their themed gardens and, later, Mrs Lort-Phillips's cottage in the grounds with its new gravel garden (Figure 47).[90] An enterprising and sociable lady, she arranged for Brookes to run a short garden design course in Jersey and introduced him to her gardening friends. This resulted in eleven commissions by 1978 (Figure 48) and a further five from 1980 to 1990, including historic Samarès Manor. Brookes was enchanted by the range of plants that could be grown in the warm microclimates of Jersey – *Agapanthus*, *Mimosa*, azaleas, *Wisteria*, numerous varieties of *Camellia*, and the Jersey lily (*Amaryllis belladonna*) – enjoying the challenge of a new growing environment and often working with local nurseryman David Ransom.[91]

In addition to writing and designing, Brookes continued teaching throughout the 1970s, firstly at the Royal Botanic Gardens, Kew, where he taught horticulture students every Friday afternoon, and then at the Inchbald School, 7 Eaton Gate, London SW1. Jacqueline Thwaites (now Duncan)

Figure 47 (above left) Exotic planting in the gravel garden at La Colline, Gorey, Jersey (1977).

Figure 48 (above right) A combination of ground moulding and elegant steps was used to create a sheltered terrace area at Bandinel Farm, St Martins, Jersey (1974).

had established the School in 1960, the first interior design school in Europe, expanding its remit in 1972 to also provide the first modern garden design school.[92] Brookes was brought in as studio tutor for the ten-week courses in early 1974, under Pat Matthews, the Director of Garden Design Studies. Excited to be involved, Brookes travelled from Devon to London several days a week, having moved from Oxfordshire to Valley Farm, Trusham (near Newton Abbot in Devon), the previous year.[93] When Matthews left the following year, Brookes was appointed Director, his enthusiastic approach and inspirational teaching style quickly developing a flourishing and highly regarded course. In a period still dominated by the elegant but, nonetheless, essentially conservative and flower-centred gardens of Percy Cane, Russell Page and Lanning Roper, promotional literature for the School (written by Brookes) reflected his radical views on the nature of garden design.[94] He emphasized to his students that the designer's remit was to create a garden to 'reflect its owner's way of life and tastes' rather than being 'an expression of a particular designer's work', but also that it should be at one with its surroundings. Describing landscape as 'a type of sculpture – a manipulation of space, heights, levels and contours – in earth, hard materials and planting', he developed his earlier concept of the garden as an abstract art form.

Brookes's views on design were, however, in tune with other, earlier, modernist designers who also recognized the fundamental link between art and landscape. James Rose (1913–91), active in North American garden design from the late 1930s and, like Brookes, an admirer of Thomas Church, saw landscape design as outside sculpture – 'sculpture which is large enough and perforated to admit circulation' – believing that design emerges from the site with plants that are sympathetic to the site.[95] Roberto Burle Marx viewed a garden as four-dimensional (with time and space as the fourth dimension) and water as 'liquid sculpture', his native planting following the line of the natural topography.[96] The late 1970s also saw the emergence of the work of the Northern American landscape architect Kathryn Gustafson (born in 1951). Turning to landscape from fashion, her earlier career informed her design philosophy of reshaping or 'sculpting' the land.[97] Much admired by Brookes, she shares with him an understanding of the patterns of natural landscapes, an understanding also integral to the work of Sylvia Crowe: 'The shapes and colours of land and vegetation form patterns which can be appreciated just as one appreciates a work of art' (Figures 49 and 50).[98]

Figure 49 (below) Earth mounding, paving circles and erect trees create a living sculpture that reflects the shapes of the local topography.

Figure 50 (bottom) Brookes admired the 1970s and later work of the artist Christo. This is Christo's *Umbrellas* (1991), using yellow to reflect the hills of south California.

The combination of training young designers, writing and continuing a busy practice was a stimulating mix. In addition, based on his earlier success at the Chelsea Flower Show, Brookes persuaded Jacqueline Thwaites that the Inchbald School should enter a garden for the 1975 Show. Persuasion was also needed before the RHS allowed the exhibit to be a kitchen garden, but Brookes's potager (constructed with Gardenesque Ltd) was a success, winning the Banksian silver medal. The simple layout was included in his 1977 book *Improve Your Lot* with the comment that 'there is no reason why the vegetable garden should not become a decorative element within the overall garden pattern'.[99] The 1976 gold medal-winning exhibit for the Inchbald School was in the style of the plantswoman Gertrude Jekyll, who had designed a garden for a house by the Arts and Crafts architect Edwin Lutyens in Cheyne Walk, London SW1 (Figure 51).[100] This choice was influenced by a resurgence of public interest in the flower garden and the publication of a life of Jekyll by Betty Massingham, then occasional lecturer at the Inchbald School.[101] The third garden in 1977 was a Moorish-inspired 'exotic' garden with a series of descending, linked pools and a terrace with fountain and shade canopy, a legacy of Brookes's visits to the gardens of southern Spain (Figure 52). Constructed with Seymours of Ewell, the garden was awarded the Flora silver-gilt medal.

Improve Your Lot contained more detailed information than previous books on evolving a garden plan, construction and planting, together with case studies, lists of books, specialist suppliers, garden and building centres, invaluable sources first compiled for Brookes's garden design

Figure 51 (below left) 'A town garden after a design by Lutyens for 100 Cheyne Walk, planting in style of G. Jekyll.' Inchbald School of Garden Design Chelsea Flower Show exhibit 1976, dated 15 December 1975. The view along the Jekyll garden towards the Lutyens seat.

Figure 52 (below) 'An Exotic Garden.' Inchbald School of Garden Design Chelsea Flower Show exhibit 1977, dated 10 January 1977. The view across the garden showing the pool and fountain on the lower terrace.

students. It was eclipsed, however, by *The Small Garden* published in full colour the same year. The book was a landmark in Brookes's development as an author as it gave full scope to expression of his deeply held beliefs that garden design should be considered in both an historic and environmental context. It included an introductory section on the evolution of the garden throughout history; a discussion of garden style, with the emphasis on the vernacular; and soil and climate patterns, followed by simple instructions for developing a plan, construction and planting. New features were case studies with full plant lists and coloured planting plans, and a comprehensive chapter on planting design. It was a successful format that many of Brookes's subsequent books followed.

Notwithstanding his horticultural background, Brookes has never considered himself a plantsman, recalling that when working with Brenda Colvin 'I couldn't honestly say I knew a lot of the plants even though I put them in planting plans'.[102] He increased his knowledge through designs for his clients and through visiting Regent's Park, accompanied by a Graham Stuart Thomas book on roses.[103] On an early visit to the Chelsea Flower Show, plantswoman Beth Chatto's displays had also been a revelation: 'I was aware what planting design was all about just looking at her stands... she was working with plants sculpturally and used a bigger palette'.[104] Despite a now extensive plant vocabulary, Brookes has always regarded plants as a design tool – 'It is plants, more than anything else, which will transform a two-dimensional garden plan into three-dimensional reality' [105] – and *The Small Garden* contains the development of his early attempts to devise a scheme to simplify plant selection for garden designers (or garden owners) based on aesthetics and function rather than horticultural attributes:

> " *The first stage of planting should... establish the bones of the planted areas... The trees and large shrubs, especially those which are tall, particularly decorative or of a sculptural outline... Planting at the second level has the most functional role to fulfil; it must fill in the spaces, creating bulk in the planted areas... It will form a backdrop for the smaller, decorative plants.* " [106]

Brookes would have been familiar with the categorization of plants in this way from his days with Brenda Colvin, who had classified trees according to their form for post-war landscape architects.[107] Contemporary with Brookes, the landscape architect and garden designer Preben Jakobsen expressed similar ideas for the design of shrubs and ground cover: 'When composing a design one is essentially juxtapositioning one or several volumes against each other, creating positive and negative volumes, or solid and void spatial compartments'.[108] Jakobsen also produced a planting terminology based on the way shrubs and trees are placed in relation to each other, featuring groupings such as the sculpturally dominant, bold spiky accents, anchor domes and fillers, having some resonance with Brookes's evolving terms, expressed more simply as specials, skeletons, decoratives, pretties and infill.[109] Chapters on the use of native plants and planting in tropical lowlands or hot arid climates in the same book reflect contemporary ecological concerns, which Brookes also espoused.

By 1977 Brookes had been in private practice for nearly 14 years and had designed over 550 gardens and landscapes (excluding designs by post). He felt the need for a change from a teaching routine at the Inchbald that after four years, despite his love of encouraging future garden designers, was becoming monotonous. He therefore welcomed the opportunity of relocating to Iran to set up an Inchbald School of Interior Design for the Iran Chamber of Commerce in Tehran – despite no formal knowledge of interior design. However, after visiting Iran on a Swan Hellenic Cruise, and armed with a programme of work and slides from Jacqueline Thwaites, tremendous enthusiasm and a deep-seated confidence in his ability, in October 1978 Brookes left England for a one-year appointment in Tehran.[110] His arrival there coincided with the revolution against the Shah but, despite gunfire and the occasional bombings nearby, the enthusiasm and thirst for knowledge of the 40 (largely Muslim) students encouraged him to stay.[111]

Having previously visited Moorish Spain with the late Antony Hutt, an Islamist of some repute, Brookes relished the idea of furthering his knowledge of Islamic gardens.[112] Hutt had given him some insight into the meaning of Islam but studying the art, architecture and gardens of Iran provided a rich source of design inspiration, and he determined to write about the gardens and their history.[113] He realized that 'To the Muslim the beauty of the garden... was held to be a reflection of God', its essence being in the spirit of harmony combined with nature.[114] He saw that flowers and foliage appeared not only in gardens but on domes and minarets, carpets and embroideries, book covers and paintings, and that courtyards, terraces and paths often had richly textured and patterned surfaces of brick, stone or marble. Brookes also examined miniatures featuring gardens, where trees, flowers and streams are portrayed with pavilions, terraces and balustrades. What impressed him most was the presence of water in all formal Islamic gardens whether static in pools, shooting into the air in fountains, tumbling down chutes or flowing through canals (Figure 53). These experiences in the Islamic 'paradise' garden were reinforced by his later travels to Mughal India and Kashmir, where he discovered that water was used in even more ingenious ways (Figure 54).

Figure 53 (below) The calmness of a central pool in a shrine in Mahan, Iran (2001) . The water features of Islam inspired Brookes's later designs.

Figure 54 (right) The extravagance of the use of water at Nishat Bagh in the foothills of the Himalayas, Kashmir, is shown by the waterfalls and fountains (1979).

THE CULTURAL CONTEXT OF LANDSCAPE

Returning to London with new ideas in late 1979 without clients or a teaching post, Brookes had to re-establish himself in the world of garden design. He had retained his Shepherds Bush flat and Michael Manser offered him space in his office at Cromwell Place, London SW7, but, nonetheless, he decided to set up a design school away from London. His first thought was to move to the West Country, but a visit to a friend in West Sussex led to an irresistible proposition. While

teaching at the Inchbald School in the mid-1970s Brookes had taken students to visit the gardens of the historic West Dean Estate, near Chichester, where, in 1971, an early 19th-century flint mansion had been converted to a college. On one such trip he also visited nearby Denmans Garden, then the home of Joyce Robinson, a formidable lady, who, from 1946, with her husband, had rescued the 1.5-ha Victorian garden from its neglected state. Mrs Robinson and Brookes became firm friends, his belief that gardens should be in tune with their surroundings finding resonance with her love of native plants and dense, random plantings in gravel inspired by holidays on Greek islands – 'a glorious disarray'.[115]

Visiting Denmans on his return from Iran, Brookes found Mrs Robinson incapacitated by arthritis and having difficulty managing her garden, even with the help of her gardener, Bertie.[116] After some discussion, it was agreed that Brookes would take over the running of the garden over a four-year period (1980–84), converting neglected stable buildings with a distinctive clock tower into his home and base for a design school. He would also have the first option to buy the whole site if Mrs Robinson decided to sell. So began a year of intense activity – Brookes sold his London flat to finance the venture (supplementing money inherited from his recently deceased father), Michael Manser's newly qualified architect son Jonathan drew up plans for the building works, and Brookes lived in a caravan on-site to supervise the work. By September 1980, Clock House, as the building was named, was ready to receive its first six students (Figures 55 and 56).

The main design courses were four weeks long and 'intended to give students a professional grounding in the theory of design, the presentation of ideas to a prospective client, and their subsequent detailing'.[117] Tuition was ambitious and concerned with both design skills and horticulture. It included drafting and landscape theory, outline surveying and construction, planting design, client relations and the management of a landscape office, landscape history, soils and composts, plant recognition, taking cuttings and pruning. Shorter courses were also provided on landscape appreciation, historic gardens, the integration of the inside and out, and 'student refresher courses with daily design exercises'. In 1980 there was no formal support for garden designers and Brookes's commitment to teaching both technical

Figure 55 (top) Students working in the studio at Clock House, Denmans Garden, West Sussex.

Figure 56 (above) John Brookes discusses a design with a student.

design skills, an appreciation of natural land patterning and plant culture, and professional development was essential for his students. Many students recall him as a passionate and inspiring teacher and have taken his design principles worldwide, establishing their own practices and design schools, often with Brookes as guest lecturer, as well as a reference point for their own further development. While Brookes was in Iran, however, his design contemporaries, Rosemary Alexander, Robin Williams and others, had been marshalling support for a new society to represent garden designers rather than landscape architects. This was formed on 15 October 1981 as the Society of Landscape and Garden Architects, with Peter Rogers as chair.[118] Although continuing as a member of the Landscape Institute,[119] Brookes supported the new Society from its inception, although his practical involvement was limited, as he was still establishing his new design school and practice at Denmans.

As Brookes's commissions increased, his client base changed from being primarily urban to those with rural gardens or country estates. Thirty per cent of his designs between 1980 and 1984 (34 of 111) were for London gardens, whereas in the second part of the decade this had reduced to 7.5 per cent (12 of 160). The increase in country house commissions was also influenced by the publication of *A Place in the Country* in 1984 (its release earlier that year in the USA also laying the foundation for future work there). This remarkable book is described as giving ideas for 'the garden ideal of our time: in touch with local ways, local habitats and the creative preservation of the countryside' (Figure 57).[120] Brookes had long been committed to an environmental agenda and had read with interest Rachel Carson's early warning against 'the reckless attempt to control our environment by the use of chemicals'.[121] *A Place in the Country* represented a public statement of his own concerns about the standardization of gardens by the use of identical materials supplied by garden centres, the promotion of a 'Home Counties aesthetic' by the RHS, and 'advertisements' portrayal of normal life as a suburban utopia'.[122] 'The 1930s garden ideal', he stated, '...must give way to the vernacular garden, tailored to the maintenance capabilities of today', and he suggested that to do this 'we must look more closely at nature at work':

" *Look then at the shapes created by field patterns. See how the local hills or downs roll or fold, note the placing of the trees in the valley bottom, and the way they thin out as they grow up the hill, observe the flow of water – the run of a fast stream compared to the gentle meander of a brook on chalky levels. Experience the enclosed feeling of being between hedges or totally enveloped in a wood, and then emerging into open fields. Moving from enclosure into shade and then into light, you will be conscious of form. It is to the form of a landscape, or of a garden, that one instinctively reacts, feeling that the place is an interesting one, or on the contrary that it is... just unsatisfactory.* " [123]

Figure 57 (below) The front cover of a brochure for Denmans Garden reflects Brookes's commitment to a natural planting style.

DENMANS GARDEN

Fontwell, Near Arundel, West Sussex (off A27)

Following detailed sections on regional diversity and the historic nature versus artifice debate in the design of gardens, Brookes returned to practicalities – 'the gardener, the gardener's family and how they see their place in the country'. Information on the design and planting of a country garden was included, together with specific advice on the wild garden, woodlands and shelter belts, encouraging game, grazing and predators. Tables on native tree species, shelter belt planting, hedges, wildflower planting, vegetables and herbs made this book a comprehensive resource for those keen to embrace an ecologically sound country life.

Now based in Sussex, Brookes's commissions in the county increased to 34 per cent of new work for the decade. One of the earliest was at Church Farm, Aldingbourne, West Sussex (1980), a 1.6-ha site where Brookes extended a Yorkstone terrace around the house by a zigzag gravel garden on the side adjacent to a swimming pool (Figures 58, 59, 60 and 61). A complementary

Figure 58 (above) John Brookes and gardener John Levett planting trees around the pond at Church Farm, Aldingbourne, in West Sussex (spring 1982).

Figure 59 (below) Slab stepping stones encourage movement from the terrace to the perennial border, Church Farm.

Figure 60 (bottom) View across the waterside planting of the pond at Church Farm.

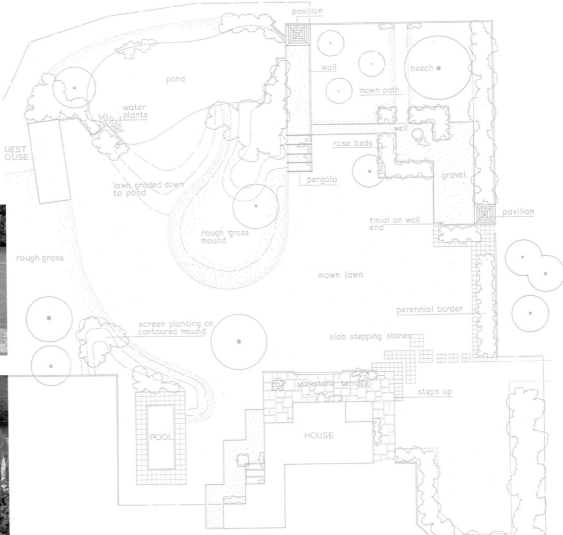

angular composition of slab stepping stones on the other side of the house formed a link to a walkway leading to a sheltered garden with rose beds, gravel areas and a pavilion. Adjacent to this, a pergola walk leads to a matching pavilion overlooking an organic-shaped pond with views to the fields beyond. Contoured mounds with low plantings of *Achillea* 'Moonshine', *Hebe* 'Autumn Glory', *Artemesia* 'Powis Castle' and *Bergenia purpurascens*, complemented by perfumed rose varieties and *Mahonia japonica*, add variety to the views across the garden, as well as providing shelter for the swimming pool area. The use of rough grass with spring bulbs and native tree species reflects the local setting. A second important commission was for the Holland family, who had bought a 16th-century property at Littlehampton, West Sussex (1981). The influence of Brookes's Iran experience is seen in the incorporation of an enclosed courtyard with a cruciform-shaped pool (Figure 62) into the garden of rooms, including gravel and vegetable gardens, a lawn on different levels and deep mixed borders, the whole integrated by intricately detailed hard landscaping.

Further afield, a third commission came from Vincent Obbard, the owner of Samarès Manor, Jersey (1982), who wished to improve the public visitor facilities of his largely 18th-century country house and 5.6-ha gardens. Brookes advised on the redesign and planting of the gardens to reduce maintenance while keeping the essence of the original design. His particular contribution was a formally laid out herb garden, reputedly one of the largest in Europe, on the site of a former rose and fruit garden (Figure 63).[124] A similar, intricate formal planting design was seen in Brookes's proposals for a new rose garden and the replanting of 17th-century St James's Square, London W1 (1984). Brookes was also involved in a number of extensive English country estates outside Sussex, which

Figure 61 (opposite right) Drawing of proposed garden layout for Church Farm, Aldingbourne, 1980.

Figure 62 (below left) The cruciform pool at Toddington House, Littlehampton, West Sussex, was one of the first inspired by Brookes's visit to Iran.

Figure 63 (below right) View across the herb garden designed by John Brookes at Samarès Manor, Jersey (1984).

gave full scope to the principles outlined in *A Place in the Country*. A notable example is Sheepdrove Farm, Berkshire (1983), where he created a gravel garden with views to downland and linked the house to the surrounding countryside by planting swathes of bluebells, winter aconites, anemones, snowdrops, crocuses and daffodils between the two. Gravel plantings included self-seeding perennials, such as Alchemilla mollis, *Sisyrinchium striatum*, *Verbascum olympicum* and *Nigella damascene*, together with *Allium cristophii*, *Iris sibirica* and *Potentilla fruticosa*. At the Manor House, Langton Long, Dorset (1984), ground contouring and a serpentine lake with native plantings of reeds, rushes, water lilies and willows firmly wedded the garden to the ancient landscape (Figure 64).

Until the 1980s Brookes's private commissions outside the UK and the Channel Islands had largely been confined to those around offices in Germany and Holland, and a few domestic gardens in France and Spain. However, in 1982 he was asked to design a private garden in rural Albertville, Alabama, the first of 32 commissions for a major body of work in the USA (Figure 65). Four years later, Janet King Poor, chair of the design committee of the Chicago Botanic Garden, where Brookes ran design workshops, followed her visit to Denmans with a recommendation to her committee that he should be asked to design a 'traditional' English garden within the Botanic Garden. In an otherwise uncompromisingly modern site, the new area was to be called the English Walled Garden. It was developed by Brookes from 1986 as a garden of rooms (with courtyard, cottage garden, a pergola walk, formal garden and sunken garden) to foster an understanding of 'Englishness' (Figure 66).[125] The success of the area as a visitor attraction later prompted other North American botanic gardens, including those at Idaho (1990) and Cleveland (1998), to also commission Brookes to redesign part of their displays.

Figure 64 (below left) Brookes's lakeside planting at Langton Long, Dorset, England, ensures the garden blends seamlessly with the surrounding countryside (2005).

Figure 65 (below right) Brookes's first commission in the USA was for a small private garden in Albertville, Alabama.

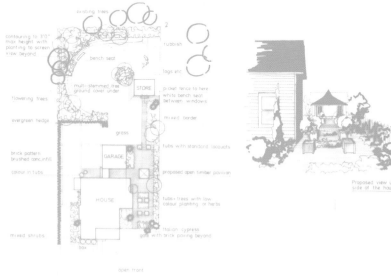

Figure 66 (above) View along the Pergola Walk to the Circular Fountain Pool at the Chicago Botanic Garden, Illinois, USA (1986).

In the last few years of the decade commissions in the USA included private gardens in Albany, New York State (1987); Lake Forest, Chicago (1988); Middleburg, Virginia (1988) and Denver, Colorado (1989). In the wake of the Chicago Botanic Garden work, Brookes was asked to design another 'English' garden in Tateshina, Japan, on a 10,000-square-metre site, where the owner Mr Eugene Yamada and his sister Kei intended to create a cultural and display centre for the Kowa Creative Art Company. Ongoing involvement with this project led to further commercial and domestic commissions in Japan during the 1990s. By 1990, Brookes had designed over 850 landscapes and gardens, including 45 outside England. His experience of designing and planting in a range of ecological regions (biomes) across the five major climatic regions had added a further dimension to his longstanding knowledge of the historic context of garden design. He was confident that with this enhanced understanding he could create gardens that people 'wanted', but which also had a sense of place: 'Although you need to interpret the basic rules of garden design, which are universal, you adapt them to local conditions. I feel I could take on a commission anywhere because I have the principles in my head'.[126]

Brookes found designers and gardeners in the USA particularly receptive to the concept of a regional landscape identity. Historically, North America had the example of natural gardening pioneers, such as the émigré Dane Jens Jensen (1860–1951) who, in 1939, wrote 'We shall never produce an art of landscaping that is worthwhile until we have learned to love the soil and the beauty of our homeland'.[127] Wherever he designed, Jensen explored the local flora so that he could create ecologically appropriate plant associations. Although in tune with Jensen's ideals, his purist approach to planting has less appeal to Brookes than the use of a mix of native and exotic plants, such as that used by the modern American landscape architects, Wolfgang Oehme and James van Sweden. In contrast to American thinking, Brookes considered that the British gardener of the late 1980s still clung to fantasies of an early, more 'gracious' age and was not yet ready to abandon his herbaceous borders.

Throughout this period of expansion and the rigours of long-distance travel, Brookes continued to teach garden design – at Clock House, the Kew School of Garden Design and at La Napoule Art Foundation in the south of France – as well as writing eight books.[128] At Denmans, Joyce Robinson retired in 1984 and Brookes formed a business partnership with Michael Neve, whose financial background was essential in developing the Garden as a visitor attraction, as well as a display of Brookes's developing design and planting philosophy – a move towards a greater exploration of the interaction between native and introduced plants and how things grow in the wild.

THE MATURE WORK

From the beginning of 1990 Brookes worked on a new book for Dorling Kindersley, the international publisher with whom he had developed a successful working relationship. *John Brookes' Garden Design Book*, published in 1991 in association with the Royal Botanic Gardens, Kew, contained the fruits of his 35 years' experience of garden-making, running a design practice and teaching.[129] Exploring design principles – 'An understanding of the way shapes relate to each other'[130] – explaining drawing techniques and, for the first time, detailing Brookes's practical approach to planting,[131] it quickly became a standard textbook for both professional and amateur garden designers. Although acknowledging that 'It is... plant material... that excites many garden designers, for in their mind's eye the static pattern takes life and the imaginative juices start to flow', he warned against becoming too absorbed in the details of a decorative planting scheme at an early stage in the design process – 'There lies the route to a restless garden with little unity of thought between concept, plan and planting'.[132] Based on the use of plants as a third 'sculptural' dimension of a garden's design, Brookes proposed building a 'framework' of plants comprised of five key plant categories:

Figure 67 (top) William Robinson advocated the use of wild and native species that would need little maintenance in his book *The Wild Garden* (1870).

Figure 68 (above) Wild planting in Miriam Rothschild's garden in Ashton Wold, Northamptonshire, England.

> " *The first category at planning stage is the 'specials'... that form focal points for the garden's design and are crucial to the direction of the eye within and around the site. The second category is that of the 'skeleton' planting... the green background that will ensure year-round enclosure, provide a wind screen and generally mould a garden space. The 'decoratives' are those to be seen in front of the skeleton, and after them come the 'pretties', the perennials for flower and foliage interest in spring and summer. Lastly I think of the infill plantings, the transitory splashes of colour as the seasons change, and the invaluable gap fillers for new schemes.* "

This system of plant selection could be adapted to all planting styles, climatic and geographic regions. Several years later, in *Planting the Country Way* (1994), Brookes moved to the specifics of designing and planting in accord with regional landscape heritage in the British Isles.[133] Proposing 'the coming together of tamed with wild' – and inspired by the Victorian garden writer William Robinson's concept of the 'wild' garden (Figure 67)[134] and the naturalist Miriam Rothschild's 'careless ordered' approach to gardening (Figure 68),[135] both of which mixed local wildflowers with exotic plants – Brookes criticized the modern 'manicured garden... overly striped lawn... completely free of daisies... neat little clumps of glaucous or gold conifer edged with heather'. He described how Britain's moorlands, wetlands, downlands and woodlands had evolved, providing guidance on creating a design 'expressive of its site' and planting using native species or, at least, 'plants in their rightful places – sites where they will grow naturally with no need for the intensive cultivation

and maintenance demanded by more exotic species'.[136] Denmans is celebrated for this approach (Figures 69 and 70) and has provided inspiration for many neighbouring garden owners, with 46 per cent of Brookes's English commissions in the period 1990–95 being for sites in Sussex.

Brookes's design for the gardens of Slinfold Manor, West Sussex (1990), an 18th-century English Heritage listed building once isolated from its agricultural landscape by a walled garden on the north side and a formal avenue on the south, demonstrates his instinctive desire to reconnect a garden to its setting. The straight drive became serpentine, part of the garden wall was replaced with a ha-ha to allow views to the surrounding fields, native and other complementary species were introduced around an existing pond and new lake, and additional trees were used to create woodland and boundary planting (Figure 71). Waterside planting included *Ligularia* 'Gregynog Gold', *L. przewalskii*, *Viburnum opulus* (guelder rose), *Iris siberica*, *Gunnera manicata* and *Hosta sieboldiana*, with shelter provided by evergreen shrubs such as *Virburnum rhytidophyllum*, *Prunus lusitanica* (Portuguese laurel), *Sambucus nigra* (common elder) and *Elaeagnus* x *ebbingei* cultivars. Informal planting was continued in areas around the house (Figure 72). Similarly, lakeside plantings and informal tree groups were used at historic Ecclesden Manor (1992) to visually merge the garden and landscape. On other country sites, Brookes uses traditional orchard-style plantings of fruit or other small trees to facilitate the transition from garden to landscape, as at Wiggonholt, West Sussex (1994), where rows of fruit and nut trees were planted in rough grass within an existing flint-walled enclosure.

Figure 69 (above left) An example of 'planting the country way' at Denmans Garden, West Sussex.

Figure 70 (above right) A colourful intermingling of informally grouped plants at Denmans Garden.

Travelling, designing and lecturing worldwide increased Brookes's commissions outside England, reaching 23 per cent (93 of 400) of his new work for the period 1990 to the end of 2006.[137] Requests from clients in mainland Europe continued (including Belgium, Switzerland, Cyprus and Austria), but he was increasingly commissioned to design gardens in the Americas, Australia and Japan and, occasionally, in Russia, India and Poland. El Choique Viejo (1991) was an early commission in Argentina, one of a number in South America, which later paralleled the setting up of design schools, first in Chile and then Argentina. Set on a flat, windy plain south of Buenos Aires and partly sheltered by a mature eucalyptus wood, Brookes has planted the 0.8-ha site at El Choique with grasses (*Bromus brevis*, *Cortaderia selloana*, *Paspalum dilatatum*, *Spartina ciliate*, *Sporobolus rigens*, *Stenotaphrum secundatum*) and native spring flowers integrating it with the surrounding landscape (Figure 73). In contrast, the almost vertiginous site at San Isidro (2002) offered scope for the creation of pools and a waterfall (Figure 74).

Frequently asked to create 'English-style' gardens in countries with different climatic conditions and historic backgrounds, Brookes took the opportunity offered by participation in a conference in Melbourne in 1994, entitled 'Gardens for Tomorrow', to promote regional diversity in design.[138] He wrote a passionate and well-argued article in *Landscape Australia* the following year:[139]

Figure 71 (above left) The abundant informal waterside planting at Slinfold Manor, West Sussex, contrasts with the smooth lawns and mature trees around the gazebo.

Figure 72 (above right) The rigid formality of Brookes's steps at Slinfold Manor is complemented by informal planting.

" *It is all too easy, with international travel and with readily available media coverage in its many forms, to overlook the very special qualities of the region in which we live – its history, its natural flora and fauna, its cultivations and constructions. One reacts against the other to produce local culture, and each is very special, giving names to communities, forms to buildings and enclosures, all of which mould our daily lives, often unconsciously... we need to keep our ear to the ground, to detect the rhythms of what happens naturally, and let the form of the new garden develop from it... We need to be aware of our underlying geology, for on top of that everything builds up, soil, vegetation, minerals, crops, villages, cities and so on.* "

Four commissions in New South Wales followed, including the design for a modernist-style house at Sutton Forest, in which lush flower and shrub borders are complemented by a formally planted orchard of apple, pear and walnut trees. The integrity of Brookes's work and his passion for designing in harmony with local conditions are re-stated in two recent publications, *The New Garden* (1998) and *Garden Masterclass* (2002), in which the garden owner (and designer) is encouraged to 'discover the essence of our own particular place and work with it'.[140] Brookes finds stimulation in the challenges presented by owners' requirements and the constraints and opportunities of the site, working with local architects, landscape architects and project managers to achieve a satisfactory solution. By working with gardeners and local nurserymen he can ensure that planting plans are based on ecologically sustainable specimens, which also meet his design requirements concerning form and colour.

Figure 73 (below left) The view across the plain at El Choique in Argentina (1991).

Figure 74 (below right) The steep site at San Isidro in the Buenos Aires hills gave Brookes the opportunity to create pools and a waterfall.

Such close collaboration has been fundamental to *grands projets* such as an estate on the borders of New England in the USA (1998) and Zespol Palace Park in Poland (1999). Just west of the New England border, Brookes has transformed the 243-ha estate surrounding a late 19th-century house into a modern-day landscape park (Figure 74). The brief was to open the house to the landscape, to create vistas and views and a series of garden rooms to be enjoyed at all seasons of the year. The project has involved earth moving, tree transplanting, planting of mature shrubs and trees and the creation of a lake, implemented by water feature expert Anthony Archer-Wills, with whom Brookes often works.[141] At Zespol Palace Park, the owners commissioned Brookes after reading a Polish translation of his *Garden Design Book*. Here, the 8-ha grounds are the setting for a restored Palladian-style mansion, where Chopin is reputed to have played the piano, commemorated in the garden by a bust of the composer. The development of the gardens has centred on the creation of intimate garden 'rooms' with views over the lawns, lakes and woodland with garden buildings, eye-catchers and winding paths (Figure 75).

Figure 74 (above) A granite pool set in a bastion of a newly created ha-ha at an estate on the New England border, USA, has views over the adjoining fields.

From the 1990s, Brookes had travelled more; he had run courses at the Kew School of Garden Design, at East Lambrook Manor, Somerset, (the home of the late plantswoman Margery Fish) and at Clock House; he had designed award-winning show gardens; and he had written seven books. He was now also actively involved in the Society of Garden Designers, holding study days at Denmans and chairing conferences. Brookes became vice chair in 1995 and chair in 1996, a three-year appointment, which provided opportunities to campaign for not only a higher standard of training for garden designers, but also a better understanding on the part of the general public on the role of the designer: 'One of the functions of the Society is, I believe, to monitor this training process and to ensure that future generations of garden designers are both inspiring and practical enough to be consulted on design work'.[142]

Brookes was also, by this time, the joint-owner of Denmans (Joyce Robinson had died in 1996) and was working with his business partner Michael Neve on plans to enlarge the scope of the garden and improve visitor facilities. Brookes's intense schedule necessitated relying on his assistants and associates to help with new work, with book illustrations and the production of design proposals, construction drawings and planting plans. Duncan Heather acted briefly in this capacity before setting up his own design school in 1991,[143] while landscape architect Michael Zin worked with Brookes as his associate until 1998. His place was taken for a short while by Andrew Duff, who joined Brookes in 1998 on completion of his design degree, leaving to set up his own practice the following year.[144] Kate Fallon followed for a short period, Brookes's current assistant Peter Gillespie joining him in 2002. Initially working in the garden as well as the design office,

Gillespie now has a sound grounding in the John Brookes style and produces his own design proposals as well as working on drawings for Brookes. In particular, he appreciates Brookes's ready grasp of the key elements of a landscape: 'The speed at which he works is amazing. He immediately establishes a connection between the architecture of the house, the garden and the surrounding landscape. After only a brief walk around the garden he can sit down with the client and start sketching a design, producing a unique design that works'.[145]

Brookes remains as committed and passionate about garden design in the 21st century as in the 1950s. He regularly travels abroad to monitor ongoing projects in South America and the USA and continues to take on new work in England, ranging from the gardens and parkland on an 18th-century Oxfordshire estate (2004) and a garden project for a Chichester hospice (2006) to a courtyard in Hampshire (2006), reminiscent of his 1960s town gardens. Current commissions continue to include non-residential landscapes, most recently those around the new offices of Taylors of Harrogate (2006), where an elegant organic-shaped planted gravel garden with seven fountains juxtaposes linear plantings of *Camellia sinensis* on contoured mounds and beds of subtropical plants with palms.

Brookes's lectures and articles continue to focus on local distinctiveness and his concern that 'So much of the detail and diversity in our everyday lives and landscapes has vanished and standardisation, increased mobility, mass production, global communication, fad and fashion are all helping to further erode local differences'.[146] He is a supporter of Common Ground and local organizations to preserve the West Sussex downland, and works closely to encourage education on the value of the vernacular landscape. Brookes promotes 'garden' art or land art as a way of re-establishing a link with the natural landscape: 'The artist uses earth, stone, water and other natural materials to mark, shape and build, to change and restructure landscape space with a sensitivity and a care arising from an awareness of ecological responsibility'.[147] He cites Alison Crowther, Andy Galsworthy and Peter Randal-Page as artists working in this way – creating 'of the land itself' and not just using the landscape as a setting for art – and encourages designers to embrace a similar philosophy: 'I have a growing disquiet that in the quest for newness and originality, designers are losing touch with the earth which should be their anchor'. The publication of *Small Garden* (a revision of the 1989 book *The New Small Garden*), however, also demonstrates continued interest in the 'room outside', albeit using 21st-century styles and materials. A revised edition of *Room Outside* is also scheduled for publication in 2007, nearly 40 years after Brookes first began to change the way people thought about their gardens. He remains as visionary and as outspoken in his views in his eighth decade as when he was a radical young landscape designer in the 1960s.

Figure 76 (above) Zespol Palace Park, Poland. The view from the rose-filled flower garden through a metal pergola to the south side of the house (2006).

The Gardens
Case Studies

Penguin Books Courtyard

LOCATION: London, England
DATE: 1964

In the early 1960s, Allen Lane, founder of Penguin Books Ltd, by then firmly established as a British institution (it had become a public company in 1961[1]), commissioned the architects John Spence & Partners to design a new canteen at its factory site on Bath Road, Harmondsworth, Middlesex, in west London. Spence's extension to the Penguin Books complex was on vacant land at the north end of the site and 'because of the orientation and the bleakness of the surrounding flat fields it was decided to set the building close to the north boundary with the principal windows facing onto an enclosed courtyard'.[2] In addition to the courtyard seen from the staff canteen, another courtyard was visible from a committee room (the directors' courtyard). A covered walkway led from the factory along two sides of the courtyard to the canteen, from where wide, glazed doors opened onto the garden area (Figures 1.1 and 1.2). John Spence asked the architect Theo Crosby, co-editor of *Architectural Design*, to recommend a landscape designer for the courtyard areas. Crosby, familiar with Brookes's innovative design concepts, particularly in his treatment of the courtyard of Michael Manser's

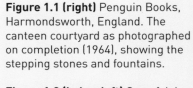

Figure 1.1 (right) Penguin Books, Harmondsworth, England. The canteen courtyard as photographed on completion (1964), showing the stepping stones and fountains.

Figure 1.2 (below left) One of John Brookes's original sketches for the canteen courtyard.

Penguin Books Courtyard

modernist house, Golden Grove in Surrey, a few years earlier, recommended him to Spence. Brookes's brief was to design the layout and planting of the two courtyards and advise on landscaping the main entrance front along the Bath Road.

By 1964 Brookes had developed his design, initially conceived, he recalls, before he had visited the site. As at Michael Manser's house, he based his design for the canteen courtyard on the building module, creating a strong rectilinear pattern that resembled the abstract paintings of the artist Piet Mondrian's 'strong colours in a grid' period of the 1920s (Figure 1.3). Brookes later described the stages involved in the garden design process, recommending the study of modern paintings 'to see how areas of colour and texture can be counter-positioned to form a balanced whole' (Figure 1.4).[3] Mondrian believed that horizontal and vertical lines, initially based on a grid, were the best means to achieve and convey harmony in art. He introduced strong colours into the individual sections of the grid, enclosing each section with bold vertical and horizontal lines to increase 'their special quality, their atmosphere and visual impact'.[4] Like Mondrian, Brookes also provides structural integrity to his designs using a grid to produce the pattern of spaces that are later assigned function – as, for example, paving, planting beds and water features. He recalls:

> " *I saw from my time at* Architectural Design *that there's a discipline within the design of a building and I thought why can't that also work outside? I was aware of Mondrian's paintings and, indeed, quite a few of Sylvia Crowe's designs on which I had worked had a touch of Mondrian in them. The press liked the idea that the Penguin garden had a relationship to the square shapes of a Mondrian painting. It was an early example of a new way of designing a garden space... and the first of mine to get notoriety! It was*

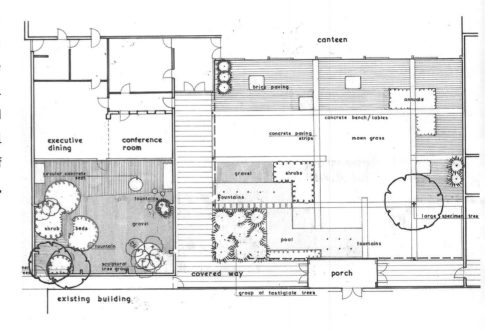

Figure 1.3 (top left) Piet Mondrian, *Composition with Large Blue Plane, Red, Black, Yellow, and Gray* (1921).

Figure 1.4 (top right) Brookes's design was influenced by the form of the Penguin Books building and by Mondrian's abstract painting.

Figure 1.5 (above) Plan of Penguin Books directors' and canteen courtyards, 27 January 1964.

Figure 1.6 (right) View from the canteen to the terrace, with one of Brookes's multipurpose concrete blocks on the terrace (1964).

Penguin Books Courtyard

John Brookes Garden and Landscape Designer

Figure 1.7 (left) Jets of water form a focal point when the courtyard is viewed from the canteen (1964).

Figure 1.8 (below) John Brookes's planting plan for the canteen and directors' courtyards, 1964.

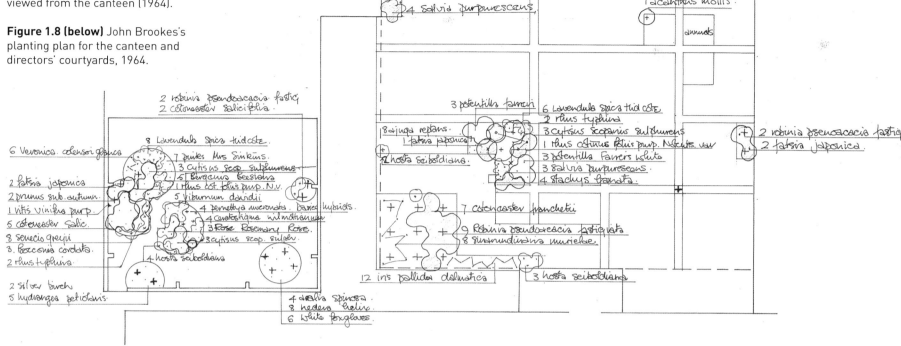

a combination of a use of different materials, a squared pattern, a terrace, sliding doors and room outside, as well as plenty of planting. The planting was typical of what I used at the time, but I'd be using larger blocks now. It seemed to catch the spirit of the time." [5]

On the published plan, the canteen courtyard consists of geometric shapes of water, planting, paving, grass and white gravel chippings, the blocks divided by textured concrete slabs (600 x 600mm) in the manner of Mondrian's horizontal and vertical lines (Figure 1.5). From the start, the brief included a paved area outside the canteen for sitting out in warm weather, and Brookes added concrete blocks with vertical shuttering which not only formed part of the design but could be used as tables or benches (Figure 1.6). Water was included to give movement and interest to the space in the form of a pool (460mm deep) with

a line of fountains which formed a focal point from the canteen windows (Figure 1.7). Stepping stones continued the linear pattern across the water.

A large ash tree was planted in one section of the courtyard before the site was enclosed, and Brookes's design needed to accommodate that. His overall planting rationale was to include blocks of planting that 'would divide up the area so that everything was not immediately visible' (Figure 1.8).[6] Forming a backdrop to the pool were sizeable plantings of *Robinia pseudoacacia* 'Fastigiata' (now 'Pyramidalis') and *Sinarundinaria murielae* (bamboo) to produce height and density, underplanted with the contrasting forms and texture of *Cotoneaster franchetii*, *Iris pallida dalmatica* and *Hosta sieboldiana*. The central planting bed, also bordering the water, continued the exotic and 'jungly' atmosphere with *Fatsia japonica*, the large pinnate leaves of *Rhus typhina* (stag's horn sumach) and colourful fruiting panicles of *Rhus cotinus*

f. *purpureus* (now *Cotinus coggygria*) 'Notcutt's Variety'. Their seasonal 'gaudiness' formed a contrast to the softer colours of lavenders, rock roses, *Potentilla*, *Salvia* and *Stachys lanata* chosen as underplanting. The terrace area was planted with shrubby aromatic herbs (*Lavandula spica* 'Hidcote', *Rosmarinus officinalis* 'Miss Jessopp's Upright' and *Salvia purpurea*), while a few beds were left for annual planting with 'instructions left that self colours only should be used in them, on pain of death!'[7] A report on the courtyard notes that 'After completion of hard landscape work by the building contractor – the soft work, including the specimen tree, amounted to approximately £513'.[8]

The canteen courtyard featured in the architectural and landscape press as an example of 'cutting edge' design gaining, in Brookes's words, 'a certain notoriety; for its abstracted shapes had not been generally accepted as a garden form at that time'.[9] The director's courtyard was a smaller space (Figure 1.9), designed for viewing from the committee room rather for than sitting in. Structure was provided by gentle mounding with silver birches, fastigiate *Robinia*, *Fatsia japonica* and *Rhus* and a rich mosaic of flowering and evergreen shrubs beneath. The plan for the entrance of the Penguin Books site (Figure 1.10) was a simple formal mixture of chippings and ground-cover plants in rectangular blocks. Brookes's evocative sketch of the view from the main road shows the contrast of the low beds and upright, evergreen trees. There were already planes and sycamores nearby, but a new, formal yew hedge was alternated with vertical, metal railings.

Brookes was asked to review the courtyards and advise on a 'facelift' in 1988.[10] He commented that the canteen area had 'a very run down feeling' but, as the structure of the garden remained intact, his suggestions focused on the cutting back of existing plant material, replanting and upgrading of the pool:

" *The pool area, while remaining the same in outline, might now be lined with a black butyl rubber liner. This would entail lifting the surrounding coping stones and removing*

View from the main road.

the stepping stones to install the liner. The stepping stones would then be built upon the rubber, which would be retained by replacing the copings. **"**

He also suggested that the paving through the grass should be lifted and relaid level and that the *Robinia*, which had outgrown their space, should be replaced with shrubs. The central planting also needed to be replaced (except for the *Fatsia japonica*) and Brookes suggested a formal but romantic look of 'bedding roses – all one colour, to sustain interest throughout the summer'. He warned, however, that 'small infills of annuals should be avoided, though spring bulbs, lilies and tobacco plants might be used to filter through the rose plantings'. Ten years later the courtyard's design retained its 'Mondrian' structure, although the planting had been simplified to reduce maintenance. With the move of the Penguin Books offices to central London in 2001, however, the site of Brookes's celebrated courtyard has been sold for development.

Figure 1.9 (above) View from the executive dining room into the directors' courtyard. Pencil and ink sketch, 1964.

Figure 1.10 (below) John Brookes's sketch of the proposals for alterations to the entrance to the Penguin Books building, undated, *c.*1964.

Bryanston Square

LOCATION: London, England

DATE: 1965

By 1964 John Brookes had moved to a mews house near Montagu Square, London W1, an early 19th-century square twinned with Bryanston Square to its west (Figure 2.1).[1] The fashionable terraced houses of the squares were built by David Porter for the Portman Estate to designs by Joseph Parkinson, district surveyor for Westminster. Montagu Square, named after Mrs Elizabeth Montagu, a wealthy resident, was completed in 1811 and Bryanston Square, named after the Portman family seat in Dorset, around 1821. The façades of the buildings on the east and west sides of Bryanston Square were designed by Parkinson to mirror each other (although they were subsequently altered), and the square itself was aligned on Marble Arch to the south and Wyndham Place to the north. St Mary's Church (1823, designed by the architect Sir Robert Smirke) at the northern end of Wyndham Place also formed an eye-catcher to the north.[2] The houses face onto a garden square for the use of residents, its maintenance managed by a residents' society set up by an Act of Parliament in 1813.[3]

Figure 2.1 (right) View from above of Bryanston Square, London, England (1967).

Bryanston Square

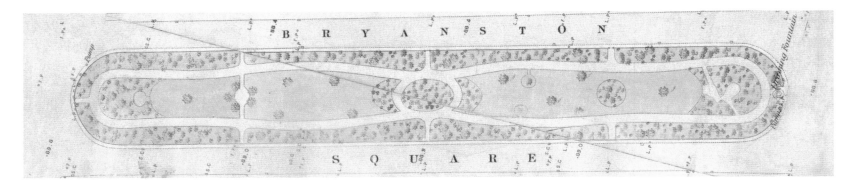

John Brookes Garden and Landscape Designer

06506072

The railed communal garden still contains the early 19th-century London plane trees (*Platanus* x *hispanica*), but the dwarf weeping ash in the middle of the lawn, once described as resembling 'a gigantic umbrella or toad-stool', has gone.[4] Potter's 1832 survey of Marylebone shows a symmetrically undulating perimeter path, while a cast-iron water pump in the form of a Doric column at the north end of the garden dates from the early 19th century. At the south end, a memorial drinking fountain by William Pitt Byrne was erected in 1862 (Figure 2.2). Twentieth-century additions include benches made *c.*1954 from the timbers of Admiral Lord Jellicoe's flagship and a brick garden store (obstructing the view north to St Mary's Church) (Figure 2.3).

Figure 2.2 (opposite top) Undulating paths around the perimeter are shown on the 1870 ordnance survey map.

Figure 2.3 (opposite) View across Bryanston Square looking north, towards St Mary's Church, showing the garden store (1967).

Figure 2.4 (above) Experimental sketches of shapes for the design of Bryanston Square, 1965.

Figure 2.5 (right) Sketch of the view across Bryanston Square, looking north, 1965.

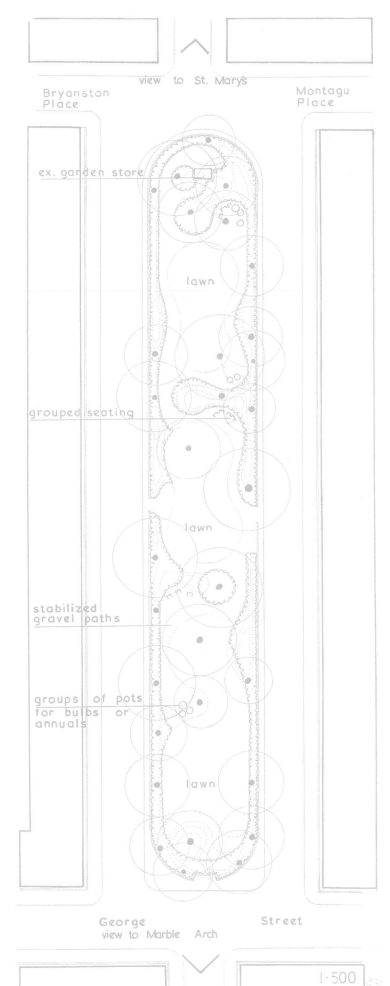

Bryanston
Place

view to St. Mary's

Montagu
Place

ex. garden store

lawn

grouped seating

lawn

stabilized
gravel paths

groups of pots
for bulbs or
annuals

lawn

George
view to Marble Arch

Street

1·500

When Brookes was commissioned to redesign the garden in 1965, his brief was to make it 'interesting for the tenants of the Square to look at', particularly from their first-floor reception rooms, and with 'enough character or privacy for them to want to use it'.[5] He also noted that the square was frequently used by nannies with children in prams and he wanted to create a meandering walk for them. Inspired by the shadows of the plane trees, Brookes based his design on 'a swirly pattern', reminiscent of the organic curves used by Roberto Burle Marx, his experimentation with the underlying abstract shape being recorded in a series of sketches (Figure 2.4). He presented his design to the garden committee, with accompanying sketches (Figures 2.5 and 2.6):

" *The design for the garden provides a strong curving pattern which has interest in itself when viewed from above. This was evolved round the existing large trees with grass in areas getting most sunlight. Bays in the curving path pattern offer seats and pots for strong annual colour, both making focal points within the layout. Surrounding shrub beds have been gently contoured and planted with a large proportion of evergreen shrubs to eventually provide some privacy...The object of the planting was not to produce a flower garden but a green one with points of colour emphasis. The dappled light coming through the leaves of the original London planes produces very pleasing light and shade effects.* "[6]

Figure 2.6 (left) Plan for the design of Bryanston Square, 1965.

Figure 2.7 (opposite) The organic curves of the path viewed from a first-floor room of a house on the square.

Work commenced the following autumn, continuing until spring 1967. This was an important, and a large, project for Brookes at this time (he recorded the contract price as £3,699. 7s. 8d), particularly as it involved 'a certain amount of mounding using some sort of industrial waste [pulverized fuel ash], quite new at the time – it was an early mounding venture'. New planting on the boundary was of evergreen shrubs, such as *Cotoneaster*, *Viburnum tinus* and *Fatsia japonica* with some underplanting of *Vinca minor*, ivy, *Anenome* and daffodils. The innovative design was considered a success but the design did not remain intact for more than a few years (Figures 2.7 and 2.8), Brookes recalling with disappointment: 'I moved out of London (1969) and the next thing I heard was that they didn't like the wiggly paths and they'd straightened them up again!' The parallel path edges remain, and modern planting is low key for ease of maintenance with a range of shrubs and perennials (Figure 2.9).

Figure 2.8 (opposite) The pattern of Brookes's serpentine paths, seen from a countoured mound, is highlighted by sun filtering through the tree canopies (1967).

Figure 2.9 (above) In spring and summer Bryanston Square remains abundant with trees, shrubs and a large proportion of planting envisaged by John Brookes in 1965 (2006).

Fitzroy Square

LOCATION: London, England
DATE: 1972

The East side of Fitzroy Square

As a young landscape designer in the 1960s working in the London office of Brenda Colvin and Sylvia Crowe, Brookes was first introduced to the architect and landscape architect Geoffrey Jellicoe and his wife Susan. They encouraged him to establish his own garden design practice, worked together on the ILA committees and promoted his early work. Jellicoe remained Brookes's mentor and, when he was commissioned to prepare a landscape design for the development of Fitzroy Square in the early 1970s, he asked Brookes to work with him on the redesign of the communal garden (Figures 3.1 and 3.2).

Figure 3.1 (opposite) Residents relax on Brookes's grassy undulating mounds in Fitzroy Square (1983).

Figure 3.2 (above) View of Fitzroy Square's east side with two women walking in the foreground. James Peller Malcolm, 1807.

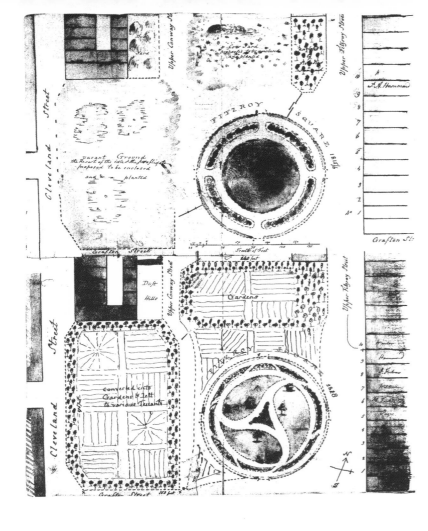

Fitzroy Square, London W1, was first laid out in the 1790s as a speculative housing development for wealthy residents on land owned by Charles Fitzroy, Lord Southampton, who commissioned the architect Robert Adam to provide designs.[1] Adam died in 1792 when only the stone-faced houses on the east and south sides had been completed, which left the Square vulnerable to invasion by 'the idle and profligate'.[2] Although the railed, circular communal garden with shrubberies and perimeter walk was planted by 1798, by 1815 contemporary descriptions refer to the surrounding land as being used as a 'cow yard', a 'yard for dust', a 'play-ground of children of the lowest classes' and 'generally covered with stagnate pools of water, serving to make the air unhealthy'.[3] Plans were made to improve the land by draining it and creating gardens 'ornamented with trees', while the communal garden was redesigned with serpentine paths, new trees and shrubs (Figure 3.3).[4]

Despite these improvements, the writer Charles Knight later described Fitzroy Square as 'the monument of failure... with great architectural pretensions',[5] a view evidently not held by the many artists and writers, such as George Bernard Shaw and Virginia Woolf, who later lived there, enjoying its Bohemian atmosphere. The garden was maintained by a committee out of rates levied on the residents by St Pancras Borough Council. Bomb damage to the Square during World War Two (later repaired) was followed from the late 1960s by disruption caused by construction of the new London Underground Victoria line, the first deep-level underground line to be built across central London since the beginning of the 20th century. The local authority took the opportunity to pedestrianize Fitzroy Square and, in 1972, Geoffrey Jellicoe was commissioned to draw up the landscape plans. His composition of paving slabs confined by a strong grid of granite setts not only retained the grand scale of Adam's original design, but also linked the classical façades of the houses on all four sides.

Jellicoe's hard landscaping also provided a foil to the naturalistic central garden remodelled by John Brookes. As in Brookes's earlier work in Bryanston Square and other private gardens close to London's Georgian squares, plans for the garden of Fitzroy Square needed to take into account the design and planting restrictions imposed by existing mature plane trees. Brookes's early proposals focused on creating an open, undulating landscape with grassy banks for sitting and sunbathing, while additional shrub planting under the planes on the perimeter provided the residents with privacy (Figures 3.4, 3.5 and 3.6). Detailed planting plans include structural blocks of *Taxus bacatta* and *Prunus Laurocerasus* juxtaposed with showy, flowering shrubs, such as *Ceonothus impressus*, *Philadelphus* 'Beauclerk', *Buddleia davidii* 'White Profusion', *Choisya ternata* and *Camellia*. These were underplanted with lower-growing plants, including white *Veronica*, *Hosta sieboldiana*, *Bergenia cordifolia* and *Senecio* (now *Brachyglottis*) *greyii*, with hundreds of

Figure 3.3 (opposite) The plans of Fitzroy Square gardens and environs before and after 19th-century improvements. Watercolour dated 1818.

Figure 3.4 (above) Banks of flowering shrubs create intimate areas in the square (1980).

Figure 3.5 (left) Informal shrub planting on the perimeter provides a green space all year round (1983).

road · hut · shrubs · shrub bed · road

Section across square

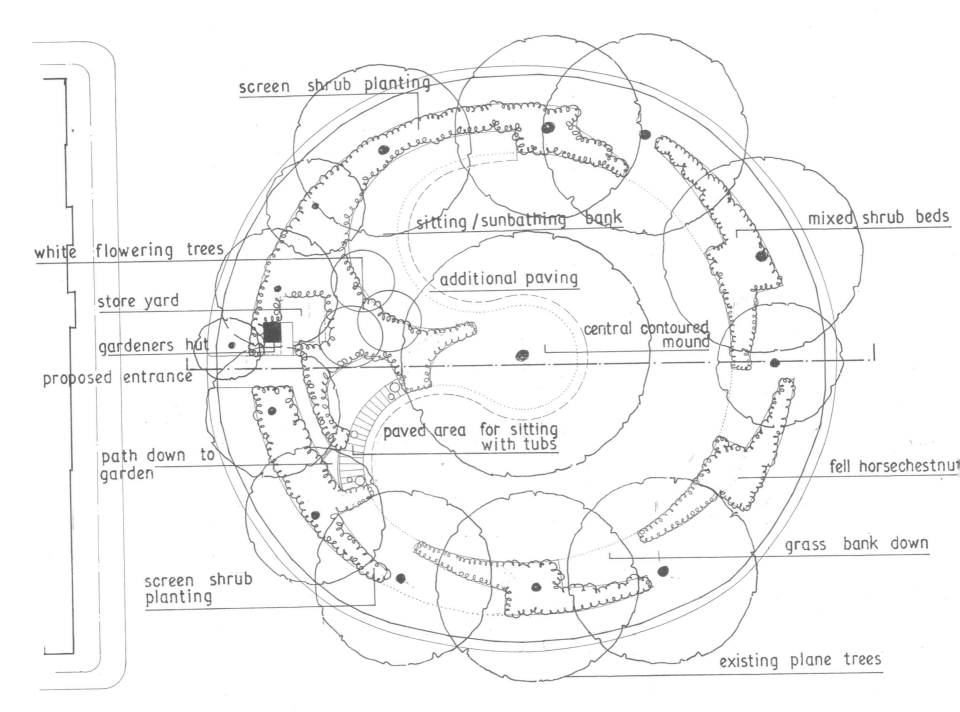

screen shrub planting

sitting / sunbathing bank

mixed shrub beds

white flowering trees

additional paving

store yard

central contoured mound

gardeners hut

proposed entrance

paved area for sitting with tubs

fell horsechestnut

path down to garden

grass bank down

screen shrub planting

existing plane trees

John Brookes Garden and Landscape Designer

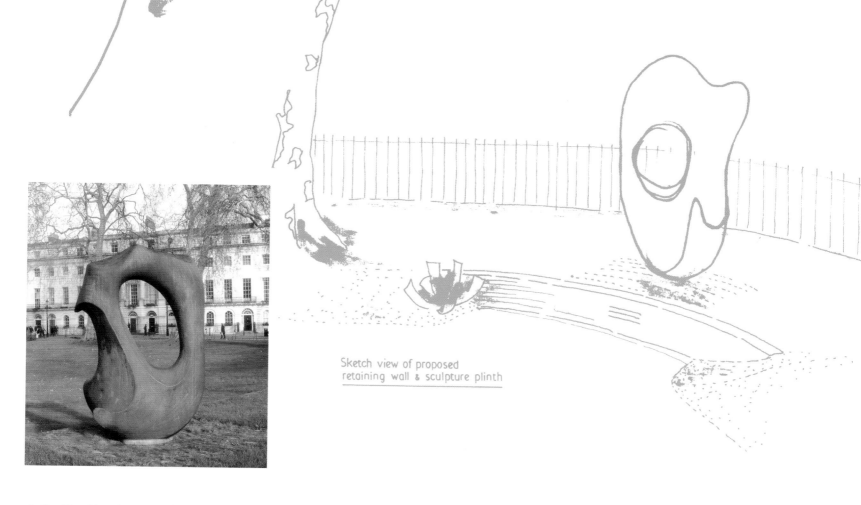

Sketch view of proposed
retaining wall & sculpture plinth

daffodils, *Narcissus* and *Crocus* studding the grassy mounds to provide a spring display. Denser shrub planting inside the proposed entrance to the garden on the north side of the Square (including *Pyracantha atalantioides*, *Cotoneaster lacteus*, *Hydrangea* 'Hortensis' and variegated holly) also housed a garden store and service area, screened from the main garden by a contoured mound. A curved gravel path led down to a paved area with tubs of plants, and the facility to seat larger groups to accommodate corporate activities and the lunchtime picnics of the employees of the increasing number of offices in the Square. Based on an underlying pattern of concentric circles, ground contours, formal planting beds and drifts of bulbs are mingled to create an informal garden landscape.

As the project neared completion, Brookes and Jellicoe discussed further alterations to the garden to allow the placing of an abstract sculpture, *View* by the Czech artist Naomi Blake,

Figure 3.6 (opposite) 'Fitzroy Square, W1. Sketch landscape plan', dated (erroneously) '28 August 1967', *c*.1977.

Figure 3.7 (above left) *View*, Naomi Blake's sculpture (2007).

Figure 3.8 (above right) Sketch view of proposed retaining wall and sculpture plinth, dated 7 February 1977.

to celebrate the Queen's Silver Jubilee in 1977. Brookes reshaped the mounds on the south side of the garden (where a plane tree had already been removed), designing a low retaining wall of old stock bricks into a bank above and beyond which the sculpture would sit. The sculpture was uplit through a grille (for safety reasons) and additional bulb planting and a simple complementary planting of *Euphorbia characias* subspecies *wulfenii* were proposed. An uninterrupted view of the sculpture from across the garden and from outside the railings in Fitzroy Square is provided for both residents of and visitors to London's best-preserved Georgian square (Figures 3.7 and 3.8).

Denmans

LOCATION: Fontwell, West Sussex, England
DATE: 1980

John Brookes had first visited Joyce Robinson and her garden at Denmans, six miles east of Chichester, in the 1970s when he was teaching at the Inchbald School in London (Figures 4.1 and 4.2). At that time, he arranged weekend visits to buildings of interest for students on the Interior Design Courses, and regularly took them to West Dean College on the outskirts of the West Sussex county town. One weekend, noticing that the garden at Denmans was open to the public, he visited for the first time and was enthralled, recalling that it was 'rambly, different to anything I'd seen'. It was, indeed, 'different', representing, at that time, more than 35 years of passion and devotion on the part of Joyce Robinson, her husband Hugh and their gardener Albert (Bertie) Reed.[1] From their marriage in 1925, the Robinsons had farmed

Figure 4.1 (left) The organic curves of the sweeping gravel path, lawn areas and planting emphasize the natural feel of the garden at Denmans in West Sussex, England (2006).

Figure 4.2 (right) Informal planting groups characterize John Brookes's own garden at Denmans.

Figure 4.3 (below) Joyce Robinson's own architectural plantings at the entrance to the walled garden.

Figure 4.4 (bottom) One of Joyce Robinson's gravel stream beds winds down the garden's slopes.

Figure 4.5 (opposite) Plan showing the different areas at Denmans Garden when John Brookes arrived in 1980.

and run market gardens in West Sussex, but had little experience of ornamental gardening. Needing more land for their expanding business, in 1946 they bought the Westergate Estate, near Fontwell, once the home of the Denman family, but by then a dilapidated 34-ha site with a 14-bedroom house, cottages, stables, farm buildings and agricultural land.

The Robinsons moved into a cottage (previously the gardeners' bothy) on the east side of the lane from the main house, adjoining a walled kitchen garden, the greenhouses and farmland. 'So there we were in this unexpected place', Joyce Robinson recalled, 'with its atmosphere of an earlier age, its stables with a clock, a coach house, a lime walk in the park and a cedar of Lebanon planted about 1800; a cricket pitch for the staff with a pavilion and a donkey-pulled roller to go with it'.[2] They named it Denmans, selling Westergate House to a local firm in 1948.[3] The market garden of fruit and flowers quickly expanded, but Joyce Robinson also wanted to start a 'real' garden and thought the site around the cottage ideal: 'It stood in an old apple orchard, surrounded by a walled garden complete with a Victorian conservatory. The whole garden sloped gently south on a free-draining, slightly alkaline soil. What more could I want? Here then was my canvas'.[4] The canvas was at first 'a wilderness of waist-high weeds', but with the help of friends, garden visits and observation of 'nature's way of using colour and variations of height and distance',[5] Joyce developed into a knowledgeable plantswoman with innovative ideas on plant associations and planting 'in sympathy with the whole natural scene'.[6]

Over the years, trees, winter-flowering shrubs and evergreens were gradually added to existing plantings to form the structure of the new garden, providing a backdrop for the shape and texture of architectural plants such as *Acanthus*, *Phormium tenax*, giant thistles and *Verbascum broussa* (now *Verbascum byciferum*) (Figure 4.3). Lawns around the house gave way to longer grass with a mown path leading to a flowering meadow, where the garden appeared to merge with the fields beyond. Self-seeding plants which colonized naturally – 'self-sown patches of beauty' – were much loved by Joyce Robinson,[7] and were the inspiration in 1969 for the creation of a 'gravel garden using water-worn gravel from the sea bed' with views down to the fields (Figure 4.4).[8] Planting included old-fashioned double primroses, hellebores, *Chionodoxa luciliae*, forget-me-nots, violets, *Epimedium*, *Euphorbia*, *Erythronium*, *Omphalodes verna*, *Salvia argentea*, *Kirengeshoma*, *Liriope muscari*, *Veraetrum nigrum* and ferns.

When space allowed, she created two gravel stream beds and a dry water hole 'wandering down a shallow slope' with 'a large flat water-worn stone across the stream as a stepping stone to reinforce the illusion':[9]

> " *The water hole through which the stream flows is about thirty feet wide and circular. Around the perimeter we threw up a low bank of soil to form a channel which was left unplanted to emphasize the flow of water. Larger rounded sea-bed stones were thrown up unevenly against the bank and we planted only things that might be found growing in a dry stream bed; grasses, iris, thistles, mint, willow and elder. Under the banks and in the gravel everywhere I planted violets, water forget-me-nots, musk and lamiums.* "

This was the garden that so intrigued John Brookes in the late 1970s and became the setting for his home and design school (based at Clock House) from 1980 (Figures 4.5, 4.6 and 4.7).

Between 1980 and 1984 Brookes gradually took over responsibility for the garden with the still active, but decreasing, involvement of Joyce Robinson and Bertie.[10] During this period the garden (and plant sales area[11]) continued to be open to visitors most afternoons from March to October, and the Clock House students used it as a design and planting resource. In 1983, with a thriving garden design school and increasing visitor numbers,

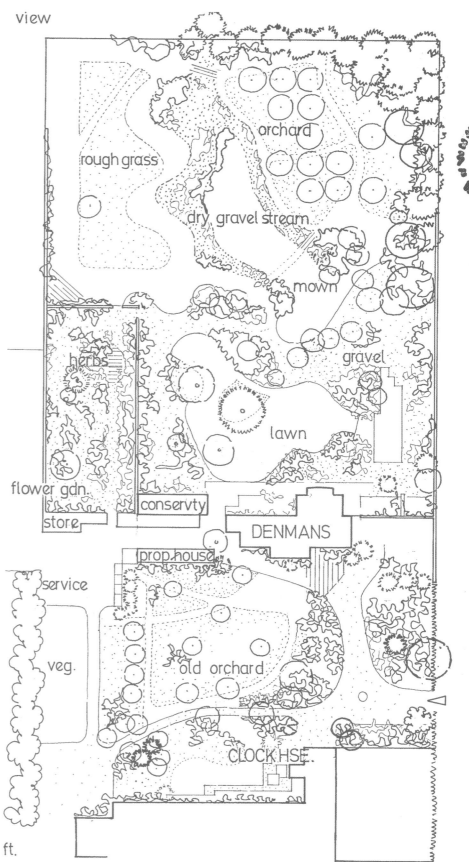

Brookes formed a business partnership with Michael Neve, initially to manage the design school finances. In January 1985 Mrs Robinson retired to cultivate a cottage garden around her house at Denmans, leaving the main garden 'in the capable hands of John Brookes' (Figure 4.8).[12] From then onwards, Neve's financial acumen and gardening interests were key to the development of Denmans as a viable business proposition. Not only did he deal with financial matters relating to Brookes's design consultancy and school, but he implemented plans to convert the 'cow barn' into a café and shop with adjoining toilets (1985), and to expand the plant sales. A collection of rare breeds of poultry and waterfowl was also developed, primarily for sale but also as an added attraction.

Figure 4.6 (above) The newly converted Clock House, with Brookes's iconic pergola creating a room outside (1980).

Figure 4.7 (right) The completed terrace area for the Clock House, where concrete slabs and setts are used to divide the space visually (1980).

Figure 4.8 (top right) Joyce Robinson tours the garden in her motorized buggy.

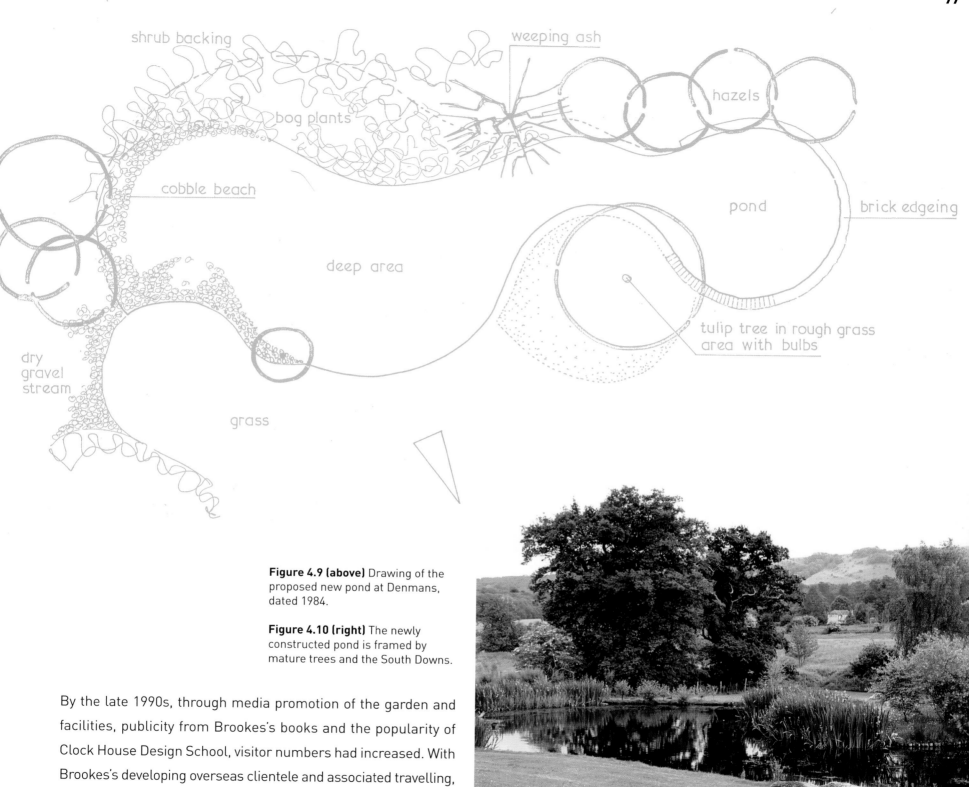

shrub backing

weeping ash

bog plants

hazels

cobble beach

pond

brick edgeing

deep area

tulip tree in rough grass
area with bulbs

dry
gravel
stream

grass

Figure 4.9 (above) Drawing of the proposed new pond at Denmans, dated 1984.

Figure 4.10 (right) The newly constructed pond is framed by mature trees and the South Downs.

By the late 1990s, through media promotion of the garden and facilities, publicity from Brookes's books and the popularity of Clock House Design School, visitor numbers had increased. With Brookes's developing overseas clientele and associated travelling, Neve's involvement in the running of the garden, as well as Denman's other core activities, was crucial.

Brookes describes the 'bones' of the planting at Denmans as:

" *made up of an unlikely redwood* (Sequoia sempervirens) *with a* Koelreuteria (K.paniculata). *There are two self-seeded birches* (Betula pendula) *and, beneath them, a mass of bamboo –* Arundinaria fastuosa *and* A. variegate [now *Pleioblastus variegatus*] *– against whose feathery backdrop in winter the red stems of red-twigged dogwood* (Cornus alba) *and the yellow ones of the white willow* (Salix alba var. vitellina) *shine out. White stemmed Rubus* (Rubus cockburnianus) *and black willow* (Salix fargesii) *complete the winter look.*" [13]

Following the lead of Joyce Robinson in planting to harmonize with the surrounding landscape, from 1980 Brookes began to introduce additional native and exotic plants into the garden. He also began to develop a more organic and cohesive overall design, reshaping the grassed areas in the south garden and creating a natural-looking pool to culminate the dry gravel streams – 'a positive statement' – now with a striking sculpture by Marion Smith (Figures 4.9, 4.10, 4.11 and 4.12). Further changes were pre-empted by the 1987 storms which brought down many mature trees, creating open sunny areas which previously had been shady:

Figure 4.11 (above) Brookes's organic overall design is shown in a plan of Denmans Garden dated November 1998.

Figure 4.12 (above right) Marion Smith's fibreglass sculpture of a seated boy peers through the *Iris pseudacorus* to the shady pool (2006).

" *When I first came here I took over the garden slowly, getting used to Joyce and Bertie. Joyce thought it took 10 years to feel that I was running the garden and it certainly took 10 years for me to feel that her garden was mine! The big trees were hers, the 'bones' were in and she had done the dry gravel stream. But she was a plantswoman and a collector of plants, while I liked arranging the plants and getting the shape right. Mrs Robinson was beginning to think ecologically very early on and wanted to use Mediterranean plants to create a* glorious disarray, *but her dry gravel stream didn't seem to go anywhere so I put a pool in to finish the garden with a positive statement.* " [14]

Brookes's experiments at Denmans paralleled planting concepts used in his clients' designs and those he outlined in articles, lectures and books:

" *Over the years I've tried to simplify the garden, experimenting with plants and plant associations. First I tried native plants only but they are extremely invasive, although they looked very handsome. It was a useful exercise as plants such as box, yew, viburnum, clematis*

and butcher's broom all grow on the Downs. Next I moved into meadow planting – the prairie phase. What I enjoyed was putting plants together rather than the cultivation of them. "

A 1998 plan of Denmans Garden emphasizes the strong abstract design Brookes believes is fundamental to both the aesthetics and function of a landscape. The garden comprises a Dutch light greenhouse, the walled garden (Figure 4.13), dry stream bed, south garden by the pool (Figure 4.14), top lawn (around Mrs Robinson's cottage) and the gardens around Clock House. Visitors enter through the greenhouse, where frost-tender species, such as *Callistemon citrinus* (Crimson bottlebrush), *Passiflora caerulea* (Passion flower) and *Strelitzia reginae* (Bird of Paradise flower) have replaced the strawberries, tomatoes and flowers grown by Mrs Robinson for the London market. The adjoining flint- and

Figure 4.13 (above left) The south-facing walled garden provides a sheltered environment for native and exotic plants (1989).

Figure 4.14 (above right) Organic shapes of rough grass and bulbs in the south garden with views to the fields beyond (1987).

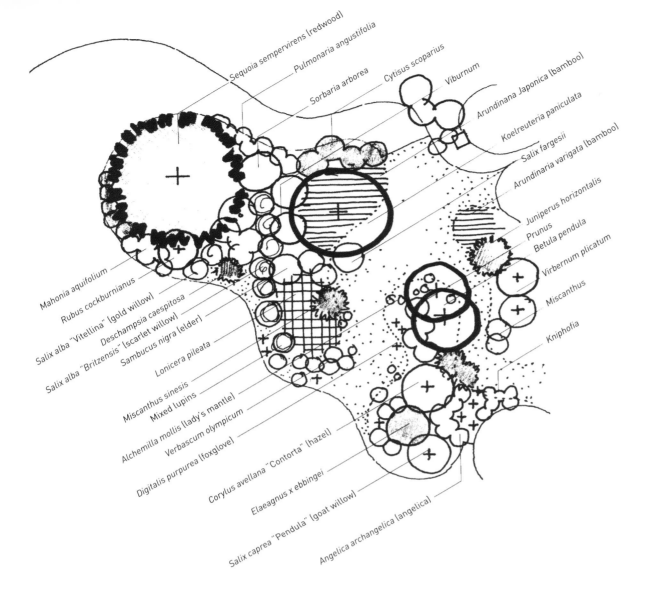

Sequoia sempervirens (redwood)
Pulmonaria angustifolia
Sorbaria arborea
Cytisus scoparius
Viburnum
Arundinana Japonica (bamboo)
Koelreuteria paniculata
Salix fargesii
Arundinaria varigata (bamboo)
Juniperus horizontalis
Prunus
Betula pendula
Virbernum plicatum
Miscanthus
Kniphofia

Mahonia aquifolium
Rubus cockburnianus
Salix alba "Vitellina" (gold willow)
Deschampsia caespitosa
Salix alba "Britzensis" (scarlet willow)
Sambucus nigra (elder)
Lonicera pileata
Miscanthus sinesis
Mixed lupins
Alchemilla mollis (lady's mantle)
Verbascum olympicum
Digitalis purpurea (foxglove)
Corylus avellana "Contorta" (hazel)
Elaeagnus x ebbingei
Salix caprea "Pendula" (goat willow)
Angelica archangelica (angelica)

Figure 4.15 (left) Plan of a wild area at Denmans specifying a mix of grasses, trees, shrubs and self-seeding plants.

Figure 4.16 (below left) Plants such as *Verbascum* are prolific self-seeders in the dry gravel stream (2006).

Figure 4.17 (below right) Informal groupings of flowers and shrubs thrive in the dry gravel streams at Denmans.

Figure 4.18 (opposite left) The organic outlines of the rough grass are mirrored by the curves of the path.

Figure 4.19 (opposite right) Brookes's terrace area, now with mature planting, remains a peaceful outdoor space.

brick-walled garden, previously the 19th-century kitchen garden, provides a sheltered, south-facing microclimate for a display of native and exotic plants with foliage and flower colour, set against a structure of clipped shrubs. Described as bursting 'with foliage masses, old-fashioned roses, perennials and herbs in glorious disarray',[15] the walled garden continues Mrs Robinson's planting style, while Brookes's intimate compartments also provide design ideas for smaller gardens.

South of the walled garden, Brookes has developed the dry stream bed as a wilder area with denser, random planting where self-seeding in gravel is encouraged. Much loved by plants such as *Verbascum bombyciferum* and *Sisyrinchium striatum*, this hot, dry area flows down to the pool set in the cool shade of the surrounding mature trees. A plan of a wild area near the pool provides an example of Brookes's loose planting style, in which self-seeders mingle with grasses, shrubs and trees (Figures 4.15, 4.16 and 4.17). In the south garden and elsewhere, Brookes has introduced bulbs and wild flowers to the swathes of rough grass to create contrasting textures, their organic outlines mirrored by the curves of the path that returns past the cottage (now Michael Neve's home) to the gardens around Clock House

(Figure 4.18). Twenty-five years after it was conceived, Brookes's terrace area with iconic pergola (now weather-beaten and covered in ivy) and bright blue Adirondack chairs remains a quintessential outdoor room, a private space for solitude and summer entertaining (Figure 4.19). Perhaps, indeed, the only part of the garden, now open daily all-year round, that he can call his own. Although he retains overall control of the direction of its development, Denmans Garden is maintained on a day-to-day basis by two gardeners, with contractors employed for regular mowing and tree work. The Garden Café, shop, plant sales and car park have been extended, and the garden draws increasing numbers of visitors, around 20,000 in 2006.[16] Brookes's assessment is that 'Denmans is ongoing!':

> " *I modified what she [Mrs Robinson] had done – and after 25 years it's sort of the same but I've done it my way... People ask what is new, but really the garden changes by evolution rather than by making dramatic statements. Those who visit the garden are getting more interested in seeing how a garden evolves and how it looks at different times of year.* " [17]

Samarès Manor

LOCATION: Jersey, Channel Islands

DATE: 1982

John Brookes Garden and Landscape Designer

By the late 1970s, following his introduction to local gardening enthusiasts by plantswoman Vi Lort-Phillips, John Brookes had completed designs for 11 Jersey gardens. In the early 1980s he ran a weekend workshop on garden design on the island, attended by Richard Adams, then newly appointed managing director of Samarès Manor Ltd, a project to develop the historic site as a financially viable visitor attraction. Adams was enthusiastic about Brookes's approach to design and suggested to Vincent Obbard, seigneur (lord of the manor) of Samarès, that Brookes might advise on the restructuring of the Manor gardens and, in particular, design a new garden to replace an early 20th-century rose garden adjacent to a new restaurant area. Brookes produced the first designs in 1982, his involvement continuing through most of the decade.[1]

Samarès (meaning salt marsh), situated in St Clement, south-east Jersey, is one of the principal feudal fiefs in the island with a documented history that dates back to the 12th century.[2] The privileges of the seigneur included running a mill to grind corn, rabbit hunting and keeping a columbier (dovecote), the latter still a prominent feature in the Manor grounds (Figure 5.1).[3] The mansion has been remodelled under different owners since the medieval house was first constructed, the architecture of the present building being early 19th century (Figure 5.2). Little is known about the gardens, however, until the early 20th century, apart from an intriguing mention in a 1670 letter from the 17th-century seigneur Philip Dumaresq to the famous diarist and gardener John Evelyn. Dumaresq writes that he has 'planted about a score of Cypresses from France and borders of Phillyrea...

Figure 5.1 (opposite) The medieval dovecote at Samarès Manor, seen across the exotic planting designed by John Brookes (2006).

Figure 5.2 (below) Samarès Manor with planting beds developed by John Brookes, but which have since been replanted (2006).

Figure 5.3 (above left) The existing rose garden, underplanted with herbs (c.1980).

Figure 5.4 (above right) The planting of the herb garden in its early stages (1983).

I have this year began a small plantation of vineyard encouraged by *The French Gardener*', a reference to one of Evelyn's works.[4] Dumaresq was also responsible for the construction of a canal to drain the swampy land around the Manor, the 1-mile water body to the sea also providing a route by boat to the nearest town.[5] In 1924, Sir James Knott, the wealthy English shipping line owner and philanthropist from near Newcastle, bought the Manor and commissioned architect and landscape designer Edward White to redesign the gardens.[6] The remains of the 17th-century canal were filled in leaving only a narrow culvert, and two large ponds with islands were constructed, one to the west of the Mansion and the second in a new Japanese garden on the north-west boundary.

John Brookes's initial brief was to redesign a sunken rose garden as a herb garden (Figure 5.3). Located on the west side of the mansion the herb garden would adjoin the patio area of a new restaurant and would also be viewed from a lily pool terrace above. Brookes was delighted with the commission as he was passionionate about herb gardens and was on the council of the Herb Society at the time, the Society's president being a Sussex neighbour.[7] The first phase of the project was to design beds of herbs according to use, as in early physic gardens – cosmetic (e.g.

woad, flax, geranium), culinary (e.g. mace, dill, angelica), medicinal (e.g. valerian, comfrey, solomon's seal) and fragrant (e.g. bergamot, tansey, roses) – backed by a deep, mixed border under a sheltering brick wall (Figures 5.4, 5.5 and 5.6). The existing turf was removed for re-use on the Royal Jersey golf course, and a grassed main path running from south to north was gravelled with low plantings of thyme and terminated at the north end by a white Lutyens seat.

The areas either side of the gravel path were quartered in traditional monastic cloister garden style, abstract designs based on the square defining the planting beds. By the following summer the beds were full of colour and fragrance and, in maturity, the plants spill over, yet are contained by, the strong grid-like design (Figures 5.7 and 5.8). The second phase was to continue the herb planting to the south end of the sunken garden, immediately below the pool and an existing bed of exotic plantings (*Agapanthus*, *Echium*, *Phormium* and palms). Standard roses underplanted with *Stachys byzantina* and rue were incorporated into the design as an echo of the previous garden.

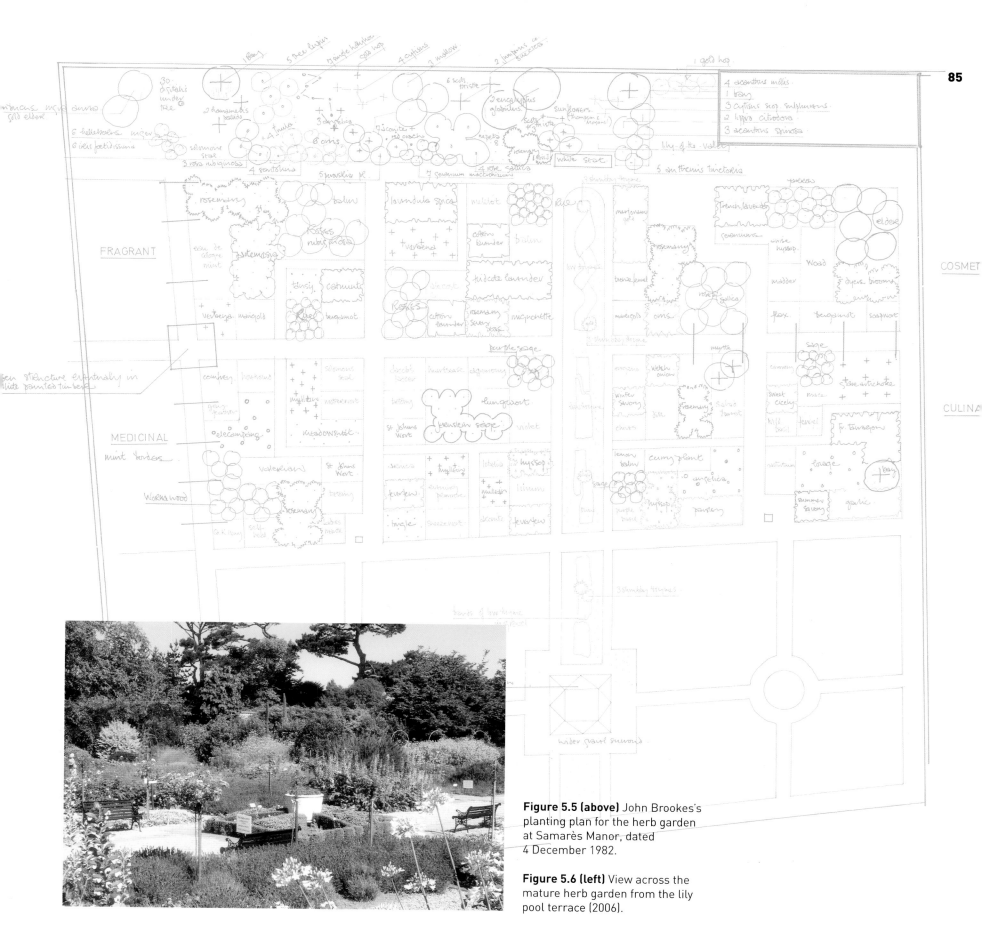

Figure 5.5 (above) John Brookes's planting plan for the herb garden at Samarès Manor, dated 4 December 1982.

Figure 5.6 (left) View across the mature herb garden from the lily pool terrace (2006).

Brookes also opened up views from the sunken garden across the parkland, on an axis with the main path through the herb garden, by removing mature plantings of *Elaeagnus* in the shrubbery.

Reshaping the planting which framed the mansion front began in the early months of 1984. Brookes's new curved beds were filled with a mix of exotic bulbs and native perennials against an evergreen foil of *Griselinia*, *Choisya ternata*, *Mahonia aquifolium* 'Atropurpurea', *Pittosporum tenuifolium*, *Elaeagnus* x *ebbingei* 'Gilt Edge', *Phormium tenax*, *Yucca gloriosa*, *Cordyline australis* and an existing palm tree. Revelling in the range of plants that can be grown in the warm Jersey climate Brookes included plantings of *Agapanthus*, *Echium*, *Helichrysum* 'Sulphur Light' and *Canna*

Figure 5.7 (below) Summer flowering in the herb garden (2006).

Figure 5.8 (right) Standard roses were retained as an echo of the early 19th-century rose garden (2006).

Samarès Manor

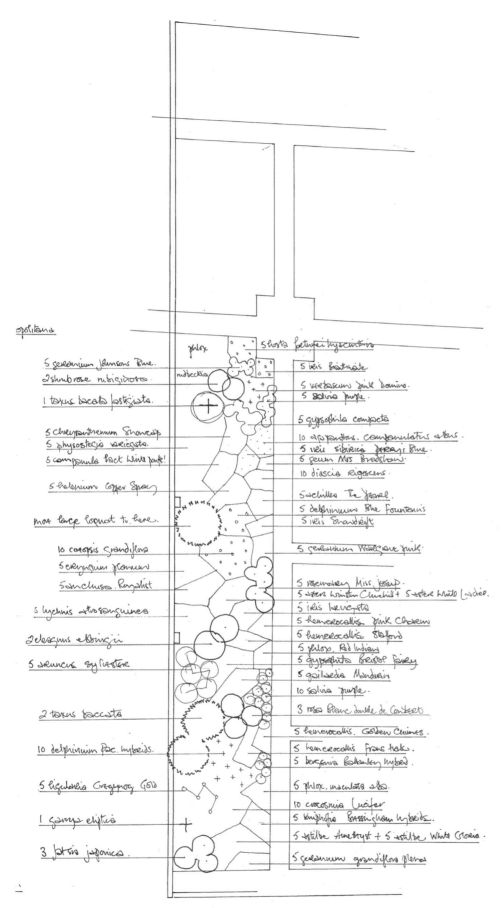

with his favoured *Euphorbia characias* subspecies *wulfenii*, *Verbascum bombycifereum*, purple and gold salvias (sage), *Kniphofia northiae* and *Alchemilla mollis*. The following year, Brookes's planting plan for the long border against the wall on the west side of the herb garden was striking in its use of flower spires to create a succession of colour from the softer blues and pinks of *Verbascum* 'Pink Domino', *Delphinium* 'Blue Fountains' and *Rosmarinus* 'Miss Jessop's Upright' to the hot *Hermerocallis* 'Golden Chimes', *Crocosmia* 'Lucifer', *Ligularia* 'Gregynog Gold' and *Kniphofia* Passingham Hybrids (Figure 5.9).

Once visitor attractions and facilities close to the house had been completed, Richard Adams and his team began to plan the development of the farmyard as an educational resource,[8] concentrating on the plant sales centre and rejuvenating the dilapidated Japanese garden. In early 1988 Brookes returned to Jersey to advise on renovation of the 1926 Japanese garden and, later in the year, replanting of trees and flowering shrubs on the northern boundary of the property. Since Japan had opened its doors in 1854, plant hunters had plundered its horticultural heritage, introducing plants such as *Magnolia stellata*, *Wisteria floribunda* and *Acer palmatum* to western gardens. Interest in Japan and its artefacts was fuelled by a series of exhibitions later in the 19th century, which featured lanterns, pagodas and other garden ornaments.[9] There were also many authoritative books on Japanese gardens, but those who could afford it sought authenticity by bringing Japanese gardeners to England to create their gardens.[10] In 1910 the Japanese-British exhibition in London included two large Japanese gardens. As its purpose was to promote trade and commerce between the two countries, it is possible that Sir James Knott, a prominent businessman, would have been aware of the garden features and plants recommended for this still fashionable style.

Sir James's Japanese garden at Samarès is reputed to have cost £50,000 and used limestone transported by ship from Cumberland, a tiered waterfall, two summer houses and many

Figure 5.9 (opposite) Planting plan for the long border in the herb garden.

Figure 5.10 (above) Early 19th-century plantings such as the *Taxodium distichum* survive in the Japanese garden (2006).

Samarès Manor

new plantings, including *Camellia*, *Magnolia*, *Rhododendron* and *Taxodium distichum* (Swamp Cypress), many still growing in the garden (Figure 5.10). By 1988 the planting was overgrown, the pool lacked definition and the buildings had been vandalized. Brookes created a gravelled, meandering path between lawns with existing specimen trees (white willows, *Metasequoia*, *Taxodium distichum* and *Catalpa bignonoides*) and clumps of

Camellia and *Magnolia* (Figure 5.11). The pool and tiered waterfall were cleared and reshaped, and the spoil from the excavations used to make contoured planted mounds on the site boundary. As in 1926, the garden 80 years later is representative of the many Japanese gardens created in the first half of the 20th century – a blend of Japanese and western features, rather than an authentic Japanese garden (Figure 5.12). A *Country Life* article pointed out

Figure 5.11 (below) Plan of the Japanese Garden, dated 4 January 1988.

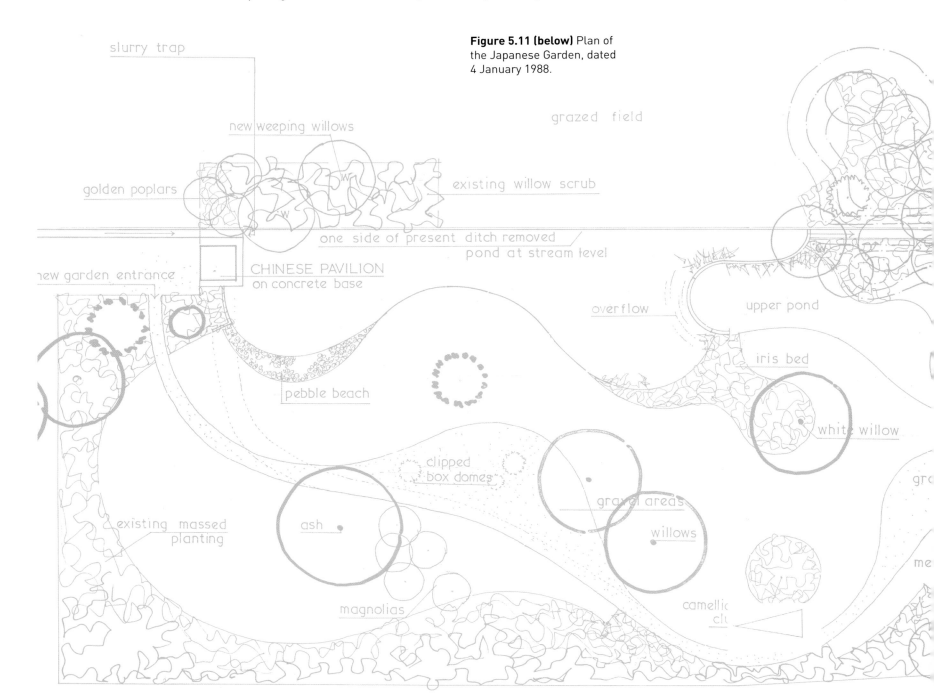

in 1915: 'The disposition of a few typical ornaments, of a bronze stork here and a stone lantern there, does not make a Japanese garden; it only makes an English garden speak with a Japanese accent.'[11] Nonetheless, whereas many of these once-celebrated Anglo-Japanese gardens are in a wild and neglected state, or have disappeared, the garden at Samarès Manor remains a well-maintained and prime visitor attraction.[12]

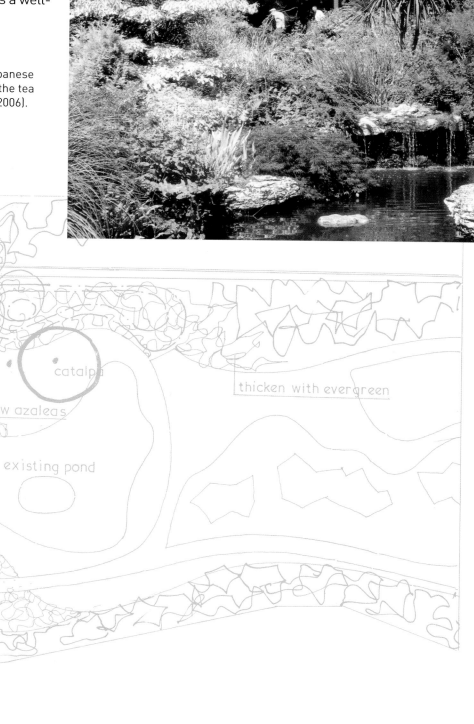

Figure 5.12 (right) The Japanese Garden with the 'ghost' of the tea house in the background (2006).

planted contoured mound
sing spoil from pool excavations

some existing scrub to remain

planted contoured mound

catalpa

thicken with evergreen

willows

low azaleas

taxodium

existing pond

fountain

azaleas

low azaleas

fountain

willow

thicken with
white flowering cherries

La Napoule

LOCATION: Cannes, France

DATE: 1985

From the early 1980s the four-week garden design courses at Clock House, Denmans, became well known as a sound grounding for those about to begin a career in garden design or, indeed, who just wanted to apply John Brookes's ideas to their own gardens. Others, already involved in landscape design, aimed to extend their skills by a greater understanding of his design philosophy. Students came not only from England but also from mainland Europe and the Americas, many returning home with both new skills and a new view of landscaping – how to 'look and see' and how to use spaces.[1] Noele Clews from New Hampshire, USA, attended one of the early courses. At the time she was also actively involved in the development of historic Château de La Napoule, west of Cannes, the first American museum abroad, created by her husband's family as a legacy for the work of sculptor Henry Clews (1876–1937):[2]

" *Nearly a century ago, two impassioned Americans left their country in search of an artist's paradise. They found a medieval castle, perched on the edge of the Mediterranean Sea, and devoted the rest of their lives to creating a haven that would nourish their artist souls.* " [3]

Figure 6.1 (right) The terrace garden after replanting, with abundant groups of *Iris*, *Echium* and rosemary.

Inspired by its location on the French Riviera with access to many cultural sites, the Château and adjoining Villa Marguerite was also to be the venue for a residential arts and cultural programme including, Noele proposed, a garden design course run by John Brookes. Brookes visited the Château, was enchanted by its magic and taught three-week courses there throughout the 1980s, introducing notable contemporary garden and landscape personalities, such as James van Sweden, Michael Laurie, Rosemary Verey and Isabelle Green. During this period he was also involved in replanting part of the 2.5-ha walled garden (Figures 6.1, 6.2, 6.3, 6.4 and 6.5).

The formal gardens at Château de La Napoule were first laid out by the architect Marie Clews, Henry Clews's wife, from 1918, when they acquired the dilapidated property as an escape from war-torn Europe.[4] Considered a brilliant eccentric, Henry had left his native New York in 1914 to pursue an artist's life in Paris, but his move to La Napoule allowed the creation of a fantasy world. He embellished the 14th-century Gothic-style castle with neo-medieval features and his own whimsical and fabulous monsters, 'sculptured demons and familiars of his visions... scaly sea monsters... beak-nosed gargoyles' (Figures 6.4 and 6.6).[5] In contrast, Marie's green garden rooms with fountains, topiary, white flamingos, peacocks and deer created a sense of tranquillity. When Henry died in 1937 he was buried in an ancient tower of the Château with, it is said, the tomb left slightly open so that his soul could escape 'To come at eventide as sprite/ And dance upon the window/ Sill'.[6] Marie was buried alongside him in 1959 having set up the La Napoule Art Foundation in 1951.

The Clews family runs the Foundation and, by the mid-1980s, Noele Clews was involved in building restoration workshops for volunteers to repair the Villa Marguerite, at risk of demolition. Brookes, on his twice-yearly visits to run design courses and

Figure 6.2 (far left) Château de La Napoule, once a medieval castle, overlooks the Mediterranean Sea.

Figure 6.3 (left) From 1918, Marie Clews created a series of tranquil garden rooms at the Château.

Figure 6.4 (above right) Henry Clew's beak-nosed gargoyles decorate the columns at the Château de La Napoule.

Figure 6.5 (right) The tower housing the tombs of Henry and Marie Clews is adjacent to the enclosed gardens with green structural planting of palms and cypresses.

La Napoule

introduce the students to French culture by visits to museums and art galleries (Figure 6.7), began to include replanting of the main garden as a student project. He also worked on the terrace garden himself:

" *We* [John Brooke with 30–40 students] *started to restore the garden on every summer and Easter course. I used to stay in a little house in the grounds that looked out over the sea with the tomb garden where Henry Clews was buried behind me. It was stepped up in a series of three terraces with three stone walls, sandy paths and one or two palms. Over the years I started planting up the terraces using exotic plants such as plumbago, palms, echiums, rosemary that I saw in the nurseries... students sometimes gave an oil jar or other contribution for the garden.* "

Figure 6.6 (below left) Marie Clews standing amongst the monster statues at the Château.

Figure 6.7 (below right) John Brookes and students at a summer school at La Napoule in the 1980s.

There are no plans for the garden, but Brookes recorded the transformation of the terrace garden from a stark pathway to a walk bordered by a succession of massed displays, including *Echium*, white *Iris* and rosemary providing a foil to the architectural cypresses and palms (Figure 6.8).

Although garden design courses are no longer part of the programme at La Napoule, John Brookes remains on its International Advisory Board and Noele Clews is now executive director, and is planning for the next major phase in the Foundation's development.

Figure 6.8 (left) The terrace garden in the early stages of replanting, with the tower containing the Clews tomb in the background (1991).

La Napoule

The English Walled Garden

LOCATION: Chicago Botanic Garden, Illinois, USA

DATE: 1986

Figure 7.1 The entrance to the Chicago Botanic Garden's English Walled Garden is through gates painted Hidcote blue (2003).

During the early 1980s John Brookes began to lecture throughout the USA, one venue on the circuit being the Chicago Botanic Garden, 32km north of Chicago in Glencoe, Illinois. Owned by the Forest Preserve District of Cook County and inspired by the concept of Chicago as a 'city in a garden', the 156-ha Botanic Garden was developed from 1963. It officially opened in 1972 and is now one of the country's most visited public gardens and an acknowledged centre for learning and scientific research, featuring 23 display gardens and three native habitats situated on nine islands surrounded by lakes.[1]

From its founding the Garden has involved leading architects and designers, beginning with the celebrated landscape architect John Ormsbee Simonds, whose masterplan with Geoffrey Rausch affirmed his belief in designing 'experiences' rather than places or things. The Garden's first building in 1977 was an Education Centre by the Modern Movement architect Edward Larabee Barnes; the 5.7-ha Japanese stroll garden (1982) was designed by Elizabeth Hubert Malott; and the recent lakeside planting is by Wolfgang Oehme and James van Sweden.[2]

Figure 7.2 (left)
Preliminary sketches
for the Chicago
Botanic Garden's
English Garden, 1986.

John Brookes's involvement began in 1986, his brief being to design a complex of English gardens (Figure 7.1) adjacent to the main building but, to his frustration, in a traditional manner: 'At last, I had thought, a modern garden to work within – and I end up doing something traditional! Because, of course, that is the way England is perceived by North Americans. For, after long discussions, I discovered it was the National Trust look that they craved'.[3] Reluctant to develop a pastiche garden in the manner of Sissinghurst Castle or Great Dixter, Brookes proposed linked garden rooms that would highlight aspects of English garden design through the centuries and convey a sense of 'Englishness':

> *To put one's finger on what constitutes an English garden is quite difficult – for the periods change. A walled garden conjures up the image of a 19th-century vegetable garden, with perennial borders, cordoned fruit, a quartered garden with a bothy and hot beds... But what of the cottage garden, the town garden, and the country garden? These are all other types and styles which come to mind. So I decided on a series of gardens, each having a change of mood.* [4]

Figure 7.3 (below) John Brookes's preliminary sketches were developed into a formal geometric design.

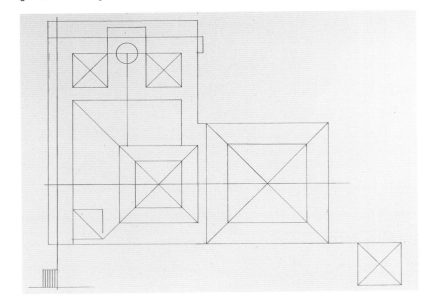

Brookes's sketches and drawings trace the development of his design concepts from early experiments with the underlying pattern (Figures 7.2 and 7.3) to the outline garden plan (Figure 7.4). Completed in early 1988, the rectilinear design on several levels takes advantage of the site's slope towards a lake:

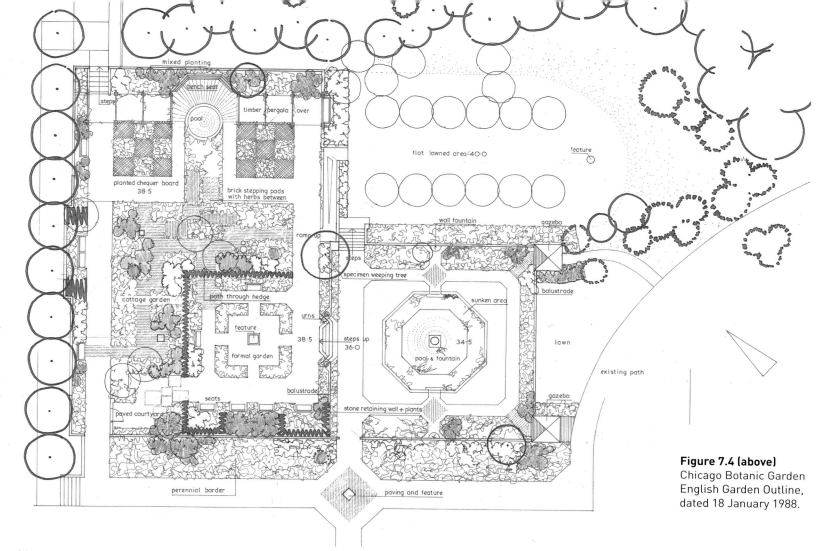

Labels within the figure:
mixed planting
bench seat
steps
pool
timber pergola over
planted chequer board 38·5
brick stepping pads with herbs between
flat lawned area 40·0
feature
wall fountain
gazebo
ramp up
steps
specimen weeping tree
cottage garden
path through hedge
urns
sunken area
balustrade
feature
38·5
steps up 36·0
34·5
lawn
formal garden
pool & fountain
existing path
seats
balustrade
gazebo
paved courtyard
stone retaining wall + plants
perennial border
paving and feature

Figure 7.4 (above)
Chicago Botanic Garden
English Garden Outline,
dated 18 January 1988.

" *The layout contained five sections, although elements of these could be sub-divided. We therefore had a small town garden, a cottage garden with a herb garden, a pergola walk and Chequer Board adjoining with a circular pool, a formal daisy garden, and at the lowest level a sunken garden with two little structures overlooking the lake, I called pepperpots.* "[5]

Creating the outline plan, however, was only the beginning of a process that involved co-operation with architects, landscape architects, contractors, nurserymen and gardeners as well as the Botanic Garden trustees. Chicago has an extreme climate with very hot summers and bitterly cold winters, which Brookes learnt not only needed to be taken into account for planting plans, but also in the preparation of construction drawings. For example,

local landscape architect Scott Byron scrutinized Brookes's drawings to ensure that they conformed to USA regulations, particularly in the use of 1-m footings in concrete throughout the site, required for even small walls because of the severe winters.

As all climbing plants (apart from some *Wisteria*) used are deciduous, the existing walls of the garden and several new brick walls were reconstructed with textured brick or had latticework panels inserted in order to break up the 'bricky' effect during the bare winter months. Internal compartments were created with 2-m-high specimens of yew, and Brookes also insisted that apple trees were sourced 'to make the bones' of the garden. To create a period feel, particularly in the formal and sunken gardens, reconstituted stone balustrades, columns, urns and finials were imported from Chilstone Garden Ornaments in Kent, England (Figure 7.5).

vation across sunken area to lake

vation up steps to small formal garden

le elevation and wall fountain in sunken garden

Figure 7.5 (above) Sketch of the proposed elevations for the sunken and formal gardens.

By September 1988, Brookes was ready to prepare planting plans for the Garden – with the reassurance from the Botanic Garden's chief horticulturalist Gaylon Gates that local hardy plants would be used for any inappropriate suggestions: 'They translated English plants into those that would survive.' Brookes also spent time with the gardener David Laubaucher discussing the English way of using plants, and comments that 'It's at this nuts and bolts stage that you realize how very different our approach to planting is – the English prefer planting near the edge of the border to soften the divide between earth and paving for instance, and the interplanting of lilies through other things'.[6]

Prior to the official opening of the Garden by Princess Margaret in October 1991, Brookes explained his rationale for the design and planting of the main areas within the English Walled Garden.[7] The entrance to the Garden is through tall wooden gates painted 'Hidcote' blue, on either side of which are 4-metre-wide mixed borders.

" *The Courtyard, approached through a creaking timber gate is intended as an urban green enclosure – the type which many an older London garden might have between street and front entrance. Usually in shade, the plants are selected for their foliage interest rather than their flower colour. A mixture of brick paving with mellow stone completes this random urban mood.* "

103

" *The Cottage Garden concept is curiously English, for its mixed flowery content is unconscious, and as you walk through its meandering brick paths its romance should be enhanced by fragrances, by butterflies and insects collecting their pollen. The plantings of the cottage garden should encompass and overwhelm the visitor in its midst, and truly represent the essence of a bygone era [Figures 7.6, 7.7 and 7.8]. [The 'tumble' of plantings included* Alchemilla mollis, Hosta, *roses,* Allium, Nepeta mussinii, Delphinium *and* Aquilegia, *many spilling over the edges of the brick paths or twining around pergolas.]* "

Figure 7.6 (above) Detail from the planting plan for the Cottage Garden, 5 September 1988.

Figure 7.7 (above right) Herbs, vegetables and flowers mingle in the Herb Garden (2003).

Figure 7.8 (right) A profusion of roses clothes the pergola in the Cottage Garden (2003).

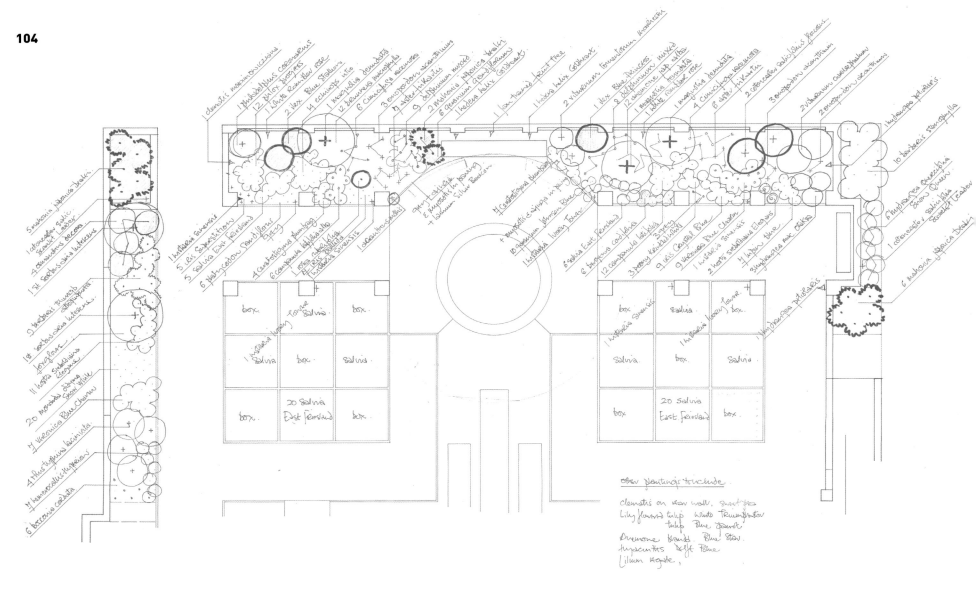

Figure 7.9 (above) Planting plan for the Pergola Garden, dated 5 September 1988.

Figure 7.10 (opposite) View across the chequer-board planting of box and grey-leaved *Artemesia* to the Pergola Garden (2003).

" *The Herb Garden is part of the Cottage Garden – the working end perhaps. But in this concept herbs are not divorced entirely, rather mingled as happened in the cottage muddle; and used as well between stepping stones so that their fragrance is released when walked upon. Herbs are used only for decorative effect, they are not segregated into categories.* "

" *The Pergola Walk is reminiscent of the gracious arcades of the Edwardian garden. The rustic timber horizontals support in their season cascades of wisteria, of rambler roses and clematis all mixed up* [Figures 7.9 and 7.10]. "

" *The Circular Fountain Pool is the central feature of the Pergola Walk. Its wide raised surround is for casual seating, and a slight deterrent to children. The fountain itself is not intended as a sculptural feature, rather the gentle flop of its water from a concealed source below water level is intended to cool the summer air, and be reminiscent of summer days in an English garden.* "

> " The Chequer Board is a series of square beds whose planting alternates between box wood and grey artemesia. Hyacinths or tulips in spring will replace the grey. This strong pattern is intended to contrast with the softer neighbouring planting, and counterpoise the geometry of the Pergola Walk.

> " The Daisy Garden is a formal flower garden enclosed eventually by high evergreen hedges. The layout will centre upon a piece of statuary, and will be planted with daisy flowers. Seating recesses surround the garden so that its colour and intimacy can be enjoyed at leisure. "

Brookes's bold use of brightly coloured flowers such *Rudbeckia* var. *sullivantii* 'Goldsturm' and *Aster* x *frikartii* creates a striking display in a contemporary version of English formality (Figure 7.11).

Figure 7.11 (above) Random plantings of mauve and blue flowers intensify the golden-yellow of plants in the Daisy Garden (1991).

Figure 7.12 (left above) The sunken pool under construction in the Vista Garden (1991).

Figure 7.13 (left below) Visitors relax in the Vista Garden (2003).

The Random Wall, between the Daisy Garden and the lower pavilion garden, is a field stone wall pierced by a flight of gracious stone steps. The wall is built on a slight 'batter' or at an angle in order that alpines like aubretia and alyssum may be grown to best advantage tumbling down its surface. Along the border at the base of the wall, pinks and small bulbs may be grown.

The Vista Garden contains an octagonal sunken pool which is reminiscent of one similar at Great Dixter in Kent – the garden of the late horticultural writer Christopher Lloyd... The pool is surrounded by a rough stone wall in which alpines and rockery subjects are grown. The effect is generally relaxed. The pool itself is planted with waterlilies, flag irises and white arum lilies [Figures 7.12 and 7.13].

Despite his initial reluctance to create an English garden abroad, the English Walled Garden is an imaginative and contemporary version of traditional English garden styles. The project has also established an educational resource for the Chicago Botanic Garden, which now produces information on 'English-style garden plants for the Midwest' and 'Design ideas for your garden from the English Walled Garden'. Brookes has since returned to the Botanic Garden to create a 'lookout' from the Walled Garden over the lake and the waterside planting of Oehme and van Sweden, which he greatly admires (Figure 7.14). The English Walled Garden was awarded the Horticultural Society of Chicago's Hutchinson Prize in 1998.

Figure 7.14 (above) The 'lookout' provides views from the enclosed English Garden across the lake (2003).

Englewood Place

LOCATION: Albany, USA

DATE: 1987

The city of Albany, situated on the Hudson River and the capital of the State of New York, lies 233km north of New York City. The city, in area 56.6 square kilometres, is the fourth-oldest continually-inhabited city in the USA and in the fourth-largest urban area.[1] Green space is at a premium, yet the area contains the only sizeable inland pine barrens (plant communities that occur on dry, acidic, infertile soils dominated by grasses, forbs, low shrubs, and scattered trees) and sand dunes in the country, and four lakes exist within its city limits. One of the largest lakes, with a surface area of just over two hectares, is in Washington Park, the 19th-century park adjoining Englewood Place, north-west of the city centre (Figure 8.1). The 32.8-ha park's design was originally conceived in 1868 as the centrepiece

John Brookes Garden and Landscape Designer

Figure 8.1 (below left) Map of
Washington Park by W.S. Egerton,
dated 1892.

Figure 8.2 (below) John Brookes's
undulating lawn and low planting
create a visual transition from the
garden to surrounding parkland (1993).

of a network of Albany parks by Frederick Law Olmsted (1822–1903), one of the USA's leading landscape architects, in a naturalistic style with serpentine roadways, wooded glades, open meadows and a lake.[2] It was opened to the public in 1871, but continued to be developed under park superintendent William S. Egerton who planted trees and flowering shrubs, created formal gardens and installed monuments and structures, including a footbridge over the lake.

The houses in Englewood Place, now part of Washington Park Historic District and on the US *National Register of Historic Places*, were built from 1879 with access to the lake circuit drive to enable residents to enjoy the Park's country atmosphere. When John Brookes first visited the converted carriage house (once attached to a turn-of-the-century house since demolished)

on a 0.5-ha plot, he was excited at the challenge of integrating a contemporary garden design with the historic landscape.[3] His first task was, therefore, to form a link between the house, the front garden and the surrounding Park (Figures 8.2 and 8.3):

" *The house had looked onto the rolling greenery of an Olmsted park. So rather than the garden design rolling up to the park, the park had to roll down to the house, with a contoured extension to screen a boundary wall on the right-hand side of a newly aligned driveway and forecourt. Bold, curving masses of plant material are in scale with the grassy sward and trees beyond. Simplicity was important, and an uninterrupted view into the park beyond.* " [4]

Figure 8.3 (left) The realigned drive at Englewood Place curves from the house and front garden to Washington Park (2003).

Figure 8.4 (above) Bold sweeps of planting on the front lawn (2003).

Figure 8.6 (right) The bluestone terrace is a cool sanctuary during the hot Albany summers.

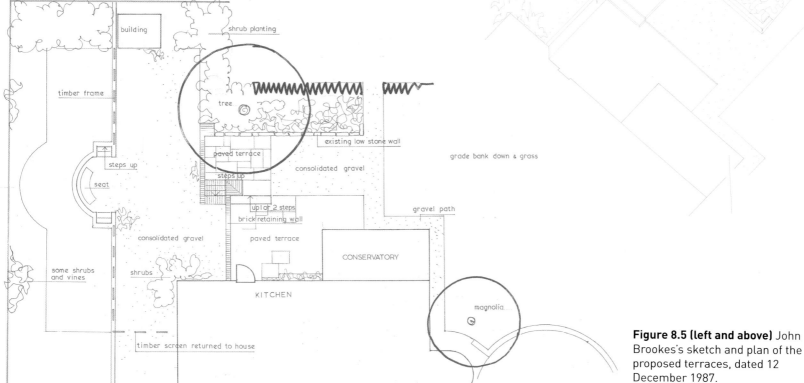

building

shrub planting

timber frame

tree

paved terrace

existing low stone wall

grade bank down & grass

steps up

consolidated gravel

seat

steps up

up 1 or 2 steps

gravel path

brick retaining wall

consolidated gravel

paved terrace

CONSERVATORY

some shrubs and vines

shrubs

KITCHEN

magnolia

timber screen returned to house

Figure 8.5 (left and above) John Brookes's sketch and plan of the proposed terraces, dated 12 December 1987.

Brookes's plans for the layout of the front garden clarify the practical steps taken to achieve his vision of an integrated landscape. These included: removing an existing rockery to ensure a smooth visual transition from lawn to park; creating a serpentine driveway to a newly gravelled forecourt in front of the house; reducing a wall to ground level beside the drive where the ground dropped down to the park; ground contouring on the same boundary to give the illusion that the park is an extension of the garden – a form of 'borrowed landscape'; and large simple

sweeps of planting, including juniper, *Perovskia* 'Blue Spire' and grasses (Figure 8.4). Albany experiences heavy winter snowfalls and this was also accommodated: 'When working with contoured shapes, it is important to remember the practicality of good drainage and particularly so in regions where there is heavy snowfall and subsequent melt... The ability to clear winter snow from the drive with ease was essential... The simple shapes of the design will make the clearance of snow more straightforward by machine'.[5]

Figure 8.7 (right) *Acer shirasawanum* 'Aureum' trees at the corners of the rectangular pool thrive in the warm courtyard.

Figure 8.8 (below right) Steps lead up to the sunny middle terrace, which provides the perfect germination ground for self-seeding plants.

Figure 8.9 (right) The gravel terrace with summerhouse, summer planting, pot and sculpture (2002).

Figure 8.10 (below) Apple trees terminate the view at the end of the top terrace (2003).

The garden to the rear and side of the house was constructed as a series of terraces, rising from a courtyard adjacent to a conservatory (Figure 8.5).The kitchen at the rear of the house originally looked towards a rather dark and dreary courtyard, the centre of the U-shaped home. Brookes recommended that the kitchen was re-orientated so that the breakfast space faced the terraces across a small balcony and the working area had views to the terraces.

The courtyard was re-designed with a bluestone terrace, the surround gravelled in a pale-coloured imported stone (Figure 8.6). A central rectangular pool was created and each corner planted with an *Acer shirasawanum* 'Aureum', these elegant, slow-growing trees with soft, yellow leaves surviving the harsh Albany winters in the warm, sheltered courtyard (Figure 8.7). Shaded by a mature *Cerdiphyllum japonicum* (katsura tree), this area has become a cool sanctuary in the heat of summer.

Planting plans included white or pale-coloured plants under the tree, drifting into the hotter colours of *Rhododendron*, day lilies, red *Aster*, *Astilbe* and *Coreopsis*, their bright hues highlighted by views through to the rolling green lawn at the front of the house. From the paved terrace, steps rise to a sunny, gravelled terrace with lush native and exotic planting (Figures 8.8 and 8.9) and then to the top terrace, also gravelled but surrounded on three sides with deep mixed borders (Figure 8.10). Brookes's planting suggestions included a profusion of flowering shrubs (including *Mahonia japonica* Bealei Group, *Weigela* 'Bristol Ruby' and *Viburnum farreri*) interwoven with the paler colours of climbing and shrub roses, *Phlox*, *Aquilegia* and other cottage garden plants. The owners have developed the garden over the years, adding a fountain on the top terrace, a summerhouse (designed by Brookes) and additional planting, making it a true 'outdoor room' to suit their lifestyle.

Barakura English Garden

LOCATION: Tateshina, Japan
DATE: 1989

Figure 9.1 (opposite) View along the gravel path, overhung with flowering shrubs, and through the rose-covered pergola.

Figure 9.2 (above) *Hemerocallis* grows wild in the fields in Nagano, Japan, near Tateshina Heights.

Tateshina Heights in Nagano prefecture, north-west of Tokyo, is a 1,200–1,600-m-high plateau extending along the north-western foot of the volcanic Yatsugatake Mountain range. The stunning landscape features hot springs, highland lakes and rich greenery, with cherry blossom and alpine plants flowering from spring to autumn each year in temperatures up to 30°C. In winter, however, temperatures drop well below freezing point (down to −20°C) and the snow-covered mountains become a popular ski resort. John Brookes was therefore surprised to receive a request to create a romantic English garden there as the setting for an English-style house under construction for Eugene Yamada and his sister Kei, a fashion, fabric and garden designer. Passionate about the British way of life, the Yamadas planned to establish a cultural centre, the Barakura English Garden, associated with their family company, the Kowa Creative Art Company (established 1950) (Figure 9.1).[1]

Brookes's first meeting with the Yamada family was in London in 1989, when they were joined by Edward Clark (of Clark Stonemasons Ltd) and Dennis Woodland (Hilliers Nursery), who were also to be involved in the project. The family also visited Brookes at Denmans Garden before he travelled to Japan. He recalls 'I flew via Alaska, eventually reaching a house in the mountains, a huge site covered in snow. How was I to make an English garden in this?'[2] On later visits, however, in more clement weather, he was able to appreciate the wealth of native species – bamboos, ferns, *Hosta*, *Geranium*, *Iris sanguinia*, *Azalea*, 'exhilarating' swathes of pale orange *Hemerocallis* and the material for a 'white garden' – *Actinidia*, *Philadelphus*, *Astilbe* and *Polygonatum* (Figure 9.2).[3]

Barakura

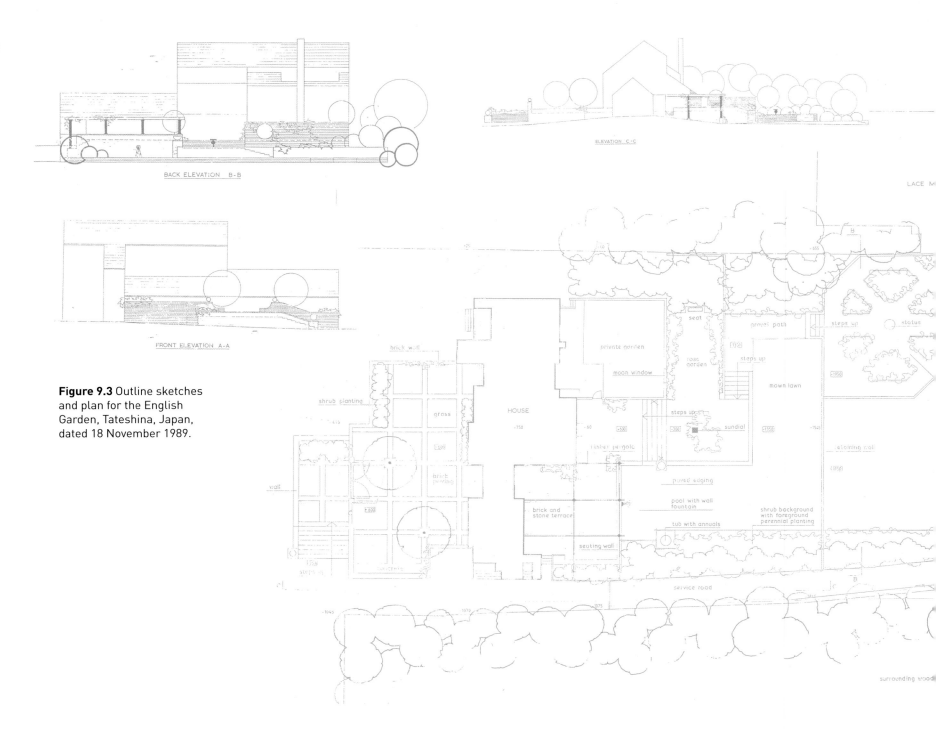

BACK ELEVATION B-B

ELEVATION C-C

FRONT ELEVATION A-A

Figure 9.3 Outline sketches and plan for the English Garden, Tateshina, Japan, dated 18 November 1989.

Brookes developed a scheme for the 10,000-square-metre site, taking advantage of the natural levels, progressing from a strong rectilinear formality around the house to informal lawns and planting beds, linked by serpentine walks (Figure 9.3). As at the English Walled Garden (Chicago Botanic Garden) begun a few years earlier, at Barakura English Garden he devised a fusion of English styles, in this case tempered by his observations of the Japanese landscape and native plant groupings. The entrance to the house (which also functions as a shop and tea room) is via a broad flight of steps to a courtyard. On the garden side of the house, a raised visitors' terrace of brick and stone with a random stone wall is surmounted by a stone and timber pergola, covered

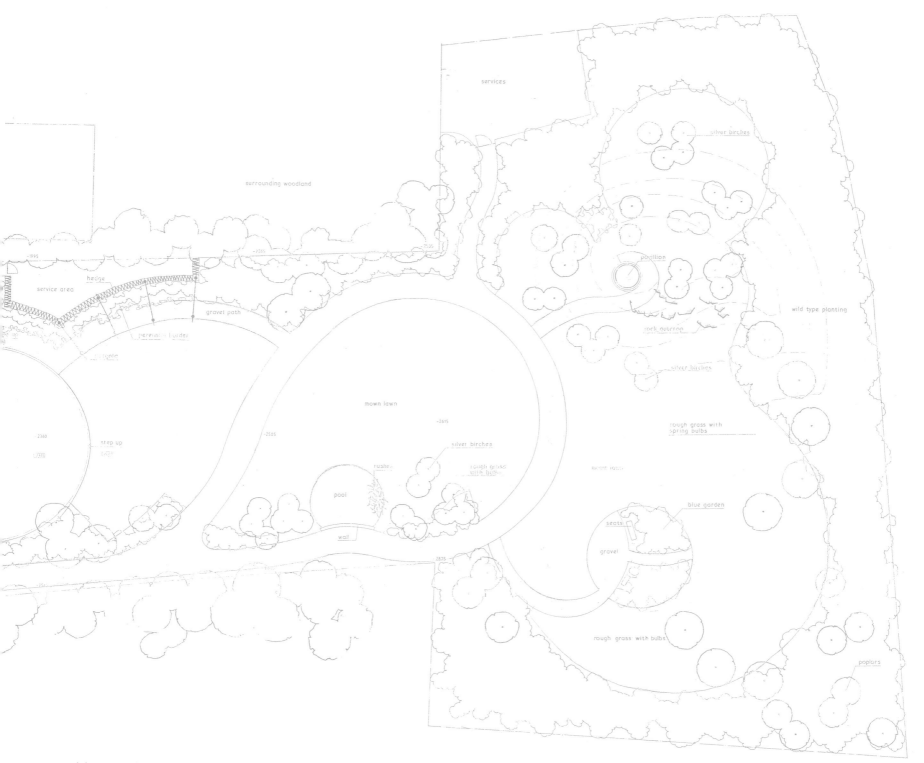

with roses in the summer months (Figures 9.4, 9.5 and 9.6). At the base of the terrace is a lily pool and further down on a lower level a planted gravel garden. Adjacent to the terrace, and accessed only from the private part of the house, Brookes has designed an enclosed garden for the owners' use with a moon window, modelled on that at the Sesshuji Temple in Kyoto. The window gives views through to the lace garden (planned to form the entrance to an unrealized lace museum) with its feathery, silver, white, mauve and pink plantings, including *Artemesia* 'Powis Castle', *Hydrangea paniculata* 'Grandiflora', *Digitalis purpurea* and *Gypsophila* 'Rosenschleier'. 'Englishness' at Barakura is perhaps most clearly encapsulated in an Edwardian-style pergola with stone pillars, solid wooden cross beams and exuberant mixed borders backed by a 1-m-high yew hedge (Figure 9.7). Seats give views over a tranquillity of mown lawns, a pool and a blue garden (with *Hebe* 'Autumn Glory', *Buddleija* 'Empire Blue', *Perovskia* 'Blue Spire', and *Rhododendron* 'Blue Peter' amongst the plants specified on Brookes's planting plan), the underlying abstract pattern here based on the circle. Inspired by native plant groups,

Brookes has also created areas of rough grass with bulbs, a Japanese-style wild flower meadow, including the yellow *Hemerocallis* of the local mountainside. At the garden boundary the designed landscape merges into the surrounding woodland by dense plantings of native bamboo, trees, such as *Betula pendula*, *Butilis* vari. *jaquemontii* and *Prunus lusitanica*, with specimen *Liriodendron tulifera* (tulip trees).

The Yamadas preferred to employ an English head gardener to ensure an 'English' approach to maintenance, but as work permit regulations limited the time each gardener could stay in Japan, the garden initially suffered from a constant change of supervision. However, now in its maturity, the Barakura English Garden has just celebrated its 25th anniversary, testament to the viability of a garden not only recognizably English in style and features, but also in tune with the local landscape (Figures 9.8 and 9.9).

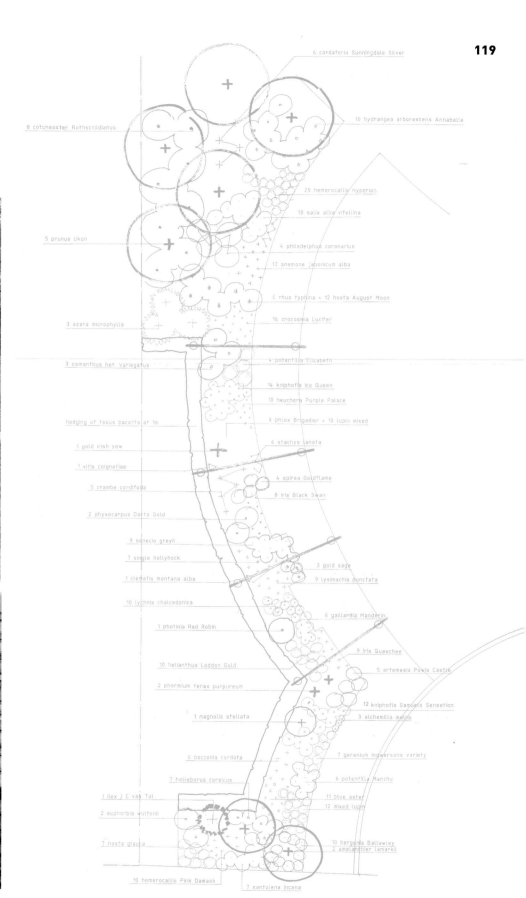

Figure 9.4 (opposite) View of the visitors' terrace from above.

Figure 9.5 (below) The visitors' terrace from below showing the random stone wall below which is the lily pool.

Figure 9.6 (bottom) Detail of the lily pool.

Figure 9.7 (right) Planting plan for the pergola garden, dated 14 December 1989.

6 cordateria Sunningdale Silver

8 cotoneaster Rothschildianus

10 hydrangea arborescens Annabelle

5 prunus Ukon

20 hemerocallis Hyperion

10 salix alba vitelina

4 philadelphus coronarius

12 anemone japonicum alba

8 rhus typhina + 12 hosta August Moon

3 azara microphylla

16 crocosmia Lucifer

3 osmanthus het variegatus

4 potentilla Elizabeth

14 kniphofia Ice Queen

10 heuchera Purple Palace

8 phlox Brigadier + 10 lupin mixed

hedging of taxus bacatta at 1m

6 stachys lanata

1 gold irish yew

1 vitis coignetiae

4 spirea Goldflame

5 crambe cordifolia

8 iris Black Swan

2 physocarpus Darts Gold

9 senecio greyii

3 gold sage

7 single hollyhock

9 lysimachia punctata

1 clematis montana alba

10 lychnis chalcedonica

6 gaillardia Mandarin

1 photinia Red Robin

9 iris Queechee

10 helianthus Loddon Gold

5 artemesia Powis Castle

2 phormium tenax purpureum

12 kniphofia Samuels Sensation

1 magnolia stellata

3 alchemilla mollis

7 geranium ingwersons variety

6 bocconia cordata

6 potentilla Manchu

7 helleborus corsicus

1 ilex J C van Tol

11 blue aster

2 euphorbia wulfenii

12 mixed lupin

7 hosta glauca

10 bergenia Ballawley

2 amelanchier lamarkii

10 hemerocallis Pink Damask

7 santolena incana

" *In the Barakura English Garden, roses of all types were on the verge of bursting open. Clematis scrambled everywhere. The intense blue of delphiniums, the stately pink heads of lupins, exotic pink and white lilies, the wonderfully variegated leaves of massive hostas and the delicately drooping blooms of various fuchsias filled the borders and terrace area with color and texture. The soil of the herb garden was totally concealed by the foliage of thyme, sage, purple and green basil, yarrow, mint, lemon balm and all the traditional herbs one expects to find in an English garden. If the temperature... and the humidity of the pure mountain air had not hinted at the exotic nature of the location, I could have been standing in a garden in Kent or Hampshire back home in the UK.* "[4]

Figure 9.8 (above) View over the English Garden during construction, where the transition from formal to informal can be traced in the path layout (1990).

Figure 9.9 (right) View over the English Garden as the planting reaches maturity.

Ecclesden Manor

LOCATION: Angmering, West Sussex, England
DATE: 1992

The new Manor of Ecclesden in Angemare (Angmering), West Sussex, was created following William's defeat of King Harold at the Battle of Hastings in 1066.[1] The land was first granted to Roger de Montgomery, who was also created Earl of Arundel for his services in the battle, but through most of the Middle Ages the Manor was in monastic ownership.[2] In 1540, following Henry VIII's dissolution of the monasteries, the estate was granted to John Palmer, but it was probably not until the following century that the current house of Ecclesden Manor was built.[3] Situated on the lower western slopes of the chalk ridge of Highdown Hill, the English Heritage listed house was described by architectural historian Sir Nikolaus Pevsner as 'a long, low, comfortable, Tudor-looking building... it takes a keen eye to spot the C17 touches'.[4] Since the 17th century, additions and alterations have been made to the house, most notably from 1918 when it was purchased by Walter Butcher, one of the principal landowners of Angmering. Following Butcher's death in 1951 the house had several owners, most recently the Holland family, who bought the property with just over 4ha of land in 1989.[5]

Following extensive work to the flint house with mellow brick dressings, mullioned windows and a plain, classical doorway set in a gabled, two-storey porch (Figure 10.1), the Hollands consulted John Brookes, who had designed their

Figure 10.1 The main entrance to Ecclesden Manor, West Sussex, England. The picture shows the extended steps and planting beds by John Brookes.

Ecclesden Manor

previous garden, on the renovation of Ecclesden Manor garden. Despite the house's history, little is recorded about the development of the garden at Ecclesden Manor and it is not included in the published works of Sussex antiquarians or artists.[6] There is, however, documentation on other Sussex houses and gardens of the 17th and 18th centuries which suggests that the garden might have been enclosed and formally laid out, possibly with topiary and water features, the latter influenced by fashionable Dutch garden styles.[7] Brookes's studies in garden history have made him aware of the meticulous processes involved in garden restoration and the subsequent maintenance involved.[8] Consequently, his modernist approach to the design of a garden or landscape attached to an historic house has always been that it 'should be completed sympathetically to the original – using the same materials – pavings or plantings – but done in a current idiom'.[9] This was the philosophy underpinning his designs for Ecclesden Manor.

Brookes proposed a formal garden, 'with lots of topiary and possibly influenced by 17th-century Dutch gardens'.[10] This is reflected in the gardens around the house, where the geometric pattern underlying the design is strengthened by the formality of box balls, herb gardens, parterres, grass plats, pleached trees, rectangular pools and a Dutch-style pavilion with a steeply sloping roof (Figure 10.2). The period ambience is also enhanced by peacocks roosting in the trees of the forecourt (Figure 10.3). The front door is now flanked by broad York stone terracing and steps extended in the flint and brick of the original narrow steps, the scale in keeping with the solidity of the building. The abundance of herb planting and potted plants complements the otherwise austere hard landscaping.

Brookes's design for the garden front (Figures 10.4 and 10.5), within an existing yew-hedged enclosure on two levels, has succeeded in creating intimate garden spaces while providing enticing views to the landscape beyond: 'The porch was reinterpreted as a pavilion to look out into the park. It looks

Figure 10.2 (right) The formal pool on the lower terrace reflects the pavilion (2004).

Figure 10.3 (top) Peacocks on the lawn of the entrance court at Ecclesden Manor (2004).

Figure 10.4 (above) The garden front at Ecclesden Manor with planting by John Brookes.

Ecclesden Manor

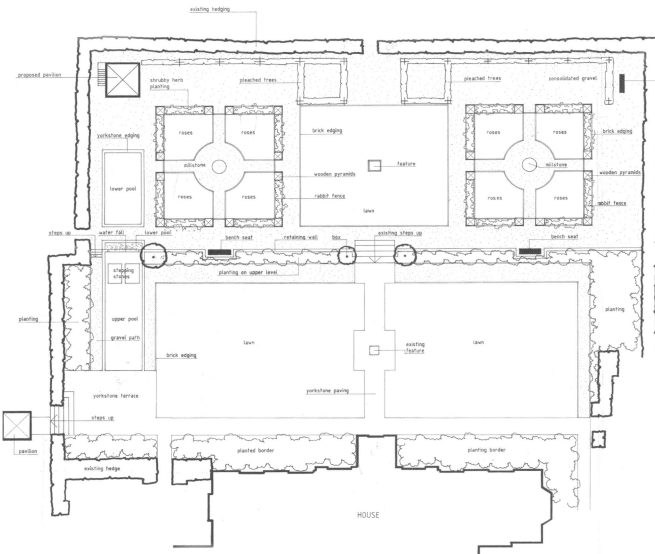

Figure 10.5 (left and below) Plan drawings for the Formal Garden, Ecclesden Manor, dated July 1993.

Figure 10.6 (bottom) View across the parterres towards the pavilion and ponds.

Figure 10.7 (opposite) Detail from drawing for the proposed screen planting, 1993.

Figure 10.8 (opposite bottom left) Brookes's informal planting at the lakeside provides a haven for wildlife at Ecclesden Manor (2004).

Figure 10.9 (opposite bottom right) The informal lake and contoured lawn provide a tranquil setting for the Manor house.

straight down to the iron gates and the lake beyond'. The austerity of the grass plats (popular in many English gardens at the time of the Civil War) is extended to the simplicity of the box-edged parterres on the lower level, with lavender now replacing the original roses as a deterrent to visiting rabbits (Figure 10.6). Haddonstone obelisks, grand stone balls and a pleached lime avenue complete the formal framework. The water garden on two levels links the terraces, the central waterfall being regulated by nozzles modelled on the ironwork on the house. Influenced by Brookes's early experiences of Islamic gardens, sited in line with the pavilion they also form a formal water body reminiscent of the Dutch-style canals of fashionable 18th-century gardens.

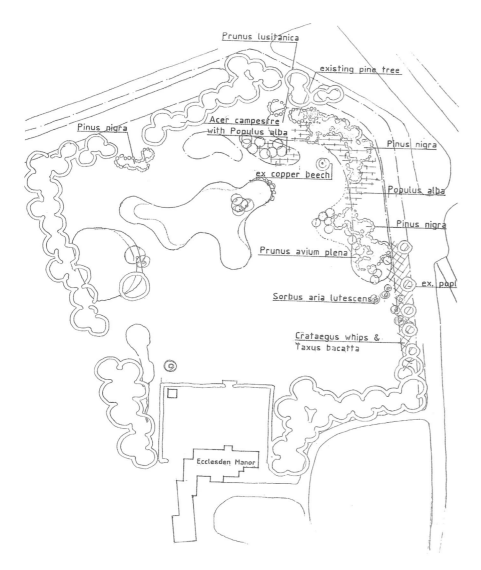

Beyond the water garden on the east side of the house, a sunny kitchen terrace adjoins sloping land, which leads up to Ecclesden Windmill, a brick tower windmill on Highdown Hill.[11] Here, Brookes advised clearing the scrub and extending existing woodland with native trees, including *Acer campestre*, *Sorbus aria*, *Alnus glutinosa* and *Quercus robur*, the new planting incorporating a lime avenue to provide boundary screening for a new lake (Figure 10.7). This more recent project was prompted by the proposed construction of the Angmering bypass with spoil from the lake excavation providing soil for ground contouring to decrease both noise and lights from the new road and to provide privacy from a footbridge. The lake, the extension of an existing pond, forms a landscape feature in scale with the grandeur of the house and gardens and forms a haven for wildlife, while the new tree-planted mounds link the garden with the surrounding countryside (Figures 10.8 and 10.9).

The garden at Ecclesden Manor received the Sussex Heritage Trust Landscape Award 2003, a scheme in which 'architects, councils, property developers and consultants compete with societies, trusts and individuals to demonstrate that with care, interest and skill, our Sussex heritage can be preserved and regenerated for the future'.

College Garden

LOCATION: Westminster Abbey, London, England
DATE: 1992

S oon after Edward the Confessor became King of England in 1042, he moved his palace to the banks of the River Thames near Thorney Island 'in the terrible place that is called Westminster'.[1] In fulfilment of a promise to the Pope in Rome, he endowed a small Benedictine monastery nearby and built a large stone church in honour of St Peter the Apostle. The abbey became known as the 'west minster', to distinguish it from St Paul's Cathedral (the east minster) in the City of London, and survived until the middle of the 13th century when Henry III began to rebuild it in the new French Gothic style. It was only completed in the early part of the 16th century, at the time of the dissolution of the monasteries, but its royal connections saved it from destruction. By 1560, however, the monks were disbanded by Elizabeth I's Royal Charter which designated the Abbey a collegiate church with a Dean and chapter of 12 canons.

Notable architects such as Christopher Wren, Nicholas Hawksmoor and George Gilbert Scott have contributed to the restoration of Westminster Abbey since that time, but there are still traces of monastic life in the Undercroft (now the Abbey Museum), originally part of the domestic quarters of the monks, the Cloisters (Cloister Garth and Little Cloister Garden) and the College Garden, named after the Collegiate Church of St Peter (Figures 11.1, 11.2 and 11.3). In early 1992, primarily with a view to developing College Garden as a commercial functions venue, John Brookes was commissioned to advise on redesign and planting schemes. He recalls 'I was thrilled to be asked. Various people had had goes at it – digging out little beds – but there was no reconciliation between the Abbey and adjoining

Figure 11.1 (top) A view from the Cloisters into Westminster Abbey College Garden, London.

Figure 11.2 (above) A view through the gate into the Little Cloister Garden at Westminster Abbey.

Figure 11.3 (right) The College Garden lawn with Westminster Abbey in the background.

College Garden

Westminster School. Much of the project was a simplification of what was already there'.[2]

The 0.8-ha College Garden is roughly rectangular in shape and on the site of the well-documented medieval Infirmarer's Garden, once used for growing medicinal herbs and foods. The garden historian John Harvey describes it 'as of outstanding importance', not only for its survival as an open space and the detailed records in the Abbey Muniment Room, but also because of the many purposes it is known to have served.[3] As well as a physic and utilitarian garden, the garden had included:

" fruit trees, a vineyard, a pool, a cider-mill, a still for distilling 'waters' from herbs, a dovecote and various houses. There were expanses of grass large enough to yield substantial amounts of hay, and... butts set up for archery... Parts of the garden were divided by hedges, palings and walls.... Posts and rails were repeatedly bought for training the vines, perhaps mainly for tunnel-arbours. " [4]

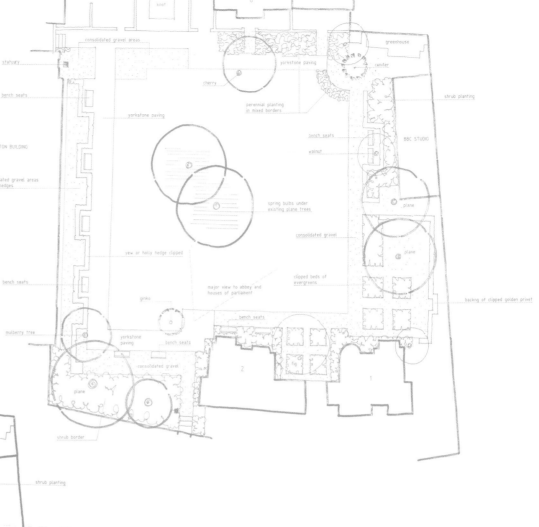

Figure 11.4 (opposite) View across the lawn with the Westminster School College Dormitory built by Lord Burlington in the 18th century to the right.

Figures 11.5 and 11.6 (right and below) Landscape proposals, dated 16 April 1992, and Landscape proposals 'Revision 1', dated 27 April 1992.

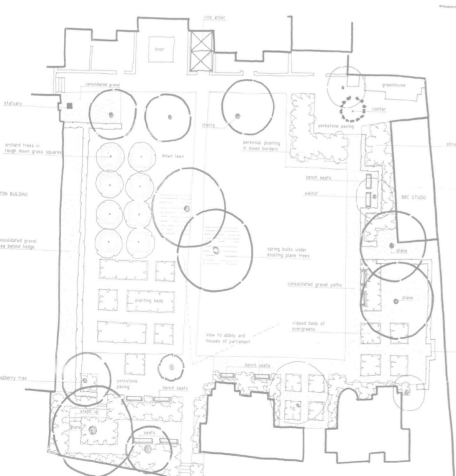

Undaunted by the site's rich history, Brookes considered his design parameters. College Garden is bounded on the east and south sides by a medieval wall with a watergate which, before the embankment, opened to the River Thames. The north side is enclosed by the great hall of Westminster School (originally the monks' dormitory) and the houses of the Abbey canons, while the west side is the School's College Dormitory, built by Lord Burlington in the 1720s (Figures 11.4). There are a number of mature trees in the Garden, including five *Platanus* x *hispanicus* (planted 1850), cherry, mulberry, fig and walnut trees and a *Ginkgo biloba* (Maidenhair tree), but also wonderful views across the roof line to the Abbey and the Houses of Parliament.

Figure 11.7 (right) Geometrically shaped beds of golden privet in the College Garden.

Figure 11.8 (left) Shrub planting with a view of the orchard trees in the lawn (1996).

When Brookes first visited the Garden, it was bisected by a stone flag path lined with wooden seats and his first drawing proposed an open central lawn with perimeter paths; his design rationale was simplicity – 'the elegant buildings could speak for themselves' (Figures 11.5 and 11.6).[5] On the west side of the Garden, clipped hedges with seat alcoves visually separate Westminster School from the Garden while on the other sides, the green architecture is echoed by hedges of golden privet, geometric beds of clipped evergreens (Figure 11.7), a knot garden and shrub and mixed beds. Spring bulbs are planted under the plane trees on the lawn. In contrast, a revised design retains the central pathway, but also draws on the historic nature of the Garden, as described by Harvey. It depicts a north-south walkway through the Garden dividing the lawn and creating medieval-style planting beds and two rows of orchard trees in rough grass squares in the west section, while the open lawn is retained on the east side. The detail of the planting beds on the perimeter remained essentially the same, although the hedge in front of the College Dormitory was simplified to a straight line (Figure 11.8).

Throughout 1993, Brookes produced detailed planting plans for an 'old-fashioned mixed border' with deep borders of shade-tolerant shrubs and ground cover under a towering plane tree to screen a concrete BBC studio in the north-east corner, and a secluded terraced area of flowering shrubs (white *Camellia*, *Pittosporum tenuifolium*, *Osmanthus decorus*, *Hypericum calycinum*) to house a dramatic statue of the crucifixion by Enzo Plazzotta (Figure 11.9). Further proposals were made the following year in response to a request for a permanent tented structure for summer functions. Based on the concept of a 'stretched' medieval-style tent in modern materials, Brookes also included an 'old garden' south of the BBC studio with a herb garden, pavilion and pergola; a 'medieval' garden with bee hives and archery lawn near the existing knot garden and a 'little topiary garden', a redesign of an existing area.

Brookes's final involvement in the Garden was several years later when he was asked to prepare plans for a new water feature. His proposal was for a narrow, planted canal running parallel to the College Dormitory flanked by mown grass. The canal would terminate at a pool on the south side of the Garden, aligned on the Crucifixion statue terrace. These designs were not implemented, however, a circular pool being constructed instead.

As with many such schemes for public or corporate concerns, changes in personnel and, presumably, financial restrictions, have meant that some of Brookes's proposals were not implemented or have been changed subsequently. For example, there is no vertical visual separation between the College Dormitory and the Garden, a boulder strip being substituted for Brookes's suggestion of a box hedge (Figure 11.10); several new cherry trees (the mature trees removed by Brookes as inappropriately placed in the 1990s) have now been planted; and a standard marquee, rather than a lighter summer structure, permanently resides on the east boundary. The underlying design

Figure 11.9 (left) The statue, *The Crucifixion*, by Enzo Plazzotta is framed by flowering shrubs on the terrace.

Figure 11.10 (right) A boulder strip replaced John Brookes's original suggestion of a box hedge for separating the College Dormitory from the Garden. Brookes's shrub planting is on the right (1997).

rationale of a simple, elegant design, easy to maintain but in scale with the surrounding historic buildings, has also become submerged in the horticulturalists' need to 'decorate with plants'. However, despite these changes, College Garden has become a popular venue for charity events and remains a tranquil space for residents and visitors, with abundant herb and bulb planting as a memory of its original function as an infirmary garden.

College Garden

Springhill Grove

LOCATION: New South Wales, Australia

DATE: 1994

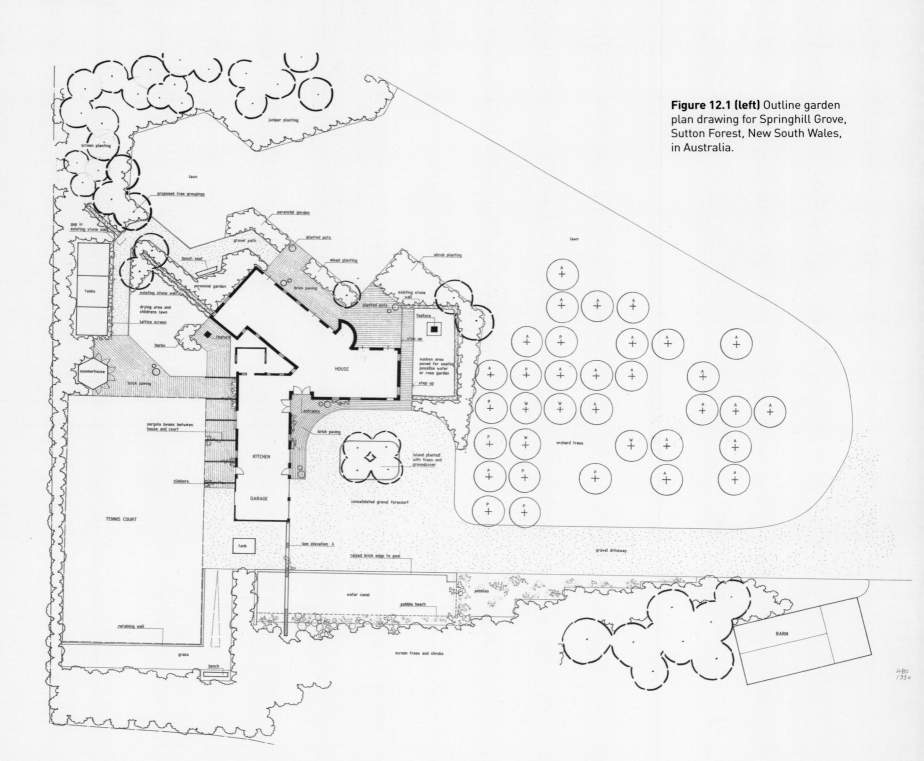

Figure 12.1 (left) Outline garden plan drawing for Springhill Grove, Sutton Forest, New South Wales, in Australia.

During the early 1990s John Brookes was invited by Landscape Publications in Melbourne, New South Wales, to speak at several conferences on garden design. His main thesis was that Australia 'is at a crossroads in its development culturally. It is now a cosmopolitan society with a European tradition meeting an Asian influx', and that Australian garden and landscape designers should now be inspired by the colours, rhythms and symbolism of their own land and history.[1] One of the delegates, a nurserywoman, had been asked to provide plants for the garden of a vineyard owner in Sutton Forrest, a town in the Southern Highlands about 130km south of Sydney, where he was building a modernist-inspired house. Taking the opportunity to discuss the project with Brookes, the nursery owner also asked him to visit the property and he was subsequently commissioned to design the garden (Figure 12.1).

New South Wales, in the south-east of the continent, is the site of Australia's first settlement by Europeans in 1788. From the early 19th century, residents of Sydney, the state capital, have built country estates to the south of the city to escape the heat and humidity of coastal summers. These Southern Highlands have an 'English feel' with rolling hills and giant pine trees, reminiscent of the 18th-century English pleasure grounds known to the first settlers. The town of Sutton Forrest is set amidst this lush green landscape, the result, as with many similar sites, of land clearing and pasture improvement over many years. The original, more extensive forest once lay between two rivers, the Bong Bong River a few kilometres north and Paddy's Creek to the south. In a temperate zone (temperatures range from 12–25°C) with marked seasonal differences, average rainfall and early morning mists, the Southern Highlands is a rich, rural, productive area renowned for the vineyards across its valleys (Figure 12.2). Brookes delighted in the colourful and varied landscape of this fertile area: 'I think that the colours, images and sounds of Australia are amazing – with red soils, gray plants, brilliant screaming parakeets overhead, and the strange call of the kookaburra'.[2]

Figure 12.2 (left) A vineyard in Hunter Valley, Southern Highlands, one of Australia's most well-known wine regions.

In 1994, during Brookes's only visit to the site, the long, low flat-roofed house, sheltered by the surrounding hills, was still under construction. Based on discussions with the owner over lunch to establish a brief, and a lengthy, solitary walk around the property and surrounding landscape, he was quickly able to visualize a design that would provide a sympathetic setting for the new house. Back home in Sussex Brookes drew an outline garden plan, the underlying abstract pattern for the main gardens being based on overlapping hexagons, perhaps inspired by the angular juxtaposition of the three parts of the house (Figure 12.3). The outline garden plan shows the approach to the forecourt as a long, gravel driveway, Brookes's much-loved orchard plantings (mainly apple trees, but with some pears and four large walnuts) in an area of approximately 500 square metres providing a strong framework on the house side. The trees are planted in rows, more thickly nearer the house to provide screening from the road and shelter for the main garden area.

The steep bank on the opposite side of the drive is planted with broad swathes of hardy shrubs, including *Cornus alba* 'Elegantissima' (a dogwood with grey-green leaves with white margins), *Prunus lusitanica* (Portuguese laurel) and the striking *Cortaderia selloana* (pampas grass), its tall, silky spikelets contrasting with the fragrant, violet-blue panicles of *Buddleija davidii* 'Empire Blue' planted above (Figures 12.4 and 12.5). Height is provided by four cherry trees and four weeping pear trees, echoing the orchard plantings nearby. Brookes's plan shows a border of pebbles at the foot of the planted bank increasing in his characteristic zigzag design to become a beach on two sides of a canal the width of the forecourt (17 x 17m). The breathtaking scale of this water feature complements the angular lines of the house, to which it is architecturally linked by a concrete ivy-covered pergola (reminiscent of 1930s modernist structures) extending across the water to the bank. Similarly on the garden side of the house a 3-metre-wide

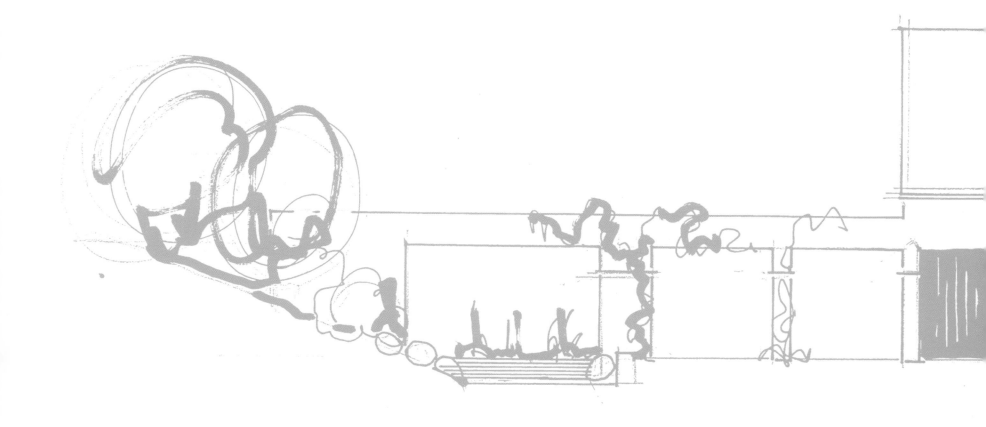

Figure 12.3 (left) Elevation drawing of the entrance courtyard at Springhill Grove.

Figure 12.4 (above left) The bold spikelets of *Cortaderia selloana* dominated the entrance to the drive at Springhill Grove.

Figure 12.5 (above right) *Buddleija davidii* 'Empire Blue', characterized by panicles of violet-blue flowers with orange eyes.

Springhill Grove

pergola (to be covered in *Wisteria sinensis*, *Rosa* 'Mermaid' and *Vitis coignetiae*) between the kitchen and tennis court extends 13m along a brick path leading to the main garden front.

The expanse of brick terrace on the garden front is relieved by box-edged blocks of lavender and rosemary alternating with primrose-coloured yellow shrub roses (*Rosa* 'Grandpa Dickson'), white tulips, *Rosa* 'Iceberg' and yellow tulips, with views across the lawns to the countryside beyond. A sunken garden adjacent to the orchard provides an alternative sheltered sitting area. A gravel path leads from the terrace to sunny perennial borders filled with the mauves, blues, pinks and soft yellows of lavender, *Achillea*, *Cistus*, *Potentilla* and *Hebe* with blocks of hot *Kniphofia* 'Fiery Fred' and *Hemerocallis fulva* hybrids (Figures 12.6 and 12.7). Groupings of *Phormium tenax* (New Zealand flax) and sweetly scented *Pittosporum tobira* provide focal points (Figure 12.8). The gravel path forms two sides of a large hexagon 15m in diameter, three further sides forming deep borders of tree and shrub plantings, enclosing an area of lawn (Figure 12.9). Here the taller boundary pines, poplars, *Amelanchier canadensis* and laurels are juxtaposed with decorative swathes of pampas grass and flowering shrubs such as *Buddleija*, *Weigela* and *Cotinus coggygria*, with purple and red dominating. A mass of low-growing junipers culminates the display.

In July 1994 Brookes sent the garden plan and three planting plans to the owner, receiving confirmation that they were approved. The plants were to be supplied by the nursery owner who had attended the conference, but there is no record of whether the plans were implemented. Notwithstanding, the ease with which Brookes was able to elicit the requirements of the owner at Springhill Grove, understand the key features of the site and respond to the pattern and topography of the surrounding landscape is his great strength. It is a well-developed natural ability also shown by his mentors Thomas Church and Geoffrey Jellicoe.

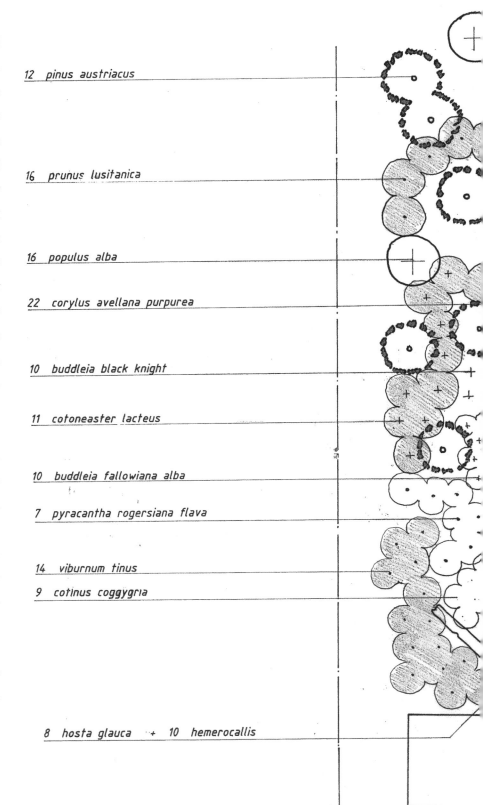

12 pinus austriacus

16 prunus lusitanica

16 populus alba

22 corylus avellana purpurea

10 buddleia black knight

11 cotoneaster lacteus

10 buddleia fallowiana alba

7 pyracantha rogersiana flava

14 viburnum tinus

9 cotinus coggygria

8 hosta glauca + 10 hemerocallis

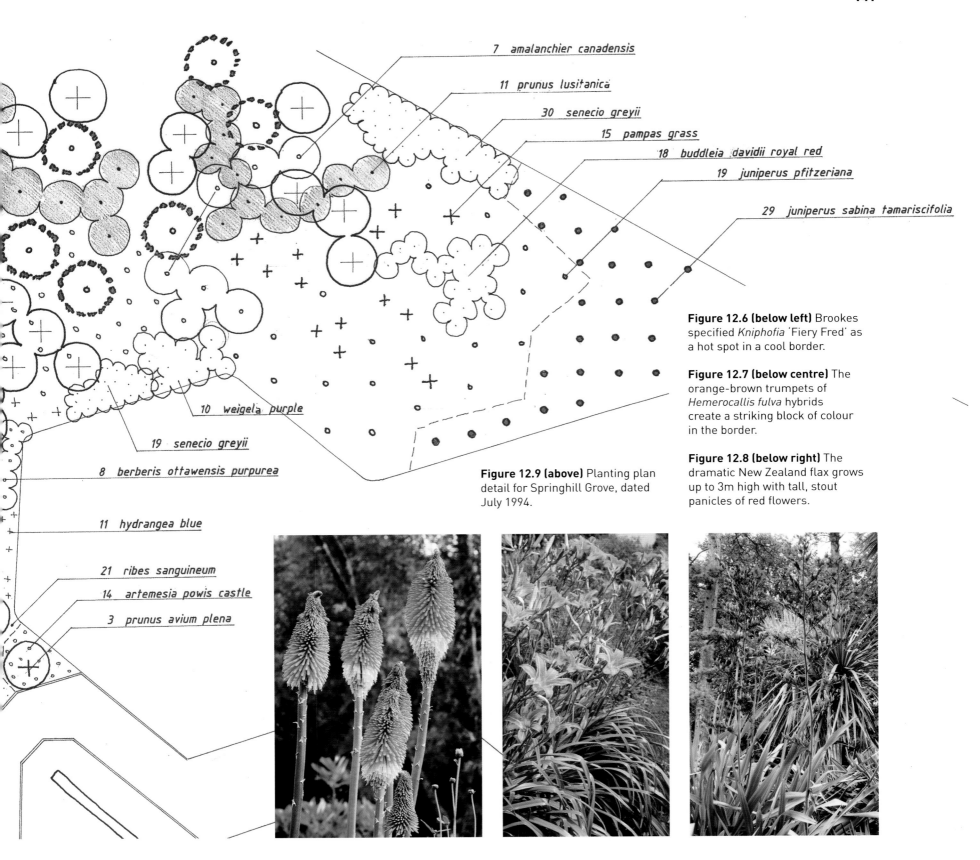

7 amalanchier canadensis

11 prunus lusitanica

30 senecio greyii

15 pampas grass

18 buddleia davidii royal red

19 juniperus pfitzeriana

29 juniperus sabina tamariscifolia

10 weigela purple

19 senecio greyii

8 berberis ottawensis purpurea

11 hydrangea blue

21 ribes sanguineum

14 artemesia powis castle

3 prunus avium plena

Figure 12.9 (above) Planting plan detail for Springhill Grove, dated July 1994.

Figure 12.6 (below left) Brookes specified *Kniphofia* 'Fiery Fred' as a hot spot in a cool border.

Figure 12.7 (below centre) The orange-brown trumpets of *Hemerocallis fulva* hybrids create a striking block of colour in the border.

Figure 12.8 (below right) The dramatic New Zealand flax grows up to 3m high with tall, stout panicles of red flowers.

The Old Rectory

LOCATION: Wiggonholt, West Sussex, England

DATE: 1994

Since John Brookes started his garden design practice in the 1960s, he has encouraged a close working relationship with his clients. His belief that knowledge of the client's expectations of a new garden and an appreciation of their lifestyle will ensure a successful design has largely been justified. He has also been rewarded by the development of a loyal nucleus of clients who, often over many years, ask him to advise on the development of the garden or to design a garden for a new house purchase, often a second (or third) home abroad. The owners of a new Arts and Crafts-style house in Wiggonholt, West Sussex, had previously commissioned Brookes to design the garden of their house in nearby Amberley. Moving nearly ten years later to an early 19th-century rectory adjoining a medieval church, they sought his advice again.[1]

Figure 13.1 (left) The stepped terraces at Wiggonholt have views over the surrounding sheep-grazed pastures (2003).

Figure 13.2 (right) Medieval Wiggonholt Church forms a focal point of the rectory garden, seen here from the entrance front of the Lutyens-style house with characteristic Arts and Crafts-style low eaves (1999).

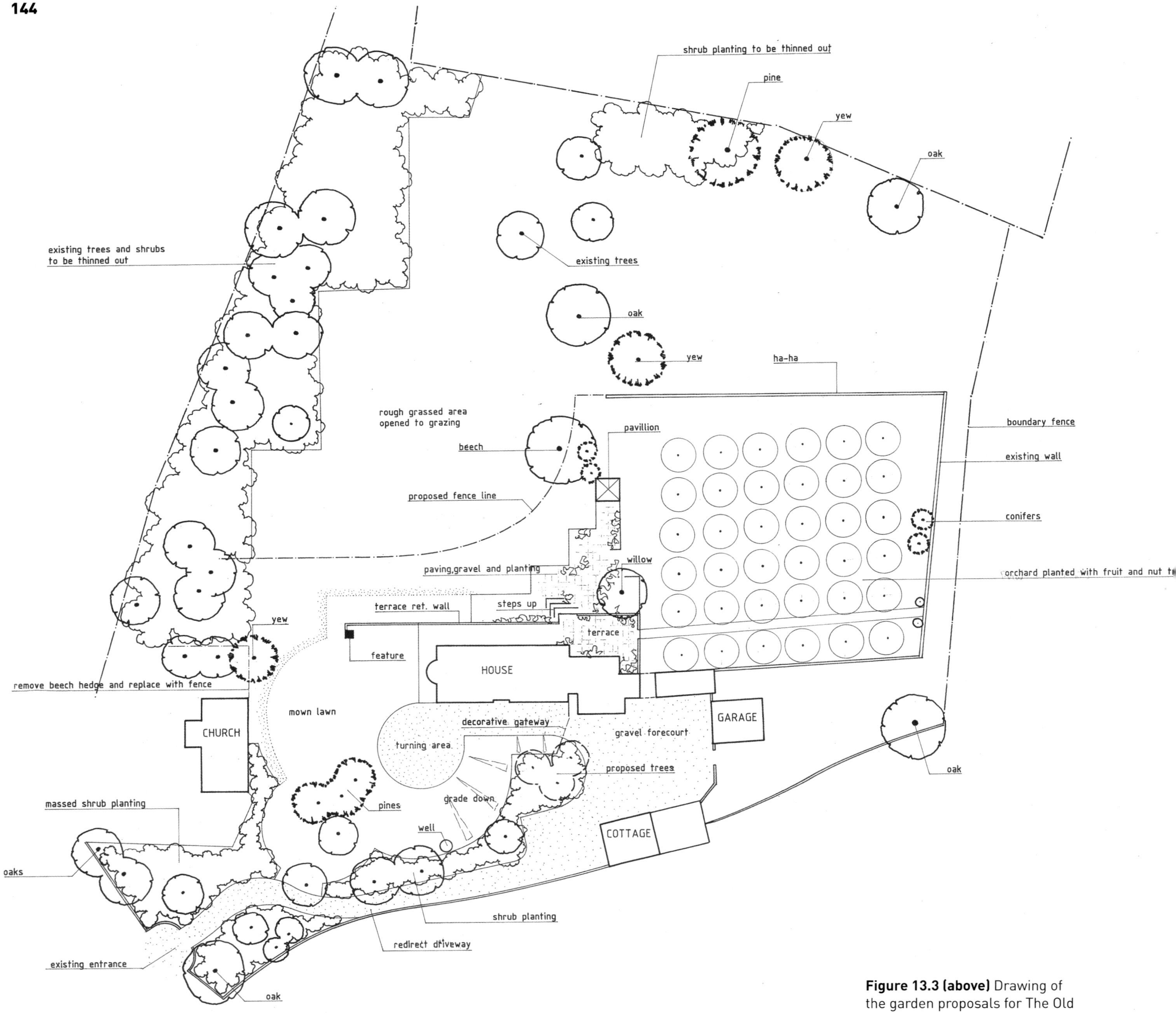

shrub planting to be thinned out

pine

yew

oak

existing trees and shrubs to be thinned out

existing trees

oak

yew

ha-ha

boundary fence

rough grassed area opened to grazing

existing wall

beech

pavillion

proposed fence line

conifers

paving,gravel and planting

willow

orchard planted with fruit and nut tr

steps up

terrace ret. wall

terrace

yew

feature

HOUSE

remove beech hedge and replace with fence

mown lawn

GARAGE

CHURCH

decorative gateway

gravel forecourt

turning area

grade down

proposed trees

oak

massed shrub planting

pines

well

COTTAGE

oaks

shrub planting

existing entrance

redirect driveway

oak

Figure 13.3 (above) Drawing of the garden proposals for The Old Rectory, dated January 1994.

Figure 13.4 (left) Views from the water terrace over the lower slopes of the garden and the hills beyond (1998).

Wiggonholt, just outside Pulborough, is an ancient parish of about 324ha, bounded on the west by the River Arun and on the east by the Pulborough to Storrington road (A283) and the River Stor. Archaeological excavation has uncovered Roman remains in the area[2] and the extant 12th-century church with a shingled bell-turret, thought to have been built for local shepherds, is evidence of its medieval history.[3] In 1848 the publisher Samuel Lewis reported that 'The church was repewed and repaired in 1839, at the expense of the Hon. R. Curzon; the rectory-house was enlarged and altered in 1838 by the incumbent, and is now a spacious residence, in the Elizabethan style'.[4] In the mid-20th century, however, the rectory had a Georgian-style makeover[5] and, when Brookes visited in early 1994, the owners had demolished the rectory completely, and were constructing in its place a house in the tradition of the Arts and Crafts architect Sir Edwin Lutyens.

At that time, the 1.6-ha sloping rectory garden had a simple layout of a York stone terrace, rose walk and shrubs around the house with a pond on the far boundary. Brookes recalls that 'They [the owners] wanted a statement without too much fuss' – they also wanted a low-maintenance garden.[6] His inspiration for the initial design in early 1994 was twofold – Lutyens's celebrated use of hard landscaping to create terraces at different levels and the position of the medieval church (Figures 13.1 and 13.2). At a later stage, on discovering that the owners had lived in Iran, where they had delighted in the sound of the water gardens there, and had read his book on Islamic gardens, Brookes added a water garden, two pools and a rill 'inspired by Islamic examples and those I have seen in Moorish Spain'.[7] Brookes's design technique is to create a module based on an architectural feature of the house (such as a bay, window or conservatory) and by overlapping and interlocking the shapes he will produce

an integrated design: 'This grid concept of evolving a garden pattern is a guide to get the designer thinking about the proportional relationship between the elements of his designs'.[8] At Wiggonholt the grid proportions were taken from the 9-metre-wide recessed bay on the garden front of the house. The underlying abstract design was based on a combination of overlapping circles (a turning area, forecourt, mown lawn with shrub borders and the boundary of a rough grassed area) and squares (the terraces, orchard and boundary planting), the latter, on plan, creating Brookes's characteristic zigzag shape (Figure 13.3).

The architectural solidity of the house is balanced by Brookes's bold treatment of the terraces, which were planned to step down to a York stone-paved seating area and pavilion towards an existing mature beech tree. The sitting area and pavilion were designed to give views over the surrounding sheep-grazed fields and the lower slopes of the garden (where Brookes had suggested sheep might also be grazed), but were not implemented (Figure 13.4). The two upper terraces feature planted gravel gardens and the water garden, the terraces being linked by broad angled steps with tiled risers – a Lutyens technique (Figures 13.5, 13.6, 13.7 and 13.8). Gravel planting included Brookes's favourite species, *Euphorbia characias* subsp. *wulfenii*, *Alchemilla mollis*, *Hebe salicifolia*, *Sissyrinchium striatum* and *Digitalis alba*, initially planted in groups but encouraged to self-seed. The rill and pools extend 16m along the top terrace, the pools being the focus of the view from the ground floor rooms (Figure 13.9). Brookes says:

Figure 13.5 (top left) Detail of gravel planting and Lutyens-inspired steps on the terraces at Wiggonholt (2003).

Figure 13.6 (centre left) The square formal pool terminates the water garden at the western end of the terrace.

Figure 13.7 (bottom left) *Sissyrinchium striatum*, *Stachys lanata*, *Verbascum* and *Euphorbia characias* subsp. *wulfenii* thrive on the sunny gravelled terraces.

Figure 13.8 (opposite) Revised outline plan of the terraces to incorporate a water garden, dated 1994.

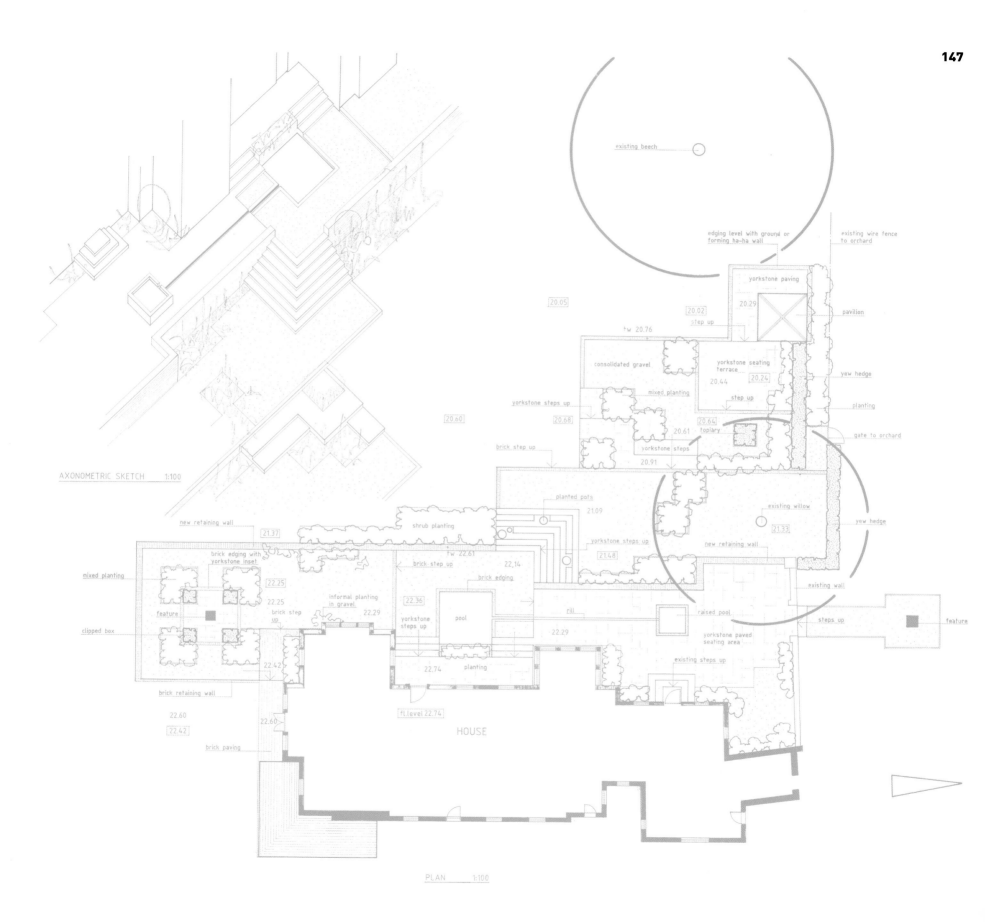

John Brookes Garden and Landscape Designer

Figure 13.9 (opposite) The Islamic-inspired water garden running along the top terrace (2003).

Figure 13.10 (left) Brookes planted the orchard with indigenous fruit and nut trees establishing a cultural link to the agricultural landscape (2003).

" *Two formal square pools are connected across the brick and gravel terrace by a narrow water channel or rill. Water appears in a gentle bubble... beneath an existing willow tree – and outside the kitchen door where meals are eaten in the summer. This pool then overflows and the rill ripples down to a larger deeper reflecting pool between the dining room and the living room.* "[9]

A small formal box-edged herb garden was added at the far end of the terrace 'to maintain the balance in the design'. The angular lines of the terrace mirrored, at a larger scale, the layout of the existing tree and shrub borders on the garden boundary.

The success of this project was marred when the retaining walls began to crack, despite having been built to British Standards specifications. They were excavated and the surveyor discovered that the builder had routed surplus water from the roof drains to the ground at the back of the walls and the heavy clay soil had prevented the water draining away. This was remedied and the retaining walls have begun to mellow as the planting matures – 'they [the owners] let the garden self-seed and ramble – glorious disarray'.[10]

Drainage was also a major consideration in the preparation of the ground in the old, partially walled kitchen garden, where the new orchard is sited, as the ancient 171-ha flood meadows at Pulborough Brooks are nearby. Since 1989, the Royal Society for the Protection of Birds has regenerated the land, restoring the biodiversity and creating a bird reserve, and around 80ha of the floodplain are inundated every winter. Drainage trenches were laid in the rectory garden and pipes inserted in the stone walls to allow surplus water to drain into the adjoining field. Based on information on suitable varieties (supplied by Horticultural Management Services, Pulborough), Brookes then planted indigenous fruit and nut trees (cob nuts, apples, pears, plums, cherries and walnuts), establishing a visual and cultural link to the surrounding agricultural landscape (Figure 13.10).

The Saltings

LOCATION: Bosham, West Sussex, England
DATE: 1997

Bosham is a small, coastal village 5km west of Chichester on an inlet of Chichester Harbour.[1] Standing on a sheltered creek, it has been settled from early times and was one of the first sites in Britain occupied by the Romans. It is close to the Roman palace at Fishbourne and, according to a local legend, Caesar landed at Bosham after capturing the Isle of Wight. The

Domesday Book lists the area as one of the wealthiest manors in 11th-century England, and the village is one of only five places that appear on the map attached to the Anglo-Saxon Chronicles.[2] In 850 AD, a church was built on the site of a Roman basilica, but in the 10th century it was replaced by the current church, dedicated to the Holy Trinity. Folklore also suggests that King Canute (who reputedly had a palace in Bosham) tried to hold back the sea from the head of the creek. Better documented is that King Harold sailed from Bosham in 1064 to meet William, Duke of Normandy, the event being portrayed in the Bayeaux Tapestry which depicts Harold, the chancel of Bosham Church and the Battle of Hastings. When

Figure 14.1 (left) Meadow planting in the orchard at The Saltings, Bosham, West Sussex, England, provides a spectacular seasonal display.

Figure 14.2 (below) Bosham village and church from across the creek (2004).

John Brookes Garden and Landscape Designer

Harold was killed in the battle, William the Conqueror took over the Manor and church of Bosham as a royal domain. By the 14th century the parish of Bosham extended to 1,214ha.

Bosham Harbour has one of the fastest-rising tides in the country and the creekside road floods each day, although for many hours at low tide the harbour bed lies exposed. Fishing and boat building have always been important trades for the village and, more recently, boating has become an important leisure activity. Described by Nikolaus Pevsner as a 'close-packed huddle of cottages at the waterside, as intricate as a Cornish village, but built to a softer Sussex colour scheme – flint, brick, tile, and tile-hanging', it is not surprising that artists and poets, such as Charles William Wyllie, Lord Tennyson and T.S. Eliot have visited or lived in the village at various times.[3] More recent residents, also attracted by the picturesque surroundings, have included a number of John Brookes's clients – 18 since his first commission there in 1972. Many have come through the personal recommendation of other village residents, as was the case in 1997 with the new owners of The Saltings, a 1926 house overlooking the creek (Figures 14.1, 14.2, and 14.3).[4]

The raised site, studded with mature pine trees, faces south-west towards the estuary into the salt-laden prevailing winds. At one stage it was also exposed to the narrow creek road, but there is now a low stone wall for protection. Without shelter from the elements, few decorative plants will grow in a seaside garden. Brookes says: 'A new garden often needs enclosing not only for privacy and screening, but for wind shelter as well. Indeed, if you live on a hill or near the sea, until you have established this enclosure there is little purpose in doing much else' (Figure 14.4).[5] Brookes's priorities at The Saltings were 'to provide enclosure and/or screening from the wind while not blocking the view'.[6] The house is accessed by a brick-edged, rolled gravel drive leading to a forecourt, continuing in a serpentine line to a secondary entrance (Figure 14.5). Brookes's outline garden plan divides the expansive gravelled forecourt

Figure 14.3 (opposite) The garden front of The Saltings with Brookes's shrub plantings framing the house and the creek as backdrop (2004).

Figure 14.4 (below) View across Brookes's planting to the creek.

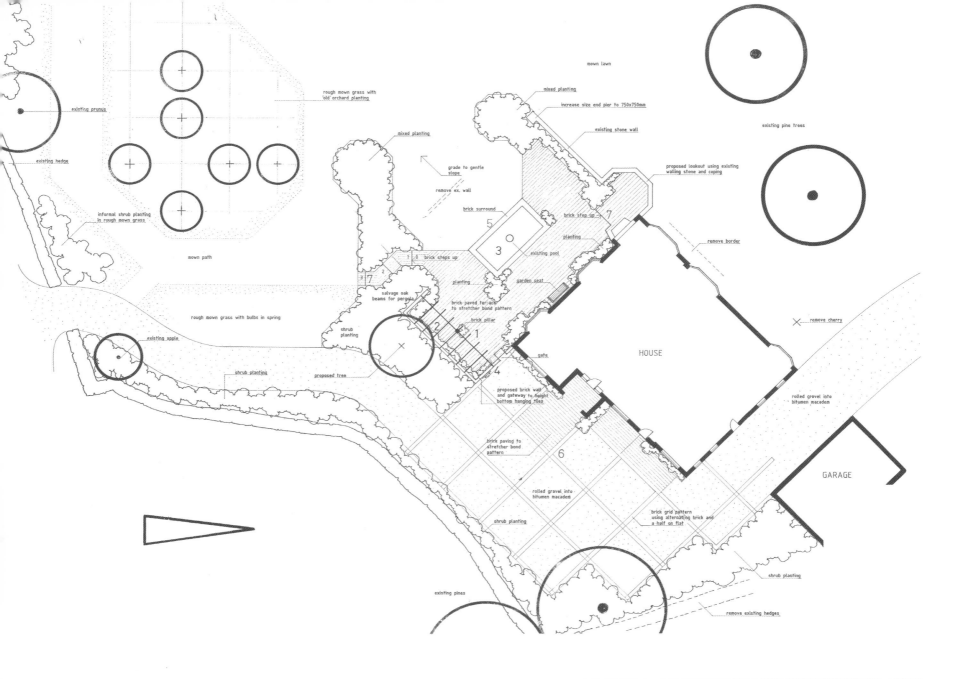

existing prunus
existing hedge
informal shrub planting in rough mown grass
mown path
rough mown grass with 'old' orchard planting
mixed planting
rough mown grass with bulbs in spring
existing apple
shrub planting
shrub planting
proposed tree
mixed planting
mown lawn
increase size end pier to 750x750mm
existing stone wall
existing pine trees
grade to gentle slope
remove ex. wall
brick surround
proposed lookout using existing walling stone and coping
brick step up
planting
remove border
existing pool
brick steps up
garden seat
salvage oak beams for pergola
brick paved terrace to stretcher bond pattern
brick pillar
planting
gate
remove cherry
HOUSE
proposed brick wall and gateway to height bottom hanging tiles
brick paving to stretcher bond pattern
rolled gravel into bitumen macadam
rolled gravel into bitumen macadam
shrub planting
brick grid pattern using alternating brick and a half on flat
GARAGE
shrub planting
existing pines
remove existing hedges

by a brick grid pattern (unrealized), a favourite detailing technique which, derived from the architecture of the building, sets the house firmly in its landscape (Figure 14.6).

At The Saltings, this large-scale grid (with modules approximately 9 square metres) is the basis for the creation of an underlying pattern of octagons. Used as concentric, tangential and overlapping shapes, Brookes demonstrates a masterly use of the technique, the angular design providing the opportunity to create intimate enclosed areas, changes in levels and stunning creekside views (Figures 14.7, 14.8 and 14.9):

Figure 14.5 (left below) Brookes's
elegant serpentine drive bordered
by the lawn, mature trees and
shrubs of the main garden (2004).

Figure 14.6 (left above) Outline
garden plan for The Saltings,
Bosham, dated October 1997.

Figure 14.7 (above) Carefully
angled brick steps draw the eye
from the terrace to the orchard
(2004).

" *The front access to the house has been screened by a wall covered with a pergola which provides shelter at the windiest time. The pergola looked onto what had been a rectangular and slightly sunken garden surrounded by grass, with a rectangular-shaped pond in the middle with a three-tiered fountain in its midst. I took off the top two layers, surrounding the pond with a terrace on three sides of brick with stone and eliminated the low surrounding walls to open the garden to mixed plantings beyond. Plant material which grows in such an exposed place is fairly limited since the wind is extremely salt-laden. Beyond the planting for shelter is a meadow garden, which thrives in the brilliant light reflected off the water.* " [7]

In contrast to the structural hardy shrub borders (including *Hebe brachysiphon*, *Elaeagnus* x *ebingii*, *Fuschi* 'Riccartonii' and *Brachyglottis greyi*) used to create shelter, screening and changing colour throughout the year, Brookes included a small orchard (near existing cherry and apple trees) east of the terrace. Set in rough mown grass with bulbs and meadow flowers, it is a spectacular feature in the spring and summer months (Figure 14.9).

Figure 14.8 (left) The pergola-covered alcove, the cross beams made from a felled oak, is a sheltered dining area in the warmer months (2004).

Figure 14.9 (opposite bottom) Brookes planted a small orchard set in rough grass to the east of the main terrace.

Casa De Campo En Oleiros

LOCATION: La Coruna, Spain
DATE: 1998

In 1998 John Brookes travelled to Spain to visit the owners of a newly constructed house and garden in La Coruna, the second largest city in Galicia in the north-west of the country. The site was high on the hillside, with views down the valley to the Bay of La Coruna and Cape Finisterre, the westernmost point of Spain, and Brookes recalls that 'there was a hell of a wind' blowing in across the Atlantic Ocean.[1] Indeed, the Ocean keeps temperatures mild and frost is rare, with average temperatures of 9ºC in winter rising to 18ºC in summer, quite unlike the hot Mediterranean climate in the south. Although in summer it is dry and sunny with only occasional rainfall, the autumn and winter months are often unsettled, with unpredictable strong winds and abundant rainfall, on average 965mm per year. Such information was of particular importance for this project as Brookes, unusually, had accepted a commission to plant a garden that had already been designed, in this case in a French formal style to complement a newly constructed two-storey, pink stucco mansion.

The owner of Casa de Campo en Oleiros, this hilltop home, had read a Spanish edition of one of Brookes's books and, living in a temperate climate, was intrigued by the possibility of

Figure 15.1 (right) The garden front from the oval lawn showing the informal planting in the mixed borders, backed by *Pelargonium* 'Balcon'.

transforming his French-style garden with English planting. The architect (who had also designed the house) had followed the contours of the land in his layout of the garden by creating a series of descending terraces that led to a formal avenue through parkland. Initially, Brookes was commissioned to replant existing beds on the terraces, but at a later stage he was given the opportunity to design and plant the parkland. His first task,

however, was to recommend yew hedges and tall plantings of trees to provide shelter from the winds. The temperate climate of Galicia facilitates the growth of a wide range of plants and Brookes's fundamental philosophy that plants should be chosen to suit the site, based on 'a reinterpretation of natural groupings, but without an exclusive use of native plant material', worked well in this context.[2]

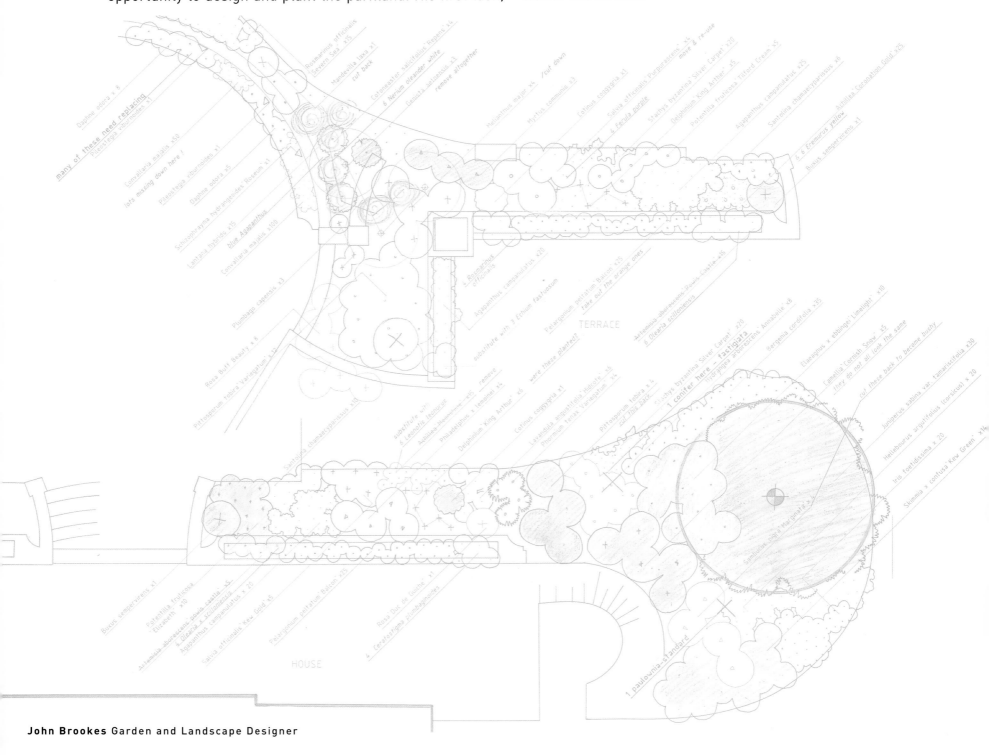

Figure 15.2 (opposite) The front garden planting plan, dated June 1998 with March 2004 revisions.

Figure 15.3 (left) Informal planting groups on the banks complement the architectural lines of the steps.

A series of seven plans traces the replanting of the terraces around the house and the oval lawn below (Figures 15.1 and 15.2). The main rooms of the house on the garden front opened onto a marble terrace, the lax informality of Brookes's planting providing a foil to this architectural flamboyance. Flowering shrubs such as *Potentilla fruticosa* 'Elizabeth', *Philadelphus x limoinei*, *Lavandula angustifolia* 'Hidcote' and *Santolina chamaecyparissus* are juxtapositioned with the bright yellow of *Salvia officinalis* 'Kew Gold', the groupings being contained by *Buxus sempervirens* and *Phormium tenax* 'Variegatum' and backed by *Pelargonium* 'Balcon'. Adjoining the south-west side of the house a second terrace, framed by sun-loving plants such as fragrant *Pittosporum tobira*, *Genista hispanica*, *Echium pininana* and rosemary, functions as a roof garden with views over the surrounding landscape. Steps lead down to a shrub-lined pergola walk and, near the garden boundary, a swimming pool, sheltered by trees and a deep shrub border.

From the terrace fronting the house, steps continue the descent of the hillside flanked by swathes of hardy colourful plants, such as *Perovskia*, *Hebe* and *Achillea* 'Moonshine', to an oval lawn, a practical demonstration that 'On any flight of steps you can break up their hardness by the introduction of plant material' (Figures 15.3 and 15.4).[3] Brookes echoed the 'Frenchness' of the garden's previous design on the broad sweep of the lawn by introducing low yew hedges between the grass and borders, and equally spaced *Hippophae rhamnoides* (sea buckthorn) planted in a circle. These bushy small trees (up to 6m high) with narrow, silvery leaves, produce yellow flowers in spring and bright orange berries in the autumn, a spiky contrast to the large-leaved shrubs such as *Loquat*, *Oleander nerium* and *Choisya ternata* planted below (Figure 15.5). Winding paths lead from this area into woodland and a newly planted orchard with spring bulbs, while two further flights of steps descend to a temple and the parkland. This lower park features a formal avenue of sweet

Figure 15.4 *Salvia officinalis* 'Kew Gold' at the top of the steps to the oval lawn.

163

chestnut trees, a remnant of the earlier design, but, with Brookes's involvement, further trees, shrubs, an orchard and vegetable garden have been added. The owner's latest project is to lay out a small golf course within the park, the designs being completed by Brookes in 2004.

As with many large projects, the work on the garden at La Coruna has been ongoing for many years to accommodate the client's finances and timescale. When John Brookes visits Casa De Campo en Oleiros every few years, he recommends the replacement of plants and advises on plans for the development of the garden until his next visit. Close co-operation with local architects, engineers, nurserymen and gardeners is essential, not just to discuss the implementation of his plans but maintenance and the English approach to gardening (Figure 15.6).

Figure 15.5 (left) Seating on the oval lawn with guyed trees and the white flowerheads of *Hydrangea arborescens* 'Annabelle' behind.

Figure 15.6 (above) John Brookes in discussion with garden staff outside the entrance gate.

A New England Estate

LOCATION: New England, USA

DATE: 1998

Driving through winding countryside lanes on the western edge of New England, the traveller might easily miss the gatehouse to this 267-ha estate. Developed by John Brookes in recent years as a modern landscape park (Figure 16.1), the setting for a late 19th-century house, this is estate building in the grand English Landscape Garden style – earth moving, tree transplanting, planting of mature shrubs and trees, and even the relocation of a house to improve the view from the pool house.[1]

Brookes was introduced to the owner of the property by Gwendolyn van Paasschen, a garden designer, who had been asked to advise on changes to a recently constructed walled garden there.[2] Van Paasschen was familiar with Brookes's work (she had attended one of his design courses at the New York Botanic Garden) and, appreciating the design potential of the landscape, requested his help.

When Brookes visited the garden he formed an immediate rapport with the owner, which has resulted in his continuing involvement in the development of the gardens and landscape away from the house, as well as the stepped terraces, his original commission.

Figure 16.1 View across a circular granite pool to the ha-ha and the mountains in the distance.

A New England Estate

" *It went on bit by bit – I sorted the terraces and front of house, then moved the road and gardener's house out of main view. I also started to reorganize the maintenance as it needed consolidation, built a large barn, Alitex glasshouse and new gardener's house. Then we started thinking about the west side of the house – we moved the orchard to allow views of the Catskill Mountains and replanted the trees to hide the barn.* " [3]

Brookes's underlying design concept was to open the house to the landscape, and to create vistas, views and a series of garden rooms to be enjoyed at all seasons, whenever the owner, his family and guests visit from the city. He recalls: 'I first saw the garden on a snowy winter day in March 1998. I looked out of the window to see a walled garden straight ahead of me... It wasn't connecting to anything else. It was like a brick ship sitting in the middle of the site'.[4] Brookes's first task, therefore, was to deal with the 'brick ship', which he did by removing a section of the walled garden to allow views from the house to a new upper terrace. Here he created an intimate space with a reflecting pool, a summer house and red garden furniture, chosen to complement a mature copper beech, now the focus of the view, the colour also being highlighted by red-purple *Angelica gigas* nearby. Passing through a door from the upper terrace, steps descend to a green and white Zen garden with a rill, relocated bubble fountains and white lilac trees underplanted with myrtle (and white tulips in spring), reflecting the ancient Moorish water courtyards of the East (Figure 16.2).

The use of water is a linking theme throughout the garden. The transition from cool Zen to hot Mediterranean is accomplished via angled steps leading down through sunny borders of citrus, jasmine and grey-leaved plants, the rill running under paving stones to splash from a lion's mouth, to a pool and then through the garden in a variety of innovative designs (Figure 16.3). To one side a dark green, wrought-iron balcony (fashioned from a dismantled pergola) gives views to the distant hills over

Figure 16.2 (left) The cool, green Zen garden is inspired by ancient Moorish water gardens (2003).

Figure 16.3 (right) John Brookes's design uses steps to direct the eye through the garden (2003).

a lush bed of purple *Buddleija*, in summer swarming with butterflies (Figure 16.4). Broad steps terminate in a formal, pleached, hornbeam garden, the focus being a honeycomb-shaped pergola clothed in mauve wisteria and other climbing plants, the structure being set on granite paving and peach-coloured bricks. The view from here to a rectangular swimming pool and pool house in a classical style continues to a simple circular granite pool set in the curved promontory (or bastion) of a newly created ha-ha with a rolling countryside view beyond.

John Brookes's approach to the design of such garden rooms as a setting for the house is also in the tradition of the late 18th-century landscape gardener Humphry Repton,[5] who, like Brookes, tried to understand not only the uniqueness of the landscape he was designing, but the architecture of the building and the personality and lifestyle of his clients:

" *The gardens or pleasure grounds near a house may be considered as so many different apartments belonging to its state, its comfort and its pleasure. The magnificence of the house depends on the number as well as the size of its rooms; and the similitude between the house and the garden may be justly extended to the mode of decoration... If in its unfurnished state there chance to be a looking glass without a frame, it can only reflect the bare walls; and in like manner a pool of water, without surrounding plantations or other features, reflects only the nakedness of the scene.* "[6]

The opportunity to further 'furnish' this home came with Brookes's next project – the entrance to the house. He had already attended to the alteration of the brick-surfaced terrace on the south and west sides of the house (Figure 16.5), the latter having an amazing downhill view (after orchard trees had been relocated) to a wide meadow in which a group of native mustang horses are run. His next project was the entrance courtyard on the north side of the

house. The original red-brick house (softened with a white wash) has been extended over the years and includes an adjoining guest house fronted by a grid-patterned courtyard. A linden avenue once led to the front door, but has been removed in recent years at Brookes's suggestion to allow views across the parkland trees to the Shawangunk Mountains. The approach drive has been hidden from view from the house by raising the level of the grassed area adjoining it. The front courtyard is divided into squares of planted and paved areas, reminiscent of Brookes's 1960s courtyard designs (Figures 16.6 and 16.7). Wide granite steps flanked by planters frame the front door. Brookes adds:

" *A pattern was evolved of limestone (echoing the same limestone used to floor the entrance hall) with a coursed granite sett infill between. A secret bench was located in one corner behind a spreading crab apple, looking towards a piece of sculpture. Flower beds are filled with*

Figure 16.4 (opposite) The lookout forms a link between the enclosed Mediterranean garden and the parkland (2003).

Figure 16.5 (above) Pots of fragrant white lilies and acidanthera decorate the terrace.

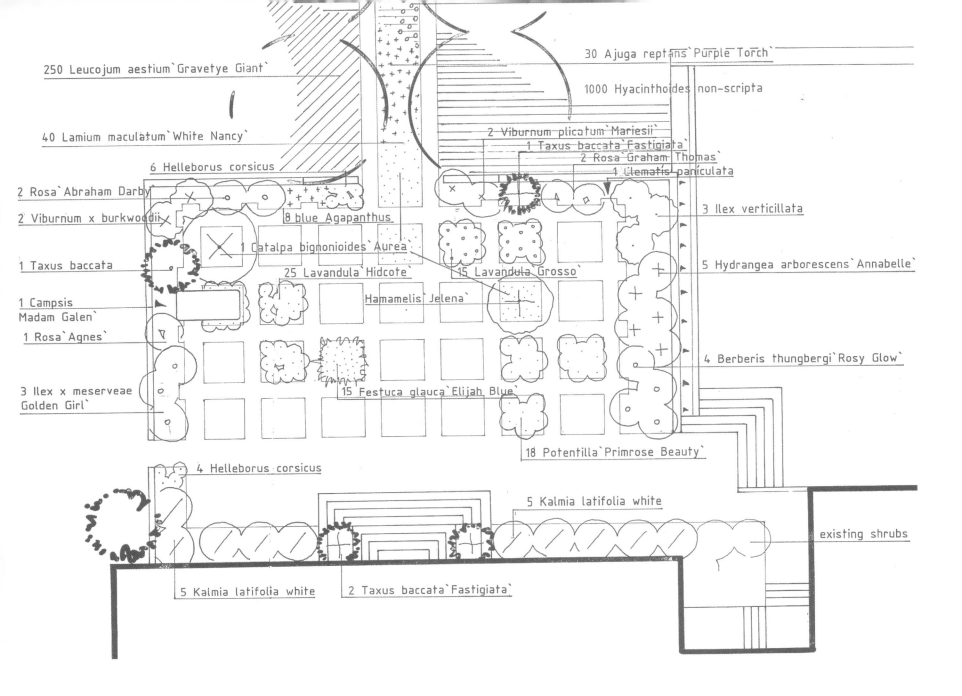

250 Leucojum aestium `Gravetye Giant`

40 Lamium maculatum `White Nancy`

6 Helleborus corsicus

2 Rosa `Abraham Darby`

2 Viburnum x burkwoodii

1 Taxus baccata

1 Campsis
Madam Galen`

1 Rosa `Agnes`

3 Ilex x meserveae
Golden Girl`

30 Ajuga reptans `Purple Torch`

1000 Hyacinthoides non-scripta

2 Viburnum plicatum `Mariesii`
1 Taxus baccata `Fastigiata`
2 Rosa Graham Thomas
1 Clematis paniculata

8 blue Agapanthus

1 Catalpa bignonioides `Aurea`

25 Lavandula `Hidcote`   15 Lavandula `Grosso`

Hamamelis `Jelena`

15 Festuca glauca `Elijah Blue`

3 Ilex verticillata

5 Hydrangea arborescens `Annabelle`

4 Berberis thungbergi `Rosy Glow`

18 Potentilla `Primrose Beauty`

4 Helleborus corsicus

5 Kalmia latifolia white

existing shrubs

5 Kalmia latifolia white   2 Taxus baccata `Fastigiata`

lavender and creamy potentilla, with a shrub backing against the wall. To minimise the height of the entrance steps to the house, planters were constructed within the steps, each one containing an Iris yew (Taxus baccata 'Fastigiata'). Wide steps link the courtyard to a grassed lawn. **7**

Once Brookes had completed the stepped terraces leading to the swimming pool he developed a masterplan to safeguard the

integrity of the whole site as an integrated landscape. Further projects since have included the extension of a pond to create two organic-shaped lakes linked by a waterfall, planted with *Euonymous alatus*, *Cornus racemosa*, *Amelanchier canadensis*, *Clethra alnifolia*, *Aronia prunifolia* 'Brilliant', *Lindera benzoin*, *Salix* and *Viburnum*. They were bounded by sculptured landforms made from excavation spoil, new kitchen gardens, an Alitex greenhouse complex and a 'barn' with a state-of-the-art propagation centre and rest facilities for the 19 stable, grounds

and garden staff. Projects under discussion are conifer-planted mounds on the property boundary to minimize noise and car lights from the road, a new wood with a rustic house, a bird sanctuary, pavilions near a tennis court and landscaping around the estate manager's house and office. By enlisting John Brookes's expertise to integrate these features into the existing garden and landscape, the owner has, indeed, found a 'best friend', as Miss Bertram called Humphry Repton in Jane Austen's satirical novel, *Mansfield Park*.[8]

Figure 16.6 (opposite above)
Planting plan for the front forecourt, showing the position of the beginning of the formal avenue, removed by Brookes to open views from the front of the house, dated February 1999.

Figure 16.7 (above) The forecourt with square planted beds of *Potentilla* and lavender (2003).

Zespol Palace Park

LOCATION: Kikol, Poland

DATE: 1998

The Republic of Poland's wealth of natural beauty – sandy beaches, lakes, rivers and lush forests – is matched by its abundance of ancient cities, medieval castles, palaces and historic houses. Since the Second World War many of these historic sites have been used as museums, government offices, agricultural institutions, colleges and hotels, only a few remaining in private ownership. Concern for the fate of these properties led to the establishment in 1976 of the Administration for the Protection and Conservation of Palace-Garden Ensembles, based at the National Museum in Warsaw.[1] By 1994, this organization had

Figure 17.1 (above) Snowfalls and bare trees in winter contrast with the colourful summer scene.

Figure 17.2 (right) The village church forms a backdrop to the flower-filled terraces (2006).

Zespol Palace Park

been integrated with the Centre for the Preservation of Historic Landscape, its remit including advising private owners on the restoration, development and care of an historic garden.[2] In 1992, Mr and Mrs Karkosik bought a neglected early 19th-century property with 8-ha garden at Kikol, in north-central Poland. The mansion, Zespol Palace Park, had been used as a workers' recuperation home during the period of Communist control and several years' meticulous restoration and redecoration were required before the landscape could be considered.

The conservation of gardens in Poland had been promoted by landscape architects Gerard Ciolek (of Cracow Technical University) and Longin Majdecki (of Warsaw Agricultural University), the latter having written the preface to a Polish translation of the publication *John Brookes' Garden Design Book*.[3]

One of the few garden design books in the Polish language at the time, it also formed part of the Karkosik's garden library. They were in tune with Brookes's approach to garden making, but were also obliged to consult the Centre for the Preservation of Historic Landscape on plans for the garden. They therefore first approached Longin Majdecki, who produced a garden plan in 1995 for a formal French-style layout, which was partly implemented (steep steps down to a lake and a shaded perennial garden) before he died in 1997. In 1998 Brookes was invited to Poland to advise on the garden's next stage of development.

Kikol is in the Kujawsko-Pomorskie region of Poland, a mainly flat province with some hills, abundant lakes and rich soil. About one-fifth of the province is wooded, mainly with conifers. The climate is mild, with a mean annual temperature of 8–9°C and only 450–590mm of rain annually, making it one of the driest areas in Poland (Figures 17.1 and 17.2). It is thought that the site of present-day Zespol Palace Park has been inhabited since the 13th century and was possibly the site of a monastery in the 14th century.[4] There is little documentation on the present house (Figure 17.3) until an 1852 plan, which shows a small lake fed from a stream, serpentine paths and a formal garden (possibly a kitchen garden). The Polish pianist and

Figure 17.3 (right) The house at Zespol Palace Park has been restored to Palladian splendour.

Figure 17.4 (left) A bust of Chopin, who was reputedly a visitor to the house, forms a focal point in the garden.

Zespol Palace Park

composer, Frederick Chopin (1810–49), is reputed to have performed at the house on a number of occasions and a monument to him has been placed in the garden by the current owners (Figure 17.4).

Although attracted by features of the surrounding agricultural area, Brookes considered the house too ornate for such simplicity to be the basis for his design:

" The Polishness of the wooded and farmed landscape through which I drive to reach this site cannot really be expressed in the garden since the house itself has such a period character. The house is approached from the east

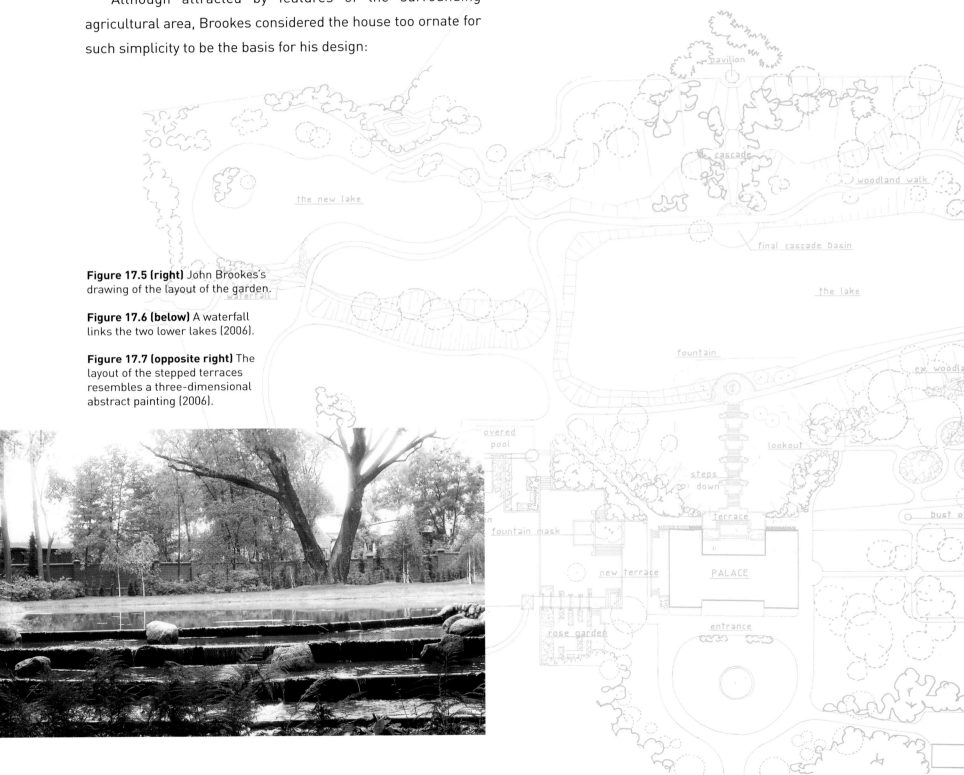

Figure 17.5 (right) John Brookes's drawing of the layout of the garden.

Figure 17.6 (below) A waterfall links the two lower lakes (2006).

Figure 17.7 (opposite right) The layout of the stepped terraces resembles a three-dimensional abstract painting (2006).

up a formal drive with a colonnaded façade in white stucco. The south terrace, occupying a hillside site, has views over the garden to a distant lake, with a foreground church. To the west the house looks down a steep incline to its own wooded lake, and to the north is a flat, partly shaded garden and a partly open flower garden.[5]

His rationale for the development of the gardens has centred on the creation of garden 'rooms' with views over the lawns, lakes and woodland (Figures 17.5 and 17.6).

Brookes's first project was on the south side of the house, which has distant views, and where he designed a terrace opening from the house with steps and further terraces downhill, culminating in the first of three pavilions which have become a motif for the garden. Comparable to an abstract painting in three dimensions, the composition is of regular, intersecting shapes filled with emerald grass, consolidated gravel, water, single-coloured rose beds and a multi-coloured flower border, punctuated by a mature *Acer negundo* (Figure 17.7). The *Wisteria*-covered pavilion (with a covered swimming pool beneath it under construction) looks onto its own flower garden. A pergola and rose garden are sited on the other side of this south façade, their backdrop being the steeple of a nearby 19th-century church.

On the forecourt of the mansion, the simple elegance of a turning circle of soft grey granite setts around a circular lawn, with concentric raised pool and fountain jets, is in marked contrast to the ornate décor of the main reception rooms and the

wooden
pavilion

water enters

bank down

ennial garden

pavilion

orchard

lime tree avenue

fountain

KIKOL PALACE
2006

Zespol Palace Park

Figure 17.8 (right) View from the house to the cascade and pavilion above (2006).

Figure 17.9 (opposite) Drawing of the flower garden planting, dated April 1999.

view through them to the tumbling waters of a cascade, surmounted by a second pavilion (Figure 17.8). Brookes placed the cascade, with its unusual hexagonal-shaped basins, on the far side of an existing lake, now the largest of three connecting lakes in the grounds. He describes the processes involved in its creation:

" *Parallel with the lake ran a deep overflow ditch and this had to be piped first, so as not to impede the cascade, but it had to be covered in earth, a minimum of 1m deep, so that the grade ran through from the lake to the bank. We decided to dig another lake in the far south-west corner of the site, and use the excavated earth to backfill the drain run... I decided that the cascade should spew out from beneath a second small pavilion located at the top of the*

hill. The water crashes into four or five basins, goes under the footpath round the lake, and ends up in a great saucer which hangs out over the lake... Earth then had to be ramped up to the basins and planted with Azaelea *and* Rhododendron *(my client's favourites).* " [6]

North of the site, Brookes echoed the open metal pavilion for climbers on the stepped terraces in his design for a flower garden (Figures 17.9). This formal garden is laid out in a traditional cruciform plan with an open metal pergola for climbers at each corner, under which simple fountains bubble. Although originally designated a rose garden, the four beds around a central fountain are now informally planted with large swathes of summer-flowering plants, including *Lavandula angustifolia*, *Hydrangea arborescens* 'Annabelle', shrub roses, *Salvia officinalis*

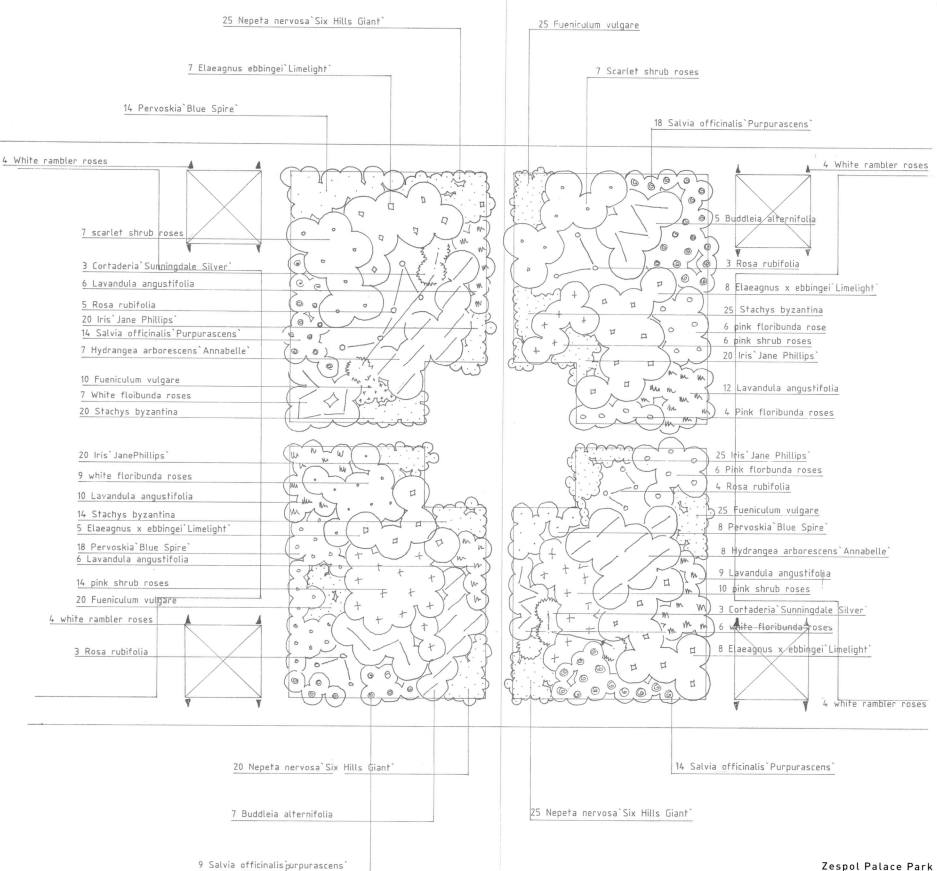

25 Nepeta nervosa`Six Hills Giant`

7 Elaeagnus ebbingei`Limelight`

14 Pervoskia`Blue Spire`

4 White rambler roses

7 scarlet shrub roses

3 Cortaderia`Sunningdale Silver`
6 Lavandula angustifolia
5 Rosa rubifolia
20 Iris`Jane Phillips`
14 Salvia officinalis`Purpurascens`
7 Hydrangea arborescens`Annabelle`

10 Fueniculum vulgare
7 White floibunda roses
20 Stachys byzantina

20 Iris`JanePhillips`
9 white floribunda roses
10 Lavandula angustifolia
14 Stachys byzantina
5 Elaeagnus x ebbingei`Limelight`
18 Pervoskia`Blue Spire`
6 Lavandula angustifolia
14 pink shrub roses
20 Fueniculum vulgare
4 white rambler roses
3 Rosa rubifolia

25 Fueniculum vulgare

7 Scarlet shrub roses

18 Salvia officinalis`Purpurascens`

4 White rambler roses

5 Buddleia alternifolia

3 Rosa rubifolia
8 Elaeagnus x ebbingei`Limelight`
25 Stachys byzantina
6 pink floribunda rose
6 pink shrub roses
20 Iris`Jane Phillips`

12 Lavandula angustifolia
4 Pink floribunda roses

25 Iris`Jane Phillips`
6 Pink florbunda roses
4 Rosa rubifolia
25 Fueniculum vulgare
8 Pervoskia`Blue Spire`
8 Hydrangea arborescens`Annabelle`
9 Lavandula angustifolia
10 pink shrub roses
3 Cortaderia`Sunningdale Silver`
6 white floribunda roses
8 Elaeagnus x ebbingei`Limelight`
4 white rambler roses

20 Nepeta nervosa`Six Hills Giant`

7 Buddleia alternifolia

9 Salvia officinalis`purpurascens`

14 Salvia officinalis`Purpurascens`

25 Nepeta nervosa`Six Hills Giant`

Zespol Palace Park

Figure 17.10 (opposite) A serpentine wooded walk replaced the original ditch on the far side of the lake (2006).

Figure 17.11 (right) Clumps of *Ligularia* brighten the lake edge (2006).

Figure 17.12 (below, right) Successful projects depend on close co-operation between the owners, designer (John Brookes third from left) and contractors.

'Purpurascens' and *Pevrovskia* 'Blue Spire'. Nearby a lawn is enclosed with freely growing briar roses. The formal luxuriance and openness of these garden rooms contrast with the informality of the woodland areas around the lakes and streams, which can be viewed from the dappled shade of a 'lookout', a hidden, decking platform high above the lake, reminiscent of the North American decks of Thomas Church. On the far side of the lake, Brookes has created a winding walk to replace the ravine or ditch originally there (Figure 17.10). In summer, deep orange *Ligularia* colour the lake's edges (Figure 17.11). On each visit Brookes walks among the mature chestnuts, oaks, beeches and pines, higher up the bank, checking which need to be removed (due to disease and overcrowding) to allow light to penetrate and create views, or where replanting is required to ensure an understorey for the future.

Outside the garden boundary a granary factory provides an industrial eye-catcher, a property which may soon be bought by Mr Karkosik for development as part of his petrochemical company. Within the current property boundary, an orchard has already been developed on previous granary land. Since his initial visit in the summer of 1998, Brookes has been given a free hand to develop the garden, visiting several times a year to check on the implementation of his plans and to leave further instructions for the local gardeners and contractors (Figure 17.12). Nearly a decade later the garden buildings, eye-catchers and winding paths entice visitors from one set piece to the next, while the juxtaposition of the formal and informal, enclosed and open, provide stimulation and surprise.

This peaceful, verdant oasis is the fulfilment of the owners' childhood dreams to own a beautiful house and garden – but, they affirm, 'Through John we have gained more than the green outdoor place we wanted, we have also acquired a passion for plants and gardens'.[7]

San Isidro

LOCATION: Argentina, South America

DATE: 2001

In 1989 two young garden designers completed their studies at the University of Buenos Aires and set up in practice together as Barzi & Casares Garden Design. Using their recently acquired qualifications as a foundation for further study of landscape design in an international context, they enrolled at the Kew School of Garden Design, London, 'one of the most prestigious design schools in Europe'.[1] Run by John Brookes until the late 1990s, the course gave them the confidence, expertise and 'a fluid and fruitful relationship' with Brookes to develop a successful design practice on their return to Buenos Aires. During the 1990s Brookes was also designing gardens in South America (Chile, Brazil and Argentina), as well as heading a garden design school with Epicentro in Chile and teaching courses for the national horticultural society in Argentina (Sociedad Argentina de Horticultura).[2] When the partnership with Epicentro ended in 2000, Brookes discussed with Martina Barzi and Josefina Casares the viability of establishing a new garden design school in Buenos Aires. Their response was enthusiastic and Pampa Infinita – John Brookes School of Garden Design in Argentina – was set up under their supervision.[3] One of the school's early students lived in San Isidro, a wealthy suburb of Buenos Aires, where, with her husband, she was planning to redesign the garden around their hillside home. Brookes was asked to advise.[4]

Figure 18.1 Steps at San Isidro, Argentina, descending to a new structure tucked into the hillside and surrounded by a tropical wild flower meadow.

San Isidro

The Republic of Argentina is an extensive country with contrasting landscapes – the central open plains, the Andes Mountains in the west and the South Atlantic coast in the east – and stretches 3,800km from north to south and 1,425km east to west. Climatic variations range from the tropical north-west, the dry temperate sierras, the fertile pampas and the cold temperatures of Patagonia on the border with Chile. The flora of Argentina reflects these variations with more than 10 per cent of the world's plant varieties growing there, with sub-tropical plants dominating in the north, prairie grasses in the central pampas and broadleaf trees and conifers in Patagonia. Buenos Aires and its environs, in the east-central part of the country, are mainly flat with two low mountain ranges, Sierra de la Ventana and Sierra de Tandil. The weather is strongly influenced by the Atlantic Ocean, resulting in hot summers and temperate winters (10–25ºC) with high humidity and abundant rain throughout the year.

The garden at San Isidro is the setting for a contemporary house on land that drops steeply with a stunning view up the delta of the River Plate. When John Brookes made his first visit in late 2001, several terraces had already been laid out around and below the house, but with no cohesive design. His first task was to integrate the existing features, including the terraces, a swimming pool and barbecue area, the existing planting in the borders and on the banks, and a number of mature trees on the main terrace

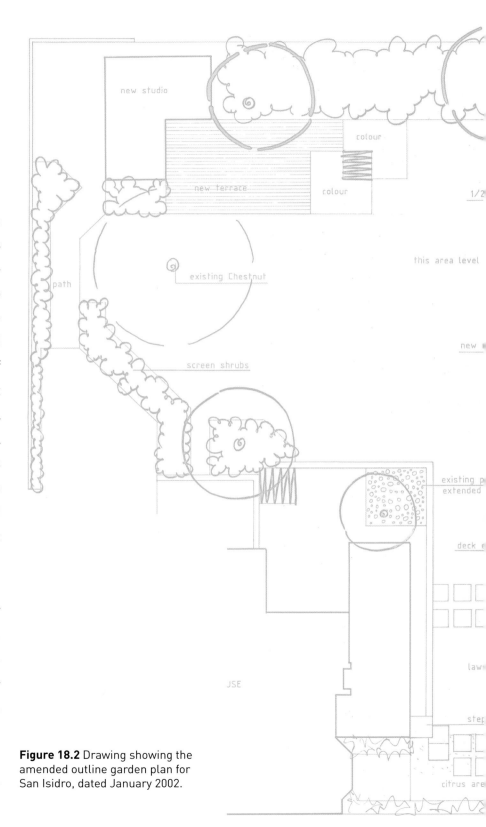

Figure 18.2 Drawing showing the amended outline garden plan for San Isidro, dated January 2002.

SECTION A-B   SCALE 1:50

steps up

stepping stone

under water planter

Cypress amongst
existing & additional planting

as many steps as necessary

−8.50

water spout

−4.0

timber steps up

terrace

wall at sit-on height

brick pattern
set in concrete
−9.0

under water level
for plants
−10.36

gravel

steps up

A

B

−9.75

existing
deck

water

stepping stones

rocks to
retain bank

all planting

retaining wall

−9.50

gravel path

existing planting

gravel path

Magnolia

tand

awn

all

swimming
pool

seat

BBQ

San Isidro

adjacent to the house. Working within these parameters, Brookes's initial proposals were to fell shade-creating trees, construct a decking terrace and plant a garden of tall clipped box in square beds of grey-leaved plants and colourful perennials. On an early plan, the underlying abstract design of overlapping squares and the architectural planting appear out of scale with the ruggedness of the landscape and lush native planting. Several months later, however, the owners decided to 'excavate out under the lawn and put in a partying place and studio for four teenage children',[5] which gave Brookes the opportunity and scope to develop an elegant design to match those of Roberto Burle Marx in neighbouring Brazil (Figures 18.1 and 18.2).[6]

Figure 18.3 (opposite) Open wooden steps wind down from the upper to the lower garden.

Figure 18.4 (top) The swimming pool terrace designed as overlapping squares of water, decking and lawn.

Figure 18.5 (above) A sunken planting bed creates the feeling of a floating deck.

The revised design creates an upper and lower garden linked by open stairways of wood decking, as though, Brookes suggests, the visitor is 'walking through plants' (Figure 18.3). The upper garden is now contained by a new retaining wall, the angular design creating a sense of spaciousness not realized in Brookes's earlier proposal.

It also comprises new intimate spaces, including a studio to the west of the house with its own decking terrace and colourfully planted beds. On the same level, the swimming pool, adjacent to, but below, the house, features a decking surround, with brick edging complementing the brick wall on the garden boundary (Figure 18.4). The deck appears to float above the lush planting area of *Iris*, juniper and massed *Strelitzia reginae* (bird of paradise), as though the water from the pool continues under the deck (Figure 18.5).

Broad steps descend from the deck with jungly plantings of *Phormium tenax*, *Yucca* and exotic lilies on the bank encroaching on the open treads. Following the contours of the land, a gravel path with a 'lookout' over the lower garden provides a shady resting place before the path continues. A winding route leads to the 'partying place' under an overhang set in a tropical 'wild flower meadow' of *Agapanthus*, *Phormium*, *Yucca*, cacti and grasses, many transplanted from other parts of the garden.

The pièce de résistance in the garden, however, is at the base of the flight of steps, where stepping stones cross a pool, into which a waterfall spills. Brookes adds: 'Coloured, rough cast walling, with the Mexican architect Luis Barragan in mind, is surrounded by a boulder and pebble beach' (Figure 18.6).[7] The path continues across the lower garden to return to the middle terrace and on, up the other side of the site.

Figure 18.6 (right) The waterfall appears to come from water flowing down the hillside.

San Isidro

Gazetteer

This comprehensive list of projects is based on drawings at John Brookes's studio at Clock House, Denmans, West Sussex, and includes ongoing projects up to the end of 2006. The list has been organized according to the date given on the earliest drawing for a project in the collection and is not necessarily the date of the commission. To preserve the privacy of owners only the house name or street together with the town or county and country are given. Drawing numbers are provided to enable future researchers to locate the drawings for specific projects in the John Brookes Drawings Archive, currently held at Clock House. Until mid-1985 each drawing was allocated a different number, but thereafter all drawings for the same project used the same prefix, e.g. 200/1, 200/2, 200/3. Brookes completed many design-only commissions, in general shown by the listing of one or two drawings in the Gazetteer. His full involvement in the implementation of a design and later development of a garden or landscape is indicated by the number of drawings listed for the project. Inconsistencies in the information provided in this Gazetteer might be attributable to missing drawings, but any other errors are the sole responsibility of the author.

DATE	SITE	LOCATION	DRAWING NUMBERS
1955	CHESHAM STREET	London SW1, England	1, 2, 3a
1955	THE SHEALINGS	Suffolk, England	3
1956	LANGLAND GARDENS	London NW3, England	4
1958	TECHWICK FARM	Surrey, England	6
1958	HOLLY LODGE	Buckinghamshire, England	17
1959	WAXWELL FARM HOUSE	Middlesex, England	8
1961	GOLDEN GROVE	Surrey, England	23
1961	FIDDLERS COPSE	London, England	25–7, 58, 63, 102, 103, 109
1961	SHIPTON UNDER WYCHWOOD	Oxfordshire, England	28–35
1961	BURLEY COTTAGE	Surrey, England	36
1962	HIGHLANDS AVENUE	Hampshire, England	37–8, 59
1962	HOMER STREET	London W1, England	39, 69
1962	SMITH HOUSE	London, England	40
1962	MONTPELIER STREET	London SW1, England	41–2, 45–6, 74
1962	BATTERSEA COLLEGE	London, England	43, 44
1962	11 UPPER PHILAMORE GARDENS	London W8, England	47, 49–55
1962	GREAT CUMBERLAND PLACE	London, England	48
1962	MANOR FARM	Oxfordshire, England	56
1962	GROVE HOUSE	Oxfordshire, England	57, 57A–F
1962	AIRLIE HOUSE	London W8, England	60, 61, 62, 64, 65, 66, 67
1963	DOGES HOUSE	West Sussex, England	68, 73, 75, 87–90
1963	QUEENSMEAD	London NW3, England	70–2, 86, 529
1963	DOWNSHIRE HILL	London, England	78
1963	PORTINSCALE ROAD	London SW15, England	79, 81
1963	MONTAGUE SQUARE	London W1, England	80
1963	ORMOND AVENUE	Middlesex, England	91
1963	WESTLEIGH AVENUE	London SW19, England	92
1963	ELVENDON ROAD	Oxfordshire, England	93, 94, 99, 100
1963	CHURCH DRIVE	Nottinghamshire, England	95
1963	THE GREEN	Surrey, England	96
1963	LONGDOWN LANE	Surrey, England	98A, 169, 181, 186–7
1963	LIVERPOOL ROAD	Surrey, England	101
1963	PLANNAIR LTD	Surrey, England	104–5, 107A, 108, 149
1963	EATON PLACE	London, England	106, 107, 110–17
1963	BLOOMFIELD TERRACE	London SW1, England	120
1964	WYNYARD HALL	Northumberland, England	123, 136–7, 141–2, 154–5, 194–200, 202, 265A
1964	ST LEONARDS SCHOOL	London WC1, England	124
1964	PARK WALK	London SW10, England	125, 161
1964	PARK VILLAGE EAST	London, England	126, 135, 140, 146B, 151, 157, 252
1964	PENGUIN BOOKS	Middlesex, England	128
1964	DRAYTON GARDENS	London SW10, England	128a
1964	UNNA HOUSE	London N2, England	130, 508, 515–6
1964	PARKSIDE	London SW19, England	131–2, 138, 147
1964	LINCOLN AVENUE	London, England	133–4
1964	MIDDLE STREET	Kent, England	139, 152
1964	BLOOMFIELD TERRACE	London SW1, England	143, 156, 163, 207, 213, 285a
1964	RECTORY ROAD	Kent, England	144–5, 148, 153, 172–2, 206, 273, 281A
1964	CAMPDEN HILL SQUARE	London W8, England	146
1964	SEYMOUR WALK	London SW10, England	150, 162, 280
1964	SCOTTS LANE	Kent, England	158, 167
1964	DARTMOUTH ROAD	London NW2, England	159
1964	PELHAM COTTAGE	London SW7, England	160, 216, 230, 233–4, 279, 282, 300, 307
1964	PATRA RESEARCH LAB	Surrey, England	164, 185
1964	MONTPELIER ROAD	London, England	165, 177–80, 192, 241
1964	CHRISTCHURCH ROAD	London SW14, England	166, 190, 191, 222–3, 251, 278a, 291a, 299, 305

DATE	SITE	LOCATION	DRAWING NUMBERS
1964	LORD NORTH STREET	London SW1, England	171, 212
1964	RINGMOOR RISE	London SE23, England	174
1964	HOLLAND PARK ROAD	London W8, England	175–6
1964	BELSIZE PARK GARDENS	London, England	182, 183, 184, 188
1964	WICKHAM ROAD	Kent, England	189, 235–40
1964	WOODLANDS	Oxfordshire, England	193, 204A
1964	ADDISON GARDENS	London SW14, England	201, 203, 215, 217, 250
1964	BALCOMBE STREET	London NW1, England	204
1964	REGAL LANE	London NW1, England	205, 214
1964	CHELSEA SQUARE	London SW3, England	208
1964	MAXBYS	Kent, England	209, 220
1964	LARCHFIELD	Surrey, England	210–11
1964	THE HEIGHTS	Kent, England	215A
1964	EGERTON TERRACE	London SW3, England	218, 219
1964	EATON PLACE	London, England	221, 224
1964	FITZJOHN AVENUE	London NW3, England	225, 231, 497, 498
1965	91 FOXGROVE ROAD	Kent, England	146a, 174a, 174b, 271, 372, 432
1965	GILDOWN	Surrey, England	229, 301
1965	BOURNESIDE	Surrey, England	232, 243
1965	THORNHILL ROAD	London N1, England	242
1965	GROVES	Sussex, England	244–9, 616
1965	NASH TERRACE	London NW1, England	254
1965	GROSVENOR SQUARE	London W1, England	255, 257
1965	LOWNDES LODGE	London SW7, England	256, 263
1965	OLD CHURCH STREET	London SW7, England	258
1965	ROYAL HOTEL	Essex, England	258A, 259–61
1965	WREN PROPERTIES	Hampshire, England	258B
1965	COOMBE LODGE	Surrey, England	262, 264, 285, 285b
1965	THE HEIGHTS	Kent, England	265–6
1965	NEVILLE TERACE	London SW7, England	267
1965	LINGWOOD	Hampshire, England	268–70, 284, 461
1965	REDINGTON ROAD	London NW3, England	272, 277, 281, 363, 474, 480–3
1965	WOODLANDS ROAD	London SW13, England	274–5
1965	WESSEX GARDENS	London NW11, England	276
1965	CHALCOT SQUARE	London NW1, England	278
1965	DALEHAM GARDENS	London NW3, England	283, 286, 444, 451, 316b
1965	CONNAUGHT SQUARE	London W2, England	287, 296
1965	LONGDOWN	Surrey, England	288
1965	ST CUTHBERTS	London, England	289
1965	MILWARDS FARM	Sussex, England	290
1965	SELBY ROAD	Nottinghamshire, England	291
1965	TREGUNTER ROAD	London SW10, England	292–4, 297
1965	STANMORE ROAD	London, England	295
1965	WATERLOOVILLE CHURCH	Hampshire, England	298, 306, 342, 351, 415–6
1965	BRYANSTON SQUARE	London W1, England	302, 308, 309, 319–35, 380, 381
1965	WEST HEATH ROAD	London NW3, England	302A, 313, 391, 426–7, 442
1965	TREMARA	Surrey, England	314, 339, 350, 413–4
1966	WYCH ELMS	Middlesex, England	303, 310, 346
1966	CAMBRIDGE STREET	London SW1, England	304, 311
1966	RIVER LANE	Surrey, England	312, 349, 352d, 368, 370–1, 373, 392, 403, 436
1966	THE VICARAGE	Buckinghamshire, England	315
1966	IMPERIAL COLLEGE	London, England	316
1966	WESTFIELD PARK	Oxfordshire, England	316A
1966	JOHN SPENCER SQUARE	London N1, England	317
1966	FINCHLEY ROAD	London NW3, England	318
1966	THURLOE SQUARE	London SW7, England	336
1966	DRUM HOUSE	London, England	337
1966	RANELAGH GROVE	London SW1, England	338
1966	HARTFIELD	Sussex, England	340, 352E, 369
1966	DALHAM HOUSE	Yorkshire, England	341
1966	SALEHURST PLACE	East Sussex, England	343, 408
1966	SWAN HOUSE	Northampton, England	344

DATE	SITE	LOCATION	DRAWING NUMBERS
1966	PEMBLEY GREEN	Sussex, England	345
1966	GOSWELL END	London, England	347
1966	CYNA COURT	London E11, England	348, 404
1966	PORTMAN SQUARE	London W1, England	352
1966	84 FOXGROVE ROAD	Kent, England	352a–c
1966	WICKHAM WAY	Kent, England	353
1966	PARK WALK	London SW10, England	354
1966	GREAT NORTH WAY	London NW4, England	355, 358, 364–5, 429
1966	BYWATER STREET	London SW3, England	359
1966	MULBERRY PLACE	Sussex, England	360, 377
1966	IMPERIAL COURT	London NW1, England	361
1966	WOODFALL	Hampshire, England	362
1966	OLD RECTORY	Berkshire, England	366, 383–4
1966	OLD RECTORY ROAD	Kent, England	367, 393
1966	MONTPELIER WALK	London SW7, England	375
1966	HAVERSTOCK HILL	London NW3, England	376, 379, 389–90
1966	BYRON CLOSE	London N2, England	378, 398–401, 484b
1966	SUSSEX LODGE	Surrey, England	385–6
1966	LITTLEWICK GREEN	Berkshire, England	387, 521A
1966	SELWOOD TERRACE	London SW7, England	388
1966	BLENHEIM & ELGIN CRESCENT	London, England	394, 395, 396, 397
1966	FORREST LODGE	Surrey, England	402, 409, 412, 754
1966	ALLIANCE BUILDING SOCIETY	East Sussex, England	405
1966	STRATFORD	London, England	406, 410–11
1966	ASTOR LODGE	London, England	406a
1966	ANCASTLE GREEN	Berkshire, England	406b, 443, 472, 473, 473/1, 487, 517a
1966	GREENACRES	Lincolnshire, England	407
1967	HAYNE ROAD	Kent, England	418, 421
1967	RECTORY ROAD	Kent, England	420
1967	ST JOHN'S WOOD PARK	London, England	422, 528A
1967	CRESCENT GROVE	London SW4, England	423, 440
1967	ST PETERS SQUARE	Oxfordshire, England	424, 462
1967	EAST MOUNT	Hertfordshire, England	425, 462
1967	BACON'S LANE	London, England	428, 393a
1967	KENSAL RISE SCHOOL	London, England	430–1
1967	FERNCROFT AVENUE	London NW3, England	433
1967	ASTOR CLOSE	London, England	434
1967	ALLISON GROVE	London, England	435
1967	SELWOOD TERRACE	London SW7, England	437
1967	EDWARDES SQUARE	London W8, England	438, 484, 504a
1967	MAYFIELDS	London, England	439
1967	LINCOMBE LODGE	Oxfordshire, England	441
1967	WITS END	Surrey, England	445, 449
1967	BELSIZE SQUARE	London NW3, England	446
1967	QUARRENDON STREET	London, England	447
1967	ROUGHWOOD OAK	Buckinghamshire, England	448
1967	FINCHLEY	London, England	450, 452
1967	STRAWBERRY HILL	Surrey, England	453
1967	HAMILTON TERRACE	London NW8, England	454–5, 457, 460
1967	REDINGTON ROAD	London NW3, England	456
1967	DRAYTON GARDENS	London SW14, England	458
1967	NORTHOOD ROAD	Hertfordshire, England	459
1967	LOCKINGTON	Middlesex, England	463
1967	GREEN HOUSE	London, England	465
1967	STONE HOUSE	London, England	466
1967	STUDDENS	Surrey, England	467
1967	BOYNTON	Hertfordshire, England	468
1967	REYNOLDS HOUSE	Surrey, England	470, 475, 499a
1967	DALEHAM GARDENS	London NW3, England	476
1967	SLOANE STREET	London SW1, England	477
1967	BEACONSFIELD GARDEN CENTRE	Buckinghamshire, England	478, 479, 486, 946b, 953, 954, 1164, 1165
1967	ALBERT STREET	London NW1, England	485
1967	THE TIDES	Middlesex, England	489
1968	WINDMILL HILL	London NW3, England	492
1968	CHARLTON END	Sussex, England	496, 499
1968	THE WEDGE	London SE3, England	500
1968	THE REST	Oxfordshire, England	501–3
1968	RYECOTES	London, England	504–5
1968	HENFIELD MILL	Buckinghamshire, England	507
1968	SCHOOL HOUSE	West Sussex, England	506
1968	LUDOVICI GARDENS	London, England	510
1968	GASPAR GARDEN	London W10, England	511, 526–7, 531–2
1968	OAST HOUSE CLOSE	Buckinghamshire, England	512
1968	LE COIN	Jersey, Channel Islands	514, 517b, 1244, 1484
1968	ILCHESTER PLACE	London W14, England	518–20
1968	SWAN HOUSE	Middlesex, England	521
1968	MERCIER ROAD	London, England	522
1968	DEAL	Kent, England	523
1968	STONE HOUSE	London NW3, England	524, 536B
1968	CHIPLEIGH	Berkshire, England	525
1968	SYON PARK GARDEN CENTRE	Middlesex, England	528, 536A, 541, 567–70
1968	MINORCA GARDEN	Minorca, Spain	530
1968	HARRODS LTD	London, England	533–5
1968	SEYMOUR WALK	London SW10, England	536
1968	HALLFARM CLOSE	Middlesex, England	537, 543, 551, 553–5
1968	ROWANTREE ROAD	Middlesex, England	538
1968	BRAKESPEAR HOTEL	Hertfordshire, England	539, 608, 609, 625
1968	BRITISH AIRWAYS	Middlesex, England	540, 585, 698
1969	TRUST HOUSE HOTEL	West Midlands, England	549–50, 559, 618, 635–7
1969	TRUST HOUSE HOTEL	Berkshire, England	552, 638a, 700
1969	OAKRIDGE AVENUE	Hertfordshire, England	556
1969	THURLOE STREET	London SW7, England	557
1969	TRUST HOUSE HOTEL	Northumberland, England	560, 626, 632, 642–4, 677–9, 682–3, 766
1969	CASTLE ROAD	Powys, Wales	561, 574, 592, 601
1969	MERRILODGE	Lincolnshire, England	562
1969	ROYCO LTD	London, England	563, 566
1969	WINGATE ROAD	London W6, England	564
1969	HYDE PARK GARDENS	London W2, England	565
1969	MAYFLOWER LODGE	London NW11, England	571, 573, 800
1969	GENNETS FARM	Sussex, England	572
1969	MINETT GARDEN	West Midlands, England	575
1969	THE WHITE HART	Wiltshire, England	578
1969	ABBOTSBURY ROAD	London W14, England	579, 580, 581
1969	TRUST HOUSE HOTEL	Leicestershire, England	582, 595–600
1969	PRIME HOUSE	Berkshire, England	583
1969	THE COTTAGE	Sussex, England	584
1969	ICI	Middlesex, England	586
1969	CASTLEMILL	Surrey, England	587
1969	ALISBY HOUSE	London, England	588, 1157, 1170
1969	HEATHFIELD	Hertfordshire, England	589
1969	ELM WALK	London NW3, England	591, 593
1969	TRUST HOUSE HOTEL	Yorkshire, England	594, 687–9, 706, 745
1970	NOTCUTT GARDEN CENTRE	Hertfordshire, England	603, 675–6
1970	ABBEY GARDENS	London NW8, England	604, 612
1970	CRESCENT GROVE	London SW4, England	605, 690
1970	WENTWORTH	Surrey, England	605E–F
1970	IVY COTTAGE	Suffolk, England	606–7, 667
1970	NOTCUTT GARDEN CENTRE	Kent, England	610–11, 639–41, 646, 648
1970	STUBBS HOUSE	Middlesex, England	613
1970	SHELDON AVENUE	London N6, England	614
1970	ASHDEN HOUSE	Kent, England	615, 627, 638, 654, 655, 656, 659
1970	KITSWELLS LODGE	Hertfordshire, England	617, 629, 649, 665
1970	ORCHARD HOUSE	Surrey, England	619, 631
1970	DORSET SQUARE	London NW1, England	622
1970	BARCLAYS BANK	London SW3, England	623, 630
1970	PUCK LANE	Oxfordshire, England	624–6, 662, 1109
1970	GAYTON ROAD	London NW3, England	628
1970	MOAT HOUSE	Surrey, England	633–4, 684
1970	SACHER COURT	Somerset, England	647
1970	FLAGSTONES	Surrey, England	658, 668, 669
1970	GREYSTONES	Gloucestershire, England	660
1970	MARYLANDS FARM	Oxfordshire, England	666B
1970	ICI	London SW1, England	671, 681, 741
1970	FOTHERINGHAM MANOR	Cambridgeshire, England	672–4
1970	FISHMONGERS HALL	London EC4, England	680
1970	NORFOLK COURT	Lancashire, England	686
1970	MEWSLADE	Glamorgan, Wales	686A, 965, 1011
1971	WATERLOO FARM COTTAGE	Sussex, England	691, 694
1971	HINCHLEY WOOD	Derbyshire, England	693
1971	TOTTERIDGE GREEN	London N20, England	695–7
1971	ST PETER'S COLLEGE	Oxfordshire, England	699, 727, 731, 739, 772, 777, 793, 811, 827, 912
1971	SHRIMPTON HOUSE	Oxfordshire, England	701, 752
1971	THE SHIPYARD HOUSE	Hampshire, England	702–3, 728, 758–62, 1277
1971	HARROW CIVIC CENTRE	London, England	704, 707–11, 714–18, 722, 734
1971	WALTON STREET	Oxfordshire, England	705
1971	SIMPSONS	London W1, England	712–3
1971	DELL HOUSE	London, England	720, 720a
1971	THE FORGE	Berkshire, England	723, 732, 733

DATE	SITE	LOCATION	DRAWING NUMBERS
1971	THAMESCOTE	Middlesex, England	724
1971	BRITISH AIRWAYS	Buckinghamshire, England	725, 735
1971	ALCAN	Berkshire, England	726
1971	ICI	Lancashire, England	729
1971	OREIL COLLEGE	Oxfordshire, England	743
1971	OLD SCHOOL HOUSE	Wiltshire, England	744, 1158
1971	CONWAY ROAD	London SW20, England	746, 763
1971	GREEN LANE	Sussex, England	748
1971	PIRA	Surrey, England	755
1971	SOMERTON	Somerset, England	756–7
1971	HAM PARK ROAD	Surrey, England	767
1971	HIGHLEGH GARDENS LTD	Cheshire, England	768–9
1972	GUILDWAY LTD	Surrey, England	771, 888
1972	COOMBE HOUSE	Oxfordshire, England	773, 774, 846
1972	FAIRVIEW HOUSE	Buckinghamshire, England	775, 798–9, 839–40, 852, 858, 961, 1012, 1025
1972	ST LUKES STREET	London SW3, England	776
1972	ELM WALK	London NW6, England	777, 860
1972	BISHAM GRANGE	Berkshire, England	779, 849, 850, 851, 866, 1317, 1339
1972	AVENUE LODGE	London, England	780, 784, 785
1972	CHURCH WAY	Oxfordshire, England	781
1972	PETERSHAM ROAD	Surrey, England	786, 801B
1972	PEMBROKE GARDEN CLOSE	London W8, England	787
1972	TEMPLEWOOD AVENUE	London NW3, England	788
1972	HIGH CLANDON	Surrey, England	789–91, 801–2, 861, 864
1972	OSLER ROAD	Oxfordshire, England	792
1972	SWAN COTTAGE	London SW3, England	795, 803–4
1972	STABLES	Buckinghamshire, England	796
1972	CHERRY LANE	Yorkshire, England	797, 837
1972	MILL HOUSE	Surrey, England	801A
1972	TUDOR LODGE	Surrey, England	806
1972	HIGHWAY HOUSE	Oxfordshire, England	807
1972	CLOVELLEY COURT	Devon, England	808
1972	WELLINGBORO MEDICAL CENTRE	Northamptonshire, England	808A, 917–8
1972	CRANBOURNE	Hampshire, England	809
1972	VOKES LTD	Surrey, England	810
1972	WATERFORD ROAD	London SW6, England	812
1972	CROMWELL PLACE	London SW7, England	813
1972	WOODLANDS COTTAGE	Buckinghamshire, England	815–9
1972	DESPATCH MOTORS	London, England	820
1972	SAINFOIN CLOSE	Oxfordshire, England	821, 847
1972	OLD FARM HOUSE	Oxfordshire, England	824
1972	NEW CROSS ROAD	Oxfordshire, England	825
1972	LIVERPOOL ROAD	London N1, England	826, 833A
1972	STANTON ST JOHN HALL	Oxfordshire, England	829–31, 865
1972	THE CITY	Buckinghamshire, England	833
1972	HOOK FARM HOUSE	Sussex, England	834
1972	WEST COMMON CLOSE	Hertfordshire, England	835
1972	CATHCART ROAD	London SW10, England	836, 862
1972	BRIDGEFOOT HOUSE	Hertfordshire, England	841
1972	MANOR HOUSE FARM	Buckinghamshire, England	842, 854–5
1972	ST CHADS	Surrey, England	844
1972	THE COP	Surrey, England	845
1972	IFFLEY	Oxfordshire, England	848
1972	GRAVEL COTTAGE	Berkshire, England	856
1972	NEWNHAM GREEN FARM	Hampshire, England	859
1972	STEELES ROAD	London NW3, England	863
1972	ALDERSHOT	Hampshire, England	867
1972	SUTTON IN ASHFIELD CENTRE	Derbyshire, England	867A–D, 1127, 1129, 1136–7
1972	SOAMES HOUSE	Surrey, England	1057
1973	BUSTO HOUSE	Sussex, England	852
1973	ALTON HOUSE	London, England	868, 870
1973	JOINT CREDIT CARD CO. LTD	Essex, England	871
1973	COOMBE LANE	London, England	872
1973	CHURCH MEADOW	Oxfordshire, England	873, 874
1973	HUDROYD HOUSE	Yorkshire, England	875
1973	BEARHURST	Surrey, England	877, 878
1973	CANDY TILES LTD	Sussex, England	880
1973	EGERTON CRESCENT	London SW3, England	881
1973	BELGRAVE PLACE	London SW1, England	883, 884
1973	THE HOUSE	Surrey, England	885, 889, 928
1973	CARLTON HILL	London NW8, England	890, 1086, 1094
1973	THE GRAIG	Hampshire, England	891, 1017
1973	THORNCROFT MANOR	Surrey, England	893–5, 1071–2, 1073A
1973	TREVOR STREET	London SW7, England	896
1973	KOHAR	Surrey, England	897

DATE	SITE	LOCATION	DRAWING NUMBERS
1973	CHESSINGTON GARDEN CENTRE	Surrey, England	898
1973	ST MARKS GROVE	London SW10, England	899, 907
1973	BROOKFIELD	Devon, England	900, 939, 946, 1068a
1973	MANCHESTER SQUARE	London W1, England	901–2, 973
1973	GOODWOOD GARDENS	West Sussex, England	903, 911, 915, 937, 945, 948, 967, 976A
1973	DENES HOLIDAY VILLAGE	Suffolk, England	904, 923–6
1973	HANDCROSS NURSERIES	Surrey, England	905
1973	RUDGEHOUSE FARM	Wiltshire, England	910
1973	VINEYARD HILL ROAD	London SW19, England	916, 930
1973	STONEBARN	Berkshire, England	920
1973	BLOSSOMFIELD ROAD	West Midlands, England	921
1973	TURN END	Hertfordshire, England	922, 1258
1973	MANOR FARM	Buckinghamshire, England	929, 957, 975, 1322
1973	POTTERS CROSS	Buckinghamshire, England	931, 944
1973	HUNTERS LODGE	Essex, England	935
1973	LYTTLETON CLOSE	London NW1, England	936
1973	SPADDON FARM	Somerset, England	938
1973	QUARKHILL FARM	Somerset, England	940
1973	OLD RECTORY	Devon, England	941, 951
1973	GROVE PARK GARDENS	London SW8, England	942
1973	PEAR TREE HOUSE	Surrey, England	942A, 955A, 1021, 1060
1973	THE SHEILING	Buckinghamshire, England	943, 964A
1973	ST JOHNS HOUSE	London, England	949–50
1973	PARKFIELD FARM	Devon, England	955
1973	CHARTER CONSOLIDATED LTD	Kent, England	955b, 955c, 966, 969–71, 1019, 1020
1974	DENTON HOUSE	Oxfordshire, England	956, 1030, 1031
1974	HORSENDEN MANOR	Buckinghamshire, England	958, 983, 1004, 1007A, 1048, 1061, 1099A, 600
1974	BISHAM VILLAGE HOUSING	Berkshire, England	959, 1008
1974	THE CELLARS	Devon, England	960
1974	GREENLANDS FARM	Wiltshire, England	962–3, 1042
1974	WORTH HOUSE	Dorset, England	964, 1016, 1032
1974	WEEVERS	Essex, England	968, 977–8, 990, 1041
1974	WALLUP HOUSE	Wiltshire, England	972, 988, 1002, 1036–7
1974	ENFIELD CIVIC CENTRE	London, England	974, 982, 986, 987, 1003, 1013
1974	NOTTINGHAM TERRACE	London W1, England	984
1974	DRUMLEE AVENUE	County Antrim, Ireland	991
1974	HOLSWORTHY HEALTH CTRE	Devon, England	994, 1006
1974	BANDINEL FARM	Jersey, Channel Islands	995, 1056
1974	LA CHASSE	Jersey, Channel Islands	996
1974	ROOK FARM	Sussex, England	997, 1009, 1038
1974	ST ANDREWS ROAD	Glamorgan, Wales	998, 1000, 1035
1974	PARKHURST ROAD	Kent, England	999, 1015
1974	FAWCETT HOUSE	Wiltshire, England	1005, 1053, 1054, 1063, 1064
1974	SUSSEX STREET	London SW1, England	1007
1974	LITTLE WALTHAM	Essex, England	1010, 1046
1974	THE SCHOOL HOUSE	Oxfordshire, England	1014
1974	SHARPHAM HOUSE	Devon, England	1018
1974	SHEPHERD CONSTRUCTION	Devon, England	1022
1974	PORTAKABIN LTD	Lancashire, England	1024
1974	STANTONBURY	Buckinghamshire, England	1026–8, 1070, 1074, 1076, 1095, 1111–3, 1128
1974	DROVERS	West Sussex, England	1039, 1052, 324/1
1974	NUNEHAM COURTNAY	Oxfordshire, England	1043–4
1974	KINGSWOOD FIRS	Surrey, England	1047, 1049, 1051
1974	HIGHER LONGCOMBE	Devon, England	1050, 1062
1974	HOBTYE	Surrey, England	1058
1974	KINGSCLERE HOUSE	Hampshire, England	1067
1974	STANSTEAD	Essex, England	1068
1975	LUCERNE ROAD	Oxfordshire, England	1075
1975	PORTAKABIN LTD	Yorkshire, England	1077–8, 1082, 1130, 1175
1975	SUTTON CENTRE	Surrey, England	1083–5
1975	L'ETOCQUET FARM	Jersey, Channel Islands	1088, 1089
1975	MAINLAND	Jersey, Channel Islands	1090–1
1975	MONTROSE GARDENS	London W6, England	1092–3
1975	BLACKMILLS PLANT DEPOT	Northamptonshire, England	1096, 1105
1975	PRIMROSE COURT	London W1, England	1097
1975	HAYES LANE	London, England	1098, 1116
1975	COOPER HOUSE	London, England	1099
1975	ST CROSS COLLEGE	Oxfordshire, England	1100
1975	COURTYARD GARDEN	Hertfordshire, England	1101
1975	DENNING CLOSE	London NW1, England	1102
1975	BARKHAM MANOR	Berkshire, England	1103, 1104, 1117
1975	MAPLES	London W1, England	1106
1975	LONDON ROAD	London NW8, England	1107–8, 1115, 1134
1975	THE OLD MANOR HOUSE	Oxfordshire, England	1110

DATE	SITE	LOCATION	DRAWING NUMBERS
1975	AQUEDUCT COTTAGE	Powys, Wales	1114
1975	CROIX AU MAITRE	Jersey, Channel Islands	1119–24, 1129b–d
1975	GREAT HASELEY	Oxfordshire, England	1125, 572A–D, 594A–B, 600
1975	LES NOUETTES	Jersey, Channel Islands	1126
1975	BATH ROAD	London W4, England	1131, 1140
1975	OLD FORGE CLOSE	Middlesex, England	1132
1975	HILL FARM	Buckinghamshire, England	1133
1975	HOLLAND ROAD	London W14, England	1135
1975	AILSBY HOUSE	Powys, Wales	1139
1976	MILTON KEYNES GARDEN CENTRE	Buckinghamshire, England	1141–2, 1147
1976	CHURCH HOUSE FARM	West Sussex, England	1143, 1146
1976	IVY WELL	Jersey, Channel Islands	1145
1976	15 UPPER PHILAMORE GARDENS	London W8, England	1148–9, 1153, 1166–9
1976	ST MARY'S LANE	Hertfordshire, England	1150–1
1976	ASHWELL	Hertfordshire, England	1152
1976	ASHLEY	London, England	1154
1976	CAMILLA DRIVE	Surrey, England	1156
1976	CREEKSIDE	Oxfordshire, England	1159
1976	LADBROKE SQUARE	London W11, England	1160
1976	BROOKFIELD	West Sussex, England	1161, 1162, 1458
1976	PRINCE OF WALES MANSIONS	London, England	1163, 1173–4
1976	PORTAKABIN LTD	Yorkshire, England	1171
1976	THE MANOR	Yorkshire, England	1177
1976	DEEP END COTTAGES	West Sussex, England	1178, 1181, 1553
1976	OLD BOTHY	Surrey, England	1179
1976	FITZROY SQUARE	London W1, England	1183, 469, 471
1977	CHELSEA SQUARE	London SW3, England	1188, 1189
1977	BROOKSIDE	County Wicklow, Ireland	1191
1977	OLD SCHOOL	Buckinghamshire, England	1192–3
1977	PIMLICO ROAD	London SW1, England	1194
1977	FLOOD STREET	London, England	1196
1977	SPRINGWOOD	Oxfordshire, England	1197–8
1977	ANCRUT HOUSE	Hampshire, England	1199
1977	SCHOOL HOUSE	Wiltshire, England	1200
1977	TEMPLECOMBE	Oxfordshire, England	1202, 1205–7, 1214, 1223–5, 1233, 1239
1977	MANOR FARM	Hertfordshire, England	1204, 1221
1977	MORTIMER HOUSE	London SW3, England	1208
1977	LA COLLINE	Jersey, Channel Islands	1209, 1234, 1235a
1977	MECHPLANT LTD	Yorkshire, England	1211
1977	DENNIS LANE	Middlesex, England	1212
1977	HOBART	London NW6, England	1213
1977	OLD SCHOOL HOUSE	Surrey, England	1215
1977	MANOR HOUSE	Buckinghamshire, England	1217–8, 1222
1977	EATON SQUARE	London, England	1219
1977	THE HOMEWOOD	Surrey, England	1220
1977	WESTBURY HOUSE	Somerset, England	1226
1977	BISHAM ABBEY	Berkshire, England	1227
1977	BROOKHAMPTON HOUSE	Somerset, England	1228
1977	BILLINGBEAR PARK	Berkshire, England	1230, 1236
1977	NEW HOUSE FARM	Essex, England	1231
1977	MANOR HALL DRIVE	London NW4, England	1232
1977	RYECROFT STREET	London SW6, England	1235, 1278
1977	IKERMAN TERRACE	London W8, England	1237
1977	MANOR FARM	Hampshire, England	1238, 1242, 1265, 1267, 1270
1977	SLEEPERS HOLT	Surrey, England	1238A, 1241A, 1252, 1259
1977	WATERY LANE STUDIO	Oxfordshire, England	1240
1978	HOTEL IMPERIAL	Kent, England	1238B, 1245–6
1978	RIVER COURT	London SE1, England	1243
1978	HYDE PARK GATE	London SW7, England	1247–8, 1254–6
1978	INISFREE	Surrey, England	1249
1978	ELSWORTHY ROAD	London NW3, England	1250, 1251, 1257
1978	LOWER BELGRAVE STREET	London SW1, England	1253
1978	THE GROVE	London, England	1260
1978	MULBERRY WALK	London SW3, England	1261
1978	OAKLANDS	Trinity, Jersey, Channel Islands	1262
1978	BLACKWELL'S	London WC1, England	1263, 1269, 1272
1978	HALDANE ROAD	London SW6, England	1264
1978	BOTTOM HOUSE	Berkshire, England	1266
1978	HOLLAND STREET	London W8, England	1269
1978	OLD SCHOOL HOUSE	Buckinghamshire, England	1271, 1273
1978	ARNISTON ROAD	Surrey, England	1274
1978	STABLE HOUSE	Warwickshire, England	1275
1978	METHERSGATE HALL	Suffolk, England	1276
1978	WATCHOUSE	London NW3, England	1279

DATE	SITE	LOCATION	DRAWING NUMBERS
1978	CHESTER TERRACE	London NW1, England	1280, 1281, 1289
1979	ELSWORTHY ROAD	London NW3, England	1282
1979	APPERT HOUSE	Paris, France	1284–5
1979	PICKETS BILL	Oxfordshire, England	1286
1979	MANOR FARM	Sussex, England	1287
1979	WOODHALL DRIVE	London, England	1288
1980	ELM PARK ROAD	London SW8, England	1291, 1296
1980	WHITE HOUSE COTTAGE	Sussex, England	1292, 1324
1980	BANKSIDE	London SE1, England	1293
1980	PARADISE FARM	Hampshire, England	1293A
1980	PUSEY HOUSE	Oxfordshire, England	1294
1980	ST PETER'S ROAD	London W6, England	1295, 1303
1980	PRIORY ROAD	London NW6, England	1302
1980	BAA	Middlesex, England	1304–12, 247/1–5, 5A, 6–8
1980	CADOGAN PLACE	London SW1, England	1315
1980	DUNSTAN'S ROAD	London, England	1316, 1322
1980	COURT HOUSE	Wiltshire, England	1319, 1320
1980	PARFREY STREET	London W6, England	1321
1980	CHURCH FARM	West Sussex, England	1323, 1340b, 1340c, 1341, 1350, 1384b
1980	SPRINGFIELD ROAD	London NW8, England	1326–7, 202/1
1980	CLARENCE DRIVE	Surrey, England	1328–32
1980	CHILSTONE	Kent, England	1333, 1334
1980	WEST HAMPNETT HOME	West Sussex, England	1335, 1408A
1980	COURTYARDS	London, England	1336
1980	ABESTERS	West Sussex, England	1337
1980	HILLSDOWN	London, England	1338, 1340C
1980	BARKHAM SQUARE	London, England	1340
1980	DENMANS	West Sussex, England	598/1
1981	GARDEN HOUSE	Hampshire, England	1340a, 1346, 1358, 138/1, 561/1–2
1981	ATHERLEIGH	West Sussex, England	1342, 1361
1981	HILLS AVENUE	Cambridgeshire, England	1343–4
1981	TOWN GREEN FARM	Surrey, England	1347, 1351
1981	LES RUETTES	Jersey, Channel Islands	1349, 1357
1981	WHITE ROCK COTTAGE	Somerset, England	1352
1981	STAPLE HOUSE	Sussex, England	1353–4, 228/1–2
1981	GREEN FARM PLACE	Norfolk, England	1355, 1360
1981	RIVER HOUSE	London W6, England	1356
1981	WOODCREST	West Midlands, England	1360A–C, 1397, 1399
1981	TODDINGTON HOUSE	Sussex, England	103/1–12, 16–22, 26
1982	MEADOW'S END	West Sussex, England	1362, 1370, 1430
1982	THE QUELL	West Sussex, England	1363, 1378
1982	REGENTS MEWS	London NW8, England	1364, 1368–9
1982	AMBERHURST	West Sussex, England	1365, 1550, 1556, 1557, 1558
1982	HARTY	Surrey, England	1366
1982	MANOR HOUSE	Surrey, England	1367
1982	THE GRANGE	London SW17, England	1371, 1373a, 1438
1982	POSTMAN'S COTTAGE	Sussex, England	1374, 1377, 1381, 1387, 246/1–5
1982	DAIRY COTTAGE	West Sussex, England	1375, 1383
1982	GROVE END ROAD	London NW1, England	1376
1982	CHALDER FARM	West Sussex, England	1379, 1419
1982	GASSONS	West Sussex, England	1380
1982	ST THOMAS STREET	Hampshire, England	1382, 1398, 1431–2
1982	LENNOX GARDENS	London SW1, England	1384
1982	DOYLEY MANOR	Hampshire, England	1385, 1388, 1391, 1394, 322/2
1982	WOODLEA	Lancashire, England	1389–90, 1402
1982	BALTIMORE AVENUE	Alabama, United States	1393, 1403, 1404
1982	BEAUFIELD HOUSE	Jersey, Channel Islands	1395
1982	SAMARÈS MANOR	Jersey, Channel Islands	1396, 1418, 1449–50, 1452, 1456–7, 1538, 194/1
1982	PARKSIDE	London SW19, England	1372–3
1983	PEMBROKE COLLEGE	Cambridgeshire, England	1400, 1409–10
1983	HENLEY PARK MANSION	Surrey, England	1401
1983	COPPER BEECHES	Hampshire, England	1405–8
1983	ETON AVENUE	London NW3, England	1411, 1415, 1416
1983	TANKARDS	Surrey, England	1412, 431/1–2
1983	NORFOLK ROAD	London NW8, England	1413
1983	SPRINGFIELD	Warwickshire, England	1414, 1422
1983	LOWER ROAD	Hampshire, England	1417, 1426
1983	HANDS GALLERY	Sussex, England	1420
1983	THE COTTAGE	Oxfordshire, England	1421, 1434, 1435, 1440, 1505
1983	RIVERSIDE	Gower, Wales	1423–4
1983	SHEEPDROVE FARM	Berkshire, England	1425, 1478, 1506, 1520, 1520A
1983	REDINGTON ROAD	London NW5, England	1427
1983	HARNIER	London, England	1428–9, 1460

DATE	SITE	LOCATION	DRAWING NUMBERS
1983	OLD RECTORY	Oxfordshire, England	1433
1983	RAVENSDON STREET	London SE11, England	1436
1983	BELMONT ROAD	London SW4, England	1437
1983	HIGH HOLBURN	London, England	1439, 1443–4
1983	LITTLE HAMPTON CARAVANS	West Sussex, England	1442, 1529
1983	EDGEWAREBY LANE	London, England	1442a, 1471
1983	OUTFIELD	Yorkshire, England	1445, 1476
1983	NEWCASTLE DRIVE	Nottinghamshire, England	1446
1983	THE CROFT	Nottinghamshire, England	1447, 1477
1983	CAMELIA COTTAGE	Jersey, Channel Islands	1448
1983	TOWNSHEND ROAD	Surrey, England	1459
1983	BLOMFIELD ROAD	London W9, England	1441, 1454, 1455
1983	HOUGHTON BRIDGE	Gloucestershire, England	1544
1984	MARLUSE FIELDS	West Sussex, England	1462, 1472, 1474
1984	MAGPIES	Buckinghamshire, England	1463
1984	SHORTHEATH ROAD	Surrey, England	1464
1984	GREENFIELD COTTAGE	Sussex, England	1465, 1500–2, 1513, 1526, 1537
1984	HOLT PLACE	West Sussex, England	1467
1984	WINDMILL HILL	London NW3, England	1468
1984	MATHAN ROAD	Surrey, England	1469, 1473
1984	FERNCROFT AVENUE	London NW3, England	1470, 166/1–3
1984	CLEEVES	Surrey, England	1471a, 186/2–5, 7–9
1984	ST JAMES'S SQUARE GARDENS	London W1, England	1475
1984	ST JOHN'S STREET	Sussex, England	1479–81, 1509, 1530
1984	GLEBE LANE	Hertfordshire, England	1482
1984	HIGHFIELD SCIENCE PARK	Nottinghamshire, England	1483, 1494, 1497
1984	LITTLE BUTTS FARMHOUSE	West Sussex, England	1487
1984	NORTHLANDS	West Sussex, England	1488, 1512A
1984	HORNDEAN ROAD	Hampshire, England	1489
1984	SOUTH STREET	London W1, England	1490–1
1984	MILL HOUSE	Kent, England	1495, 1534
1984	COTSWOLD PERFUMERY	Oxfordshire, England	1496, 1510, 1518
1984	SPRING VALLEY	Jersey, Channel Islands	1498
1984	ST PETERSBURGH PLACE	London W2, England	1499
1984	CHURCH FIELDS	Surrey, England	1503, 1504
1984	GREYFRIARS ROAD	Berkshire, England	1507–8
1984	MALVERN BUILDINGS	Somerset, England	1511
1984	KEEPERS WOOD	West Sussex, England	1512, 1516–7, 262/1, 334/1–2
1984	MANOR HOUSE	Dorset, England	1512B, 1543A–B, 1520, 1564, 133/3–4,6–8
1984	CLANDON	Surrey, England	1514, 1515, 1545
1984	STONEHAM	Hampshire, England	1519, 1546
1984	EYOT COTTAGE	London, England	1521, 1536
1984	NORDIC SAUNAS LTD	Surrey, England	1522
1984	FAWLEY COURT	Berkshire, England	1523
1984	VICARS CLOSE	West Sussex, England	1524, 1530A
1984	SHERBORNE HOUSE	West Sussex, England	1525, 1539–40
1984	STONEHAM	Surrey, England	1527, 1542
1984	RINGWOOD AVENUE	London N2, England	1528
1984	CATSLAND FARM	West Sussex, England	1535, 1541, 404/1
1985	LADYWELL COTTAGE	West Sussex, England	1543
1985	SEMLEY ROAD	Sussex, England	1547
1985	APRIL COTTAGE	Surrey, England	1548, 1563
1985	CRANE COTTAGE	Surrey, England	1549
1985	RYDONS	Surrey, England	1551, 1567
1985	SUNDIAL HOUSE	Surrey, England	1552
1985	ADSDEN HOUSE	West Sussex, England	1554, 1555
1985	PARK FARMHOUSE	Somerset, England	1555A, 1562A
1985	THE COACH HOUSE	London SE3, England	1559, 1561
1985	DARRINGTON NURSERY	Yorkshire, England	1560
1985	WARGRAVE-ON-THAMES	Oxfordshire, England	1562
1985	DELL QUAY	West Sussex, England	1565–6
1985	IBSTONE HOUSE	Buckinghamshire, England	1568–9
1985	GOODWOOD PARK HOTEL	West Sussex, England	100/1 (2)
1985	WARGRAVE-ON-THAMES	Oxfordshire, England	101/2
1985	CHARTWELL PLACE	Surrey, England	102/1
1985	GREYWELL HOUSE	Surrey, England	119/1–3
1985	SHALDON LODGE	Hampshire, England	127/1–6
1985	LA NAPOULE	Cannes, France	270a
1985	RIPLEY PARISH CHURCH	Surrey, England	838
1986	AINSWORTH AVENUE	West Sussex, England	105/1
1986	OLD PARK	West Sussex, England	109/1
1986	FAIRMILE HOTEL	West Sussex, England	110/2
1986	KINTYRE	Surrey, England	111/1
1986	SOUTH WALK	West Sussex, England	112/1–2

DATE	SITE	LOCATION	DRAWING NUMBERS
1986	BROADLANDS	West Sussex, England	113/1
1986	ANTROBUS ROAD	London W4, England	114/1–2
1986	PUCKS LANE	West Sussex, England	118/1
1986	ROOKSNEST	Berkshire, England	121/1
1986	RHYD HOUSE	West Sussex, England	122/1
1986	STEPPING STONES	West Sussex, England	123/1
1986	MILL WOOD	Hertfordshire, England	124/1
1986	SPRINGFIELD FARM	Gloucestershire, England	125/1
1986	MIDDLE OAKSHOTT FARM	Hampshire, England	126/1–5
1986	MOON HALL	Surrey, England	129/1
1986	HUNTERS COURT	Surrey, England	130/1
1986	FAVELL HOUSE	Surrey, England	131/1–5
1986	SOUTHERN CROSS	West Sussex, England	134/1
1986	CHICAGO BOTANIC GARDEN	Chicago, United States	135/1–23
1986	FLANSHAM HOUSE	West Sussex, England	136/1
1986	WARWICKSHIRE MOUNT	Surrey, England	137/1
1986	OLD BAKEHOUSE	Gloucestershire, England	140/1–6
1986	THE HERMITAGE	Surrey, England	141/1
1986	WOOLHAMPTON COURT	Berkshire, England	142/1
1986	ST MARTINS SQUARE	West Sussex, England	144/1
1986	BIRMINGHAM BOTANIC GDNS	Alabama, United States	147/1
1986	CAMDEN PARK ROAD	Kent, England	148/1–2, 4–5
1986	THE FIELD HOUSE	Somerset, England	151/1
1986	POUND PLACE	West Sussex, England	152/1
1986	CLIFTON ROAD	West Sussex, England	153/1
1986	HOOK LANE	West Sussex, England	154/1
1986	LOWER FARM	West Sussex, England	155/1
1986	HOLLY TREE HOUSE	West Sussex, England	156/1
1986	THE OLD RECTORY	Hampshire, England	157/1
1986	STANTON COURT	Gloucestershire, England	158/1
1986	CROWTHERS	Middlesex, England	159/1
1986	WILLESDON LANE	London NW2, England	160/1
1986	BOISSEVAN HOUSE	West Sussex, England	162/1
1987	CROCK'S HOLLOW	Surrey, England	110/1
1987	GREY'S CLOSE	Yorkshire, England	139/1, 4–10
1987	PONDS LANE HOUSE	Surrey, England	150/1–2
1987	SAND HOUSE	Hertfordshire, England	163/1–2
1987	COLD ARBOUR	Surrey, England	167/1
1987	SYDNEY STREET	London SW3, England	168/1
1987	HIGHWOOD ASH	London, England	169/1–4
1987	TODHURST FARMHOUSE	West Sussex, England	170/1–2
1987	CHURCH HOUSE	West Sussex, England	171/1
1987	CUTTLEBROOK HOUSE	Oxfordshire, England	172/1
1987	WOOD LEA	Lancashire, England	173/3
1987	LITTLE LONDON	West Sussex, England	174/1
1987	STOCKBRIDGE HOUSE	West Sussex, England	177/1
1987	SHAFIQ HOUSE	Malaga, Spain	178/1–2
1987	THE BARN	London NW7, England	179/1
1987	ALBERMARLE VILLAS	Hampshire, England	180/2
1987	ADAMS HOUSE	Essex, England	181/1
1987	MANOR STABLES	Oxfordshire, England	182/1–3
1987	SUSSEX SQUARE	West Sussex, England	183/1
1987	PRIORY TERRACE	London NW6, England	184/1
1987	KILQUADE HOUSE	County Wicklow, Ireland	185/1
1987	ENGLEWOOD PLACE	New York, United States	189/1–5
1988	VALLEY FARM	Hertfordshire, England	161/1–5
1988	LANGDALE	Surrey, England	176/1–3
1988	THE OLD MANOR	Surrey, England	191/1
1988	OLD ORCHARD	Hampshire, England	192/1–4
1988	OAST HOUSE	Hampshire, England	195/1
1988	TARRANT STREET	West Sussex, England	196/1
1988	MORDEN COLLEGE HOUSING	Kent, England	199/1
1988	MATSON GROUND	Cumbria, England	200/1–2
1988	RIDLANDS FARMHOUSE	Surrey, England	201/1
1988	BLACKTHORNE HOUSE	Surrey, England	203/1–2
1988	CHILWORTH FARM HOUSE	Oxfordshire, England	205/1–2
1988	DANEBURY HOUSE	Hampshire, England	207/1
1988	BOSSINGTON MILL	Hampshire, England	208/1
1988	MILL HOUSE	Suffolk, England	209/1
1988	GREAT ORCHARD	West Sussex, England	210/1
1988	ORCHARD HOUSE	Worcestershire, England	211/1
1988	COVERT COTTAGE	Gloucestershire, England	212/1–7
1988	LONG ACRES	Surrey, England	214/1–6
1988	MOONRAKERS	West Sussex, England	215/1
1988	MANOR HOUSE	Lincolnshire, England	216/1–2
1988	ST JOHNS JERUSALEM	Kent, England	217/1–2

DATE	SITE	LOCATION	DRAWING NUMBERS
1988	LONDON TRANSPORT	London, England	218/1–2
1988	THE DYKE HOUSE	West Sussex, England	219/1–3
1988	SILVERMERE	West Sussex, England	220/1–2
1988	LURGASHALL WINERY	West Sussex, England	221/1
1988	AVERNALS FARM	West Sussex, England	222/1–5
1988	WOODSTOCK ROAD	Oxfordshire, England	226/1
1988	ASHINGTON	Essex, England	227/1–8, 8A
1988	DYKE CLOSE	East Sussex, England	229/1
1988	MANOR LODGE	West Sussex, England	230/1–2
1988	LOXWOOD CHASE	West Sussex, England	231/1
1988	ELM TREE	Surrey, England	232/1–2
1988	HOME FARM HOUSE	West Sussex, England	234/1–3
1988	SHENLEY HILL	Hertfordshire, England	235/1–2
1988	CITY BUSINESS CENTRE	West Sussex, England	236/1
1988	LITTLE KINGSHILL GRANGE	Buckinghamshire, England	237/1–2
1988	CURDON HOUSE	Somerset, England	238/1–2
1988	WEST COMPTON HOUSE	Dorset, England	239/1–2
1988	CRUMP HOUSE	Kent, England	242/1
1988	GREEN CLOSE	London, England	249/1–7
1988	McCONNELL HOUSE	Virginia, United States	250/1–2
1988	EAST SPRUCE STREET	Illinois, United States	251/1, 669
1988	MALBROOK ROAD	London SW15, England	252/1–3
1988	FLINT ACRE	East Sussex, England	254/1–2
1988	FAIRWAY	West Sussex, England	255/1–4
1989	CHERRY HILLS	Colorado, United States	241/1
1989	FURZE CREEK	West Sussex, England	243/1
1989	OLD TOWN HOUSE	Oxfordshire, England	248/1–3
1989	DENTON DRIVE	East Sussex, England	253/2
1989	MINERVA THEATRE	Sussex, England	256/1
1989	CHERRY CROFT	West Sussex, England	257/1–3
1989	UPPER SHOREHAM ROAD	West Sussex, England	258/1
1989	ZERO	Bedfordshire, England	259/1–3
1989	WOODCROFT	West Sussex, England	260/1
1989	FRANKLIN PLACE	West Sussex, England	263/1
1989	TAGENTS FARM	West Sussex, England	264/1, 1A, 2–5
1989	EUROTHERM INTERNATIONAL	West Sussex, England	266/1–2
1989	SWAN WALK	London, England	267/1
1989	STONEMILL	West Sussex, England	268/1–2
1989	LITTLE HEATH ROAD	West Sussex, England	269/1–3
1989	WHYKE LANE	West Sussex, England	271/1
1989	CHANNINGS	West Sussex, England	272/1
1989	WEST WOODBURN FARM	Devon, England	274/1–5
1989	LITTLE BEALINGS	Gwent, Wales	276/1–4
1989	MAYFIELD ROAD	Surrey, England	277/1–2
1989	HIGH BARN FARM	Surrey, England	280/1–2
1989	NORTON HOUSE	West Sussex, England	281/1–2
1989	GRAYS	Hampshire, England	282/1–5
1989	THE DRUMBER	Cheshire, England	284/1–2
1989	NUTHALL ROAD HOTEL	Nottinghamshire, England	285/1
1989	STABLE COTTAGE	West Sussex, England	287/1
1989	GLENWOODS	Dorset, England	289/1–2
1989	WHARF HOUSE	Hampshire, England	290/1–6
1989	OLD WHARF	West Sussex, England	291/1
1989	BOSSINGTON HOUSE	Hampshire, England	292/1
1989	RECTORY COTTAGE	West Sussex, England	293/1
1989	MAPLE ROAD	West Sussex, England	294/1–2
1989	NORTH MANOR	West Sussex, England	296/1–2
1989	BEECHFIELD	Wirrall, England	297/1
1989	MOONRAKER	West Sussex, England	298/1–2
1989	GRAND AVENUE	West Sussex, England	299/1
1989	LOWER AVERNALS FARM	West Sussex, England	301/1–2
1989	RING HOUSE	West Sussex, England	302/1–4
1989	CLIFTON COTTAGE	London SE5, England	303/1
1989	BARAKURA	Tateshina, Japan	304/1–15, 17–20, 304A, 572/1, 581/1–2
1989	BLUE GATE COTTAGE	Surrey, England	308/1
1990	FELDON STREET	London SW6, England	275/1–4
1990	OLDFIELD HOUSE	West Sussex, England	295/1–3
1990	CLIFTON ROAD	Surrey, England	307/1
1990	IDAHO BOTANIC GARDEN	Idaho, United States	309/1–2
1990	ELANGENI	West Sussex, England	310/1–4
1990	PEEL STREET	London W8, England	311/1
1990	EAST SUSSEX GOLF CLUB	East Sussex, England	314/1
1990	THE OLD VICARAGE	West Sussex, England	315/1
1990	WALNUT COTTAGE	Berkshire, England	316/1–3
1990	PHYLLIS WOOD FARM HOUSE	West Sussex, England	317/1
1990	WITHERDENE FARM	Gloucestershire, England	318/1–5

DATE	SITE	LOCATION	DRAWING NUMBERS
1990	KENNERTON GREEN	New South Wales, Australia	319/1–2
1990	BOBERSKI PARK	Illinois, United States	320/1–7
1990	BROOK HOUSE	West Sussex, England	321/1
1990	SLINFOLD MANOR	West Sussex, England	325/1, 1A–B, 2–3, 3A, 4, 4A, 5–11
1990	CHISELHAMPTON LODGE	Oxfordshire, England	326/1–2
1990	BRAMBLES	East Sussex, England	328/1
1990	STAG LANE	Essex, England	329/1–3
1990	KIDDERPORE GARDENS	London, England	330/1
1990	POUNDSBRIDGE FARM	Kent, England	331/1
1990	WELLNAP COTTAGE	West Sussex, England	332/1
1990	HAMMERSMITH TERRACE	London W4, England	345/1–3
1990	RUSTINGTON HALL	West Sussex, England	355/1–2
1990	CHURCH HILL COTTAGE	West Sussex, England	335/1
1990	MANGERTON MANOR FARM	Dorset, England	333/1
1990	THE CROFT	Cheshire, England	336/2
1990	RIBBLESDALE PARK	Berkshire, England	340/1–2
1990	COOMBE LODGE	Berkshire, England	341/1–2
1990	HATWELL COPSE	West Sussex, England	344/1
1990	NARROWAY	West Sussex, England	346/1–4
1990	HOLLYBANK HOUSE	Jersey, Channel Islands	347/1–6
1990	WEST PARK ROAD	Surrey, England	349/1–2
1990	VICARAGE LANE	Oxfordshire, England	350/1
1990	ORCHARD HOUSE	Essex, England	351/1–3
1990	MARELLBAR FARM	Illinois, United States	353/1–3
1991	THE BARN	West Sussex, England	177
1991	DUMMERS COTTAGE	West Sussex, England	270/1–2
1991	HARESFIELD TERRACE	West Sussex, England	273/1
1991	ECKENSFIELD BARN	West Sussex, England	313/1–3
1991	HIGH TOBY	Surrey, England	343/1–3
1991	HULLASEY HOUSE	Gloucestershire, England	354/1–2
1991	ST JOHN'S SCHOOL	East Sussex, England	356/1–2
1991	EL CHOIQUE ESTANCIA	Argentina, South America	357/1–2
1991	LOS TOLDOS ESTANCIA	Argentina, South America	358/1–2
1991	HOOK LANE	West Sussex, England	359/1, 582/1–2
1991	PRIORY GATE	West Sussex, England	360/1–2
1991	AMBERLEY PLACE	West Sussex, England	361/1–4
1991	GRAFFHAM COURT	West Sussex, England	362/1–2
1991	THREE GABLES	Gloucestershire, England	363/1
1991	OAST COTTAGES	Kent, England	366/1
1991	RICHMOND COTTAGES	West Sussex, England	367/1
1991	TELEGRAPH COTTAGE	Surrey, England	368/1
1991	CHURCH FARM HOUSE	West Sussex, England	369/1–3
1991	NORTHFIELDS FARM	West Sussex, England	370/1–3
1991	THE FAIRWAY	West Sussex, England	372/1
1991	THE RANCH	Buckinghamshire, England	374/1
1991	BISHOPSGATE WALK	West Sussex, England	375/1–2
1991	BROOKGREEN STUDIOS	London W6, England	376/1
1991	MUNSTER GREEN	West Sussex, England	378/1
1991	LEWES ROAD	West Sussex, England	380/1–9
1991	EDMONDS FARMHOUSE	Surrey, England	381/1–2
1991	VIA LIDO NORD	California, United States	382/1–3
1991	WESTGATE	Devon, England	384/1
1991	SURREY RESEARCH PARK	Surrey, England	385/1–9
1991	HOMEWOOD RIDE	Kent, England	386/1
1991	PENNY FARTHING	Oxfordshire, England	387/1–3
1991	LITTLE WASHBROOK FARM	West Sussex, England	388/1
1991	BROOKFIELD HOUSE	West Sussex, England	389/1–8
1991	WINCHESTER CATHEDRAL	East Sussex, England	391/1
1991	MUTTONS BARN	West Sussex, England	392/2
1991	THE HOMESTEAD	Hampshire, England	393/1–3
1991	TOLLHOUSE CLOSE	West Sussex, England	394/1
1991	WOODLANDS	Hampshire, England	398/1–3
1991	THE MANOR HOUSE	West Sussex, England	400/1–2
1992	COLEBROOK ROAD	Hampshire, England	397/1
1992	FAWLEY ROAD	London NW6, England	401/1
1992	DUBLIN GARDEN FESTIVAL	Dublin, Ireland	403/1–2
1992	BRYANSTON SCHOOL	Dorset, England	405/1
1992	CENTRE TERRE VIVANTE	Rhône-Alps, France	406/1
1992	WESTMINSTER ABBEY GARDEN	London W1, England	408/1–10, 13
1992	ROBINS	Kent, England	409/1–3
1992	SLIPPER COTTAGE	Berkshire, England	410/1–2
1992	MANOR FARM	Worcestershire, England	412/1
1992	CRINGLEFORD HALL	Norfolk, England	413/1
1992	VON HASSELYN HOUSE	California, United States	414/1–2
1992	HABER HOUSE	New York State, United States	415/1
1992	TRENTHAM HOUSE	Hampshire, England	416/1

DATE	SITE	LOCATION	DRAWING NUMBERS
1992	COURTFIELD	London W5, England	418/1
1992	BARRYMORE	Berkshire, England	419/1–9
1992	ELLIS GARDEN	Oregon, United States	420/1–5
1992	EAST LODGE FARM	Cambridgeshire, England	421/1–2
1992	PALACE GARDENS TERRACE	London W8, England	422/1–2
1992	CUNNINGSTONE HOUSE	London W4, England	423/1
1992	VALLEY FARM	Lincolnshire, England	424/1, 3–5
1992	HAZEL COURT	Devon, England	425/1–2
1992	DOWNINGS	Hampshire, England	426/1–6
1992	UPPER BUNCTON	West Sussex, England	427/1–3
1992	ST MARKS CRESCENT	London NW1, England	428/1
1992	JODRELL BUILDING	Surrey, England	430/1
1992	RUMSTICK ROAD	Rhode Island, United States	432/1–6
1992	SKINNER HOUSE	Normandy, France	440/1–4
1993	SPRING LODGE	East Sussex, England	439/1
1993	TENTWORTH HOUSE	West Sussex, England	406/1
1993	LOWER BUNCTON	West Sussex, England	427/4
1993	GOODHEW CLOSE	West Sussex, England	434/1
1993	SULGRAVE FARM	Oxfordshire, England	435/1–3
1993	THE COURT HOUSE	Oxfordshire, England	436/1–2
1993	WIMBOURNE AVENUE	Kent, England	437/1
1993	ARGYLE ROAD	London W8, England	438/1
1993	KINGSWAY	Kent, England	441/1–7
1993	COGGESHALL HALL	Essex, England	443/1–4
1993	BARN COTTAGE	West Sussex, England	445/1
1993	OLD BRIDGE CLOSE	Hampshire, England	446/1–4
1993	WINTERBOURNE ROAD	West Sussex, England	447/1–2
1993	IMBRECOURT	Dorset, England	448/1–2
1993	RIVER COPPICE	West Sussex, England	449/1–2
1993	KINGS ARMS HILL	West Sussex, England	450/1
1993	GLEBE HOUSE	West Sussex, England	451/1
1993	HURST ROAD	West Sussex, England	453/1–4
1993	HILL RISE	London, England	455/1
1993	HAMILTON GARDENS	West Sussex, England	454/1
1993	DOBBIES	West Sussex, England	456/1–3
1993	LOWER STREET	West Sussex, England	461/1
1993	FOSSE BARN	Wiltshire, England	462/1–4
1993	CHATSWORTH DRIVE	West Sussex, England	463/1
1993	BLENHEIM GARDENS	Hampshire, England	464/1
1993	HUDSON CLOSE	West Sussex, England	465/1
1993	HARBERTON CRESCENT	West Sussex, England	467/1–7
1994	MARCH SQUARE	West Sussex, England	468/1–2
1994	THE OLD RECTORY	West Sussex, England	469/1, 3, 5–13
1994	WESTMINSTER DRIVE	Georgia, United States	470/1
1994	DERWENT CLOSE	West Sussex, England	471/1
1994	PARKLANDS	New South Wales, Australia	474/1–2
1994	HAMESFORD HOUSE	West Sussex, England	475/1
1994	PILGRIM COTTAGE	Hampshire, England	476/1–7
1994	TREVEREUX MANOR	Surrey, England	477/1–2
1994	JONES HOUSE	New South Wales, Australia	478/1–2
1994	SPRINGHILL GROVE	New South Wales, Australia	480/1–4
1994	NETHERHILL HOUSE	Hampshire, England	481/1
1994	THE WHITE HOUSE	Cambridgeshire, England	486/6–7, 487/1, 1a, 2–6
1994	HEDGEROWS	West Sussex, England	489/1–5
1994	OAKLEYS BARN	West Sussex, England	490/1–2
1994	BIDURA	New South Wales, Australia	491/1
1994	IVY COTTAGE	West Sussex, England	492/1–2
1994	SALTHILL HOUSE	West Sussex, England	493/1–3, 5–11
1994	KENTS BARN	West Sussex, England	494/1–3
1994	FORGE HOUSE	West Sussex, England	495/1–2
1994	HYDE VALE	London, England	496/1
1994	SOUTH BEACH	West Sussex, England	497/1–2
1994	EATON PLACE	London SW1, England	498/1–2
1994	CHEMIN VERT PRE	Geneva, Switzerland	499/1–2
1994	ROLLESBY	Cambridgeshire, England	501/1
1994	MARYLEBONE GATE	London, England	503/1, 3–10
1994	BANQUE PARIBAS	London, England	503/2
1995	HARGREAVES SHOW HOUSE	West Sussex, England	389/9–11
1995	RUSTINGTON HOUSE	West Sussex, England	389/12–14
1995	RUSHMANS	West Sussex, England	501/1
1995	SHEEPDROVE FARMHOUSE	Berkshire, England	502/1–3
1995	ROBARNS LAY	Surrey, England	504/1
1995	HACKERS CLOSE	Nottinghamshire, England	506/1
1995	CHANTI	West Sussex, England	507/1
1995	TUPTON PLACE	East Sussex, England	509/1–2

DATE	SITE	LOCATION	DRAWING NUMBERS
1995	MANORA	West Sussex, England	510/1–2
1995	ROWAN LODGE	London, England	511/1–2
1995	LANCASTRIAN COURT	West Sussex, England	512/1
1995	THE SQUARE HOUSE	West Sussex, England	515/1
1995	EAST DULWICH GROVE	London SE22, England	517/2, 4–5
1995	BOWLING HOUSE	Cheshire, England	518/1
1995	ADUR AVENUE	West Sussex, England	519/1–3
1995	GRAININGFOLD FARMHOUSE	West Sussex, England	522/1–2
1995	GRIFFINS	Surrey, England	529/1–3
1995	OAKMEAD FARM	Surrey, England	532/1–4
1995	WESTERGATE MEWS	West Sussex, England	534/1
1995	WHINNEY MACKAY LEWIS	London W1, England	526/1
1995	MAPLE COTTAGES	Derbyshire, England	528/1
1996	HOBERTHGASSE	Gablitz, Austria	523/1A–C, 2–3
1996	EAST WALLS CLOSE	West Sussex, England	530/2–4
1996	THE METROPOLITAN CLUB	Beirut, Lebanon	534/1
1996	GAYLES	East Sussex, England	535/1–10
1996	ELGIN CRESCENT	London W11, England	536/1–2
1996	RECTORY COTTAGE	Oxfordshire, England	537/1
1996	EAST BEACH ROAD	West Sussex, England	538/1
1996	FLINT COTTAGE	West Sussex, England	539/1
1996	WEST LANE	Hampshire, England	542/1
1996	TILSON HOUSE	Oregon, United States	543/1–2
1996	SOUTHDOWN ROAD	West Sussex, England	544/1
1996	CROWS HALL FARM	West Sussex, England	545/1–2
1996	BRAMHALL	Surrey, England	546/1–3
1996	BROOKLANDS COTTAGE	Surrey, England	547/1–2
1996	ATZENACH	Stolberg, Germany	550/1–2
1996	WARBLINGTON ROAD	Hampshire, England	551/1–6
1996	HURTWOOD HOUSE	Surrey, England	552/1
1996	PARADISE HOUSE	Devon, England	553/1
1996	RIVERSIDE HOUSE	Devon, England	554/1
1996	SUNNYHILL	Hampshire, England	555/1
1996	LONDON ROAD	West Sussex, England	556/1
1996	SOUTHAMPTON COURT	Hampshire, England	557/1–8
1997	PINE COTTAGE	West Sussex, England	514/1–3
1997	SUMMER COTTAGE	Dorset, England	521/1–2
1997	PALM BEACH HOTEL	Larnaca, Cyprus	560/1–17
1997	TYMA HOUSE	West Sussex, England	562/1–2
1997	SEMLER	Brazil, South America	563/1–3
1997	WARENNE LODGE	West Sussex, England	564/1–3
1997	SEATON ROAD	West Sussex, England	565/1–2
1997	ROEHAMPTON GATE	London SW15, England	566/1–2
1997	EATON PLACE	London SW1, England	569/1
1997	BROYLE CLOSE	West Sussex, England	571/1
1997	MISTY	West Sussex, England	573/1
1997	MANOR HOUSE	West Sussex, England	576/1–2
1997	WATLINGTON PRIMARY SCH	Oxfordshire, England	577/1
1997	OBEROI FARM HOUSE	Delhi, India	578/1–2
1997	THE SALTINGS	West Sussex, England	579/1–4
1997	THE CHERWELL SCHOOL	Oxfordshire, England	580/1
1998	THE RIDGE	Surrey, England	559/1–6
1998	NEW ENGLAND ESTATE	New England, United States	587/1–3, 5–6, 8–10, 20–4, 27–44, 46–52, 54–71
1998	SAWMILL BARN	West Sussex, England	584/1,3
1998	MILCOMBE HOUSE	Oxfordshire, England	585/1
1998	ST PANCRAS	West Sussex, England	586/2
1998	GARDENERS WORLD LIVE	West Midlands, England	588/1A, 2–3
1998	LORDSHIP LANE	London SE22, England	589/1–3
1998	SOPERS BARN	Surrey, England	590/1
1998	BERKSHIRE RECORD OFFICE	Berkshire, England	591/1–2
1998	CASA DE CAMPO EN OLEIROS	Fachada Oeste, Spain	592/2–5–9
1998	PRIORY ROAD	London NW6, England	593/1–2
1998	CLEVELAND BOTANICAL GDN	Cleveland, United States	595/1
1998	KING GEORGE GARDENS	Sussex, England	596/1
1998	HEATHERLANDS	West Sussex, England	603/1
1998	VILLAGE FARMYARD	Warwickshire, England	604/1
1998	DRAYCOTT COURT	London, England	608/1
1998	CENTRO DE DEPORTES	Chile, South America	612/1–3
1999	ST JAMES'S STREET	London SW1, England	140B/2
1999	NORTH STREET	West Sussex, England	513/1–3
1999	CASTLE LODGE	East Sussex, England	583/1–4
1999	ZESPOL PALACE PARK	Kikol, Poland	594/1–8
1999	THE DRIVE	Kent, England	606/1–2

DATE	SITE	LOCATION	DRAWING NUMBERS
1999	WESTERGATE MEWS	West Sussex, England	613/1
1999	APULDRAM HOUSE	West Sussex, England	614/1–2
1999	OUSELEY STREET	London SW12, England	615/1
1999	HESLOP ROAD	London SW17, England	615/2–4
1999	BROOMWOOD HALL	London, England	616/1–3
1999	LA PORTE	Menerbes, France	617/1
1999	PEWLEY HILL	Surrey, England	618/1
1999	LA CARMEJANE	Menerbes, France	619/1–6
1999	FOLLY FOOT FARM	West Sussex, England	621/1
1999	WILDWOOD ROAD	London NW11, England	622/1–2
1999	HOLISTIC HOLIDAYS	Lanzarote, Spain	626/1
1999	HORTON COTTAGE	Sussex, England	628/1
1999	ORCHARD HOUSE	Oxfordshire, England	629/1–2
1999	VINA APALTA ESTANCIA	Chile, South America	630/1–4
1999	CHANTRY COTTAGE	Surrey, England	632/1–2
1999	STRATHMORE CLOSE	West Sussex, England	633/1, 1A, 2, 2A
1999	HAGGENSTON HOUSE	West Sussex, England	635/1–3 (5)
1999	IWATA GRAND HOTEL	Shizuoka, Japan	636
1999	RAVENS WOOD SCHOOL	Kent, England	637
2000	ECCLESDEN MANOR	West Sussex, England	400/3–15
2000	TIMS SPRINGS	Hertfordshire, England	625/1–4, 4A
2000	DU PORT-DE-BELLERIVE	Geneva, Switzerland	639
2000	THE OLD RECTORY	Surrey, England	640/1–2
2000	PORTOLA ROAD	California, United States	643/A
2000	POND ACRE	West Sussex, England	645
2000	ROMAN CROFT	West Midlands, England	643/2, 644/1, 1A, 2-3, 4
2000	THE MANOR HOUSE	Dorset, England	646
2000	DINGLEY	Sussex, England	647
2001	WHITELOCKS	West Sussex, England	624/1–2–2A
2001	WITHDEAN ROAD	West Sussex, England	508/1–9
2001	REMENHAM PLACE	Oxfordshire, England	627/1–15
2001	WESTHOLME HOUSE	Somerset, England	642/1–4
2001	WARREN HOUSE	West Sussex, England	648
2001	NINEVAH SHIPYARD	West Sussex, England	649
2001	INGLEBY	West Sussex, England	650/A, B, 1
2001	MERMAID COTTAGE	West Sussex, England	651/1–2
2001	ELLIS BEACH HOUSE	Oregon, United States	652
2001	TORTINGTON PRIORY BARN	West Sussex, England	653
2001	RUE NOTRE-DAME DE NAZ	Paris, France	655
2001	THE POUND HOUSE	Berkshire, England	657
2001	BROOKFIELD HOUSE	Dorset, England	658
2001	KITHURST COTTAGE	West Sussex, England	659
2001	PALATINE ROAD	West Sussex, England	654/1, 1A
2001	LADY PLACE	Oxfordshire, England	660/1–2
2001	WESTONBIRT FESTIVAL	Gloucestershire, England	661/1–10
2001	CLYDE ROAD	Sussex, England	662
2001	VAN LIERDE HOUSE	Argentina, South America	663/1–3
2001	MILLSTREAM	Wiltshire, England	664
2002	BLOUNTS LODGE	Buckinghamshire, England	638/1–3
2002	CAROLINA	Berkshire, England	656/1–4
2002	BARTSCHT	West Sussex, England	665/1–2
2002	ROCK COTTAGES	West Sussex, England	666/1–2
2002	CAVENDISH AVENUE	Yorkshire, England	667/1–4
2002	BARBER MOTORSPORTS PARK	Alabama, United States	668
2002	FIFTH AVENUE	New York, United States	668/1–2
2002	NURSTED BARNS	Hampshire, England	670/1–2
2002	HOLLAM HOUSE	Hampshire, England	672/1–2
2002	ANGLING SPRING FARM	Buckinghamshire, England	673
2002	AMBERLEY COURT	Sussex, England	675/1–2
2002	OAK APPLE COTTAGE	Surrey, England	676/1–2
2002	SHOULTS RESIDENCE	British Columbia, United States	674/1–3
2003	SUAKIN	West Sussex, England	677
2003	REDHILL DRIVE	West Sussex, England	678/1–2
2003	YSTYM COLWYN HALL	Powys, Wales	679
2003	CROWDER TERRACE	Hampshire, England	680
2003	GUESSAN	Gers, France	682/1–3
2003	DAVENPORT HOUSE	West Sussex, England	683
2003	VILLA LA ANGOSTURA	Argentina, South America	684/1–2
2003	BERINSHILL WOOD	Oxfordshire, England	685
2003	SUGAR MAPLE FARM	New York, United States	686/1–4
2003	GREENBRIAR LANE	London, England	687/1–3
2003	FARM STREET	London W1, England	688
2003	SHERBURNE HOUSE	West Sussex, England	689
2003	EASTGATE MEWS	West Sussex, England	690

DATE	SITE	LOCATION	DRAWING NUMBERS
2003	DOUGLAS LAKE FARM	West Sussex, England	691/1/2
2003	ATHENA DRIVE	British Colombia, United States	692/1–3
2003	ORCHARD HOUSE	London SW19, England	693
2004	BROOK HOUSE	London, England	694/1–2
2004	FITZGERALD CLOSE	Hampshire, England	695
2004	HILL TOP	Surrey, England	696
2004	CHURCH FARM	West Sussex, England	697/1–2
2004	ST JOHN'S ROAD	Kent, England	699/1–2
2004	WOODHILL COTTAGE	Kent, England	700
2004	SLIEVE RUSSELL HOTEL	County Cavan, Ireland	701/3–4
2004	PEAR TREE HOUSE	Yorkshire, England	703/1–2
2004	ST JOHN STREET	Oxford, England	705
2004	THE LODGE	Buckinghamshire, England	706
2004	WEST BARN	West Sussex, England	708
2004	HARROWHILL	Surrey, England	709/1–5
2004	PEQUOT AVENUE	Connecticut, United States	710
2004	ROBIN HILL	Surrey, England	711
2004	FOSTER RESIDENCE	New York, United States	712
2004	THE WHITE HORSE	Kent, England	713
2004	DEPOT ROAD	West Sussex, England	714
2004	RENAISSANCE	Surrey, England	715
2004	BROOK HOUSE	West Sussex, England	716
2004	MOUNT ST JOHN	Yorkshire, England	718
2004	CHISELHAMPTON HOUSE	Oxfordshire, England	719/1–14
2004	HOTEL GOURMOND	Brazil, South America	720/1–29
2004	ROSE COTTAGE	West Sussex, England	721
2005	THE SQUARE HOUSE	West Sussex, England	722
2005	AUTUMN HOLLOW	East Sussex, England	723/1–3
2005	COLTS BAY	West Sussex, England	724
2005	TORTINGTON MANOR	West Sussex, England	725
2005	HANDLEY HOUSE	Nottinghamshire, England	726
2005	LA SERENA CHICO	Argentina, South America	727
2005	LA SERENA	Argentina, South America	728
2005	NEW FARM HOUSE	Northamptonshire, England	729
2005	HAVANT ROAD	Hampshire, England	730
2005	DUCKS HILL	Kent, England	731
2005	HOLLY TREES	West Sussex, England	732
2005	FIELD HOUSE	Worcestershire, England	733
2005	OLD POPLARS FARMHOUSE	Gloucestershire, England	736
2006	TAYLORS OF HARROGATE	Yorkshire, England	734/1–6
2006	SHAKER BAY ROAD	North Colonie, United States	737
2006	RUSKINS FIELD	East Sussex, England	739
2006	VILLA GIRASOL	Brazil, South America	740/1–2
2006	THIRLEMERE WAY	West Sussex, England	741
2006	GROVE COTTAGE	Surrey, England	743
2006	ELMHURST FARM	West Sussex, England	744/1–4
2006	THE NORTH CANONRY	Dorset, England	745
2006	CROFT END	West Sussex, England	746
2006	MALSHANGER	Hampshire, England	747
2006	ST WILFRID'S HOSPICE	West Sussex, England	749
2006	LAVENDER HOUSE	West Sussex, England	750
2006	BROME HOUSE	Kent, England	751
2006	SHOCKWAVE	West Sussex, England	752
2006	PARK STREET LANE	Hertfordshire, England	753
2006	WILBURY AVENUE	East Sussex, England	754
2006	GASSONS	West Sussex, England	755
2006	EAST ASHLING HOUSE	West Sussex, England	756
2006	MIDDLE PETT FARM	Kent, England	757
2006	NIGHTINGALES	East Sussex, England	758

Endnotes

Page 4
1 John Brookes, *Room Outside. A New Approach to Garden Design* (London: Thames & Hudson, 1969), p. 5.

John Brookes: Garden and Landscape Designer
2 Fred Whitsey, 'This Garden is "Modern" – but would you choose it?', *The Sunday Telegraph* (27 May, 1962).
3 Theo Crosby (1925–94) came to London from Johannesburg after World War II, attending art school before working in the architectural practice of modernist Maxwell Fry. He was editor of *Architectural Design* 1953–62 and was one of the organizers of the iconic exhibition *This is Tomorrow 1956*, which promoted a multi-disciplinary approach to art and architecture.
4 Michael Manser (b.1929), recognized early on as an innovative architect, established a private practice in 1961, promoting the steel and glass aesthetic of the Modern Movement in his designs. During the 1960s he regularly contributed to *Architectural Design* and was president of the Royal Institute of British Architects (RIBA) 1983–5.
5 Geoffrey Jellicoe (1900–96), landscape architect, architect and town planner, was president of the Landscape Institute 1939–49. He worked on plans for Hemel Hempstead, power stations and civic centres as well as a range of garden designs, completing schemes for over a hundred projects. He was knighted in 1979.
6 Brookes (1969), *op.cit.*, p. 5.
7 *Ibid.*, p. 25, Figure 33.
8 Brookes's aunt was Eve Standring. Her daughter, Heather, attended Chelsea Art School, becoming an illustrator and working on the women's page of the *Daily Mail* with Shirley Conran. She joined *House Beautiful* as interiors editor in 1968. John Brookes in conversation with the author, 20 April 2004.
9 Dorothy Stroud, *Capability Brown* (London: Country Life, 1950).
10 Information from Michael Brookes, 12 January 2007.
11 Michael Brookes recalls that from the age of seven John was always 'nicking bits of plants from other people's gardens' and that the family home was always full of cuttings. Michael Brookes in conversation with the author, 28 September 2004. Percy Brookes approved of this choice, advising John that the Institute of Parks Administration would need advice on roadside and other planting as part of post-war infrastructure. John Brookes in conversation with the author, 20 April 2004.
12 Christopher Tunnard, *Gardens in the Modern Landscape* (London: The Architectural Press, 1938). Revised version 1948. Tunnard (1910–79) was born in British Columbia, Canada, of English parents, but returned to England in 1928, where he studied horticulture on the Royal

Horticultural Society's course at Wisley, Surrey. He became a proponent of the Modern Movement in England, his book being an important statement of the modernist position.
13 A white, three-storey, Corbusier-inspired house of reinforced concrete designed by Connell, Ward & Lucas 1928–30 for Bernard Ashmole. For further details see Alan Powers, *Modern. The Modern Movement in Britain* (London and New York: Merrell Publishers Limited, 2005), pp. 88–89.
14 Geoffrey Chadbund worked with the Surrey firm of L. R. Russell Ltd, Richmond Nurseries, Windlesham. He later wrote a book on flowering cherries with line drawings by John Brookes. See Geoffrey Chadbund, *Flowering Cherries* (London: Collins, 1972).
15 John Brookes in conversation with the author, 20 April 2004.
16 John Brookes in conversation with the author, 20 April 2004.
17 The profession of landscape architecture was formally established in Britain on 11 December 1929 with Thomas Mawson as its first president. The name of the organization was the British Association of Garden Architects, but within two months the name was changed to the Institute of Landscape Architects.
18 Brenda Colvin (1897–1981) was ILA president 1951–3 and produced a number of books for landscape professionals, most notably *Land and Landscape* (London: John Murray, 1947) and (with Jaqueline Tyrwhitt) *Trees for Town and Country* (London: Lund Humphries, 1947). Sylvia Crowe (1901–97) was ILA president 1957–9. By 1960 she had written *Tomorrow's Landscape* (London: Architectural Press, 1956); *The Landscape of Power* (London: Architectural Press, 1958); *Garden Design* (London: Country Life, 1958); and *The Landscape of Roads* (London: Architectural Press, 1960). See also Geoffrey Collens and Wendy Powell (eds.), *Sylvia Crowe* (Reigate: Landscape Design Trust Monographs, 1999) for an evaluation of Crowe's work.
19 An article on this early period of John Brookes's work was first published in 2005. See Barbara Simms, 'Rooms Outside: 1960s London Gardens by John Brookes', *The London Gardener* 10 (2005), pp. 79–88.
20 Brenda Colvin, 'Gardens to Enjoy', *Gardens and Gardening: The Studio Gardening Annual 1952*, p. 10. See also 'Begin your London garden now', *Evening News* (March 1927) – interview with Brenda Colvin.
21 Thomas Church, 'The Small California Garden, A New Deal for the Small Lot', *California Arts and Architecture* 43 (May 1933); *Gardens are for People* (New York: McGraw-Hill, 1955). See also Marc Treib (ed.), *Thomas Church, Landscape Architect: Designing a Modern California Landscape* (San Francisco: William K. Stout, 2004) for a review of the life and work of Church (1902–78).
22 A number of publications have described Burle Marx's work, which was centred on his native Brazil. See for example Marta Iris Montero, *Burle Marx: The Lyrical Landscape*

(London: Thames & Hudson, 2001). First edition in Spanish 1997.
23 Michael Laurie (1933–2002) later became Professor of Landscape Architecture at the University of California, Berkeley, where he knew Thomas Church and was a contributor to a revised edition of *Gardens are for People* (1983). With thanks to UOC at Berkeley Library for providing information on Laurie.
24 Anthony du Gard Pasley (b.1929) was a pupil with Brenda Colvin whilst studying landscape architecture at University College, London, under Peter Youngman. He became an associate with Sylvia Crowe in 1964. A skilled plantsman, he left to establish his own practice in 1970, has written widely and taught at the English Gardening School, Chelsea, London SW1. With thanks to Anthony du Gard Pasley for information on life in the Colvin-Crowe office in interview with the author, 22 July 2005.
25 Crowe (1958), *op. cit.*, pp. 166, 171.
26 Sylvia Crowe, 'Presidential Address', *Journal of the Institute of Landscape Architects* (November 1957), p. 4.
27 John Brookes in conversation with the author, 20 April 2004.
28 An early example is Colvin's proposal for Dr Walker's garden at Thatcham, Berkshire, which includes garden areas on different levels, rough grass with bulbs and a gravel play space. Drawing no. 414/4. Dated October 1957 and signed JAB. Landscape Institute Archives. See Jeremy Dodd, 'Chelsea Flower Show, 1958', *Journal of the Institute of Landscape Architects* (August 1958), p. 5.
29 Colvin (1952), *op. cit.*, p. 10.
30 *Ibid.*, p. 10. See also Brenda Colvin, 'Planting as a medium of design', *Journal of the Institute of Landscape Architects* (August 1961), pp. 8–10.
31 John Brookes is colour blind and his difficulty in differentiating the subtle variations of colour may have made him more responsive to the form and texture of plants.
32 Jellicoe developed the concept of the unconscious mind as both inspiration for and understanding of landscapes. In particular, he was drawn to the works of Paul Klee, whose organic shapes he felt explored the world of the 'subconscious'. See *Studies in Landscape Design* Vol. 1 (Oxford: Oxford University Press, 1960); Vol. 2 (1966); Vol. 3 (1970) and other works by Geoffrey Jellicoe for further discussion of his ideas.
33 John Brookes in conversation with the author, 14 May 2004.
34 Willem de Kooning (1904–97) was one of the major figures of Abstract Expressionism. Mark Rothko (1903–70) developed a new form of abstract painting, characterized by a formal use of colour, shape, balance, depth, composition, and scale.
35 Susan and Geoffrey Jellicoe, *Modern Private Gardens* (London: Abelard-Schumann Ltd, 1968), p. 9. The book was reviewed by Brookes in *Journal of the Institute of Landscape Architects* (August 1968), p. 34.

36 In conversation with the author, 14 May 2004, Brookes also cites the following books as influential: Marjory Allen and Susan Jellicoe, *The New Small Garden* (London: Architectural Press, 1956) and Elizabeth Beazley, *Design and Detail of the Space Between Buildings* (London: Architectural Press, 1960). In the early 1960s Rachel Carson, *Silent Spring* (Boston: Houghton Mifflin, 1962) and Elizabeth Kassler, *Modern Gardens and the Landscape* (New York: Museum of Modern Art, 1964) also informed his design principles.
37 John Brookes in conversation with the author, 14 May 2004.
38 Brookes also did the drawings for Marjorie Allen, *Design for Play* (London: Housing Centre Trust, 1962).
39 At this time there were only four courses (Reading, London, Durham and Leeds) training landscape architects. See Sylvia Crowe, 'Presidential Address', *op. cit.*, pp. 3–5, 20. Brookes attended the London evening course from September 1957 and was awarded the Certificate in Landscape Design on 1 March 1960. With thanks to Wendy Butler, University College London Records Office for this information. Brookes's special study focused on the Festival Gardens created as part of the 1951 Festival of Britain on the south bank of London's Thames, a project which he discussed with the garden designer Russell Page, who had contributed to the planting design.
40 With thanks to Annabel Downs (archivist) and Kate Lander (head of library and information services), Landscape Institute, 33 Great Portland Street, London W1 for making these and other records available.
41 See, for example, John Brookes, 'Churchill College. A landscape review of exhibition designs', *Journal of the Institute of Landscape Architects* (November 1959), pp. 8–9.
42 For example, Brookes's contribution to an open ILA discussion is included in the Journal: 'Mr Brookes thought [the term] "landscape designer" more suitable than "landscape architect", because the profession was really concerned with design involving something living, organic and moving – entirely different from building design'; 'Collaboration between the architect and the landscape architect', *Journal of the Institute of Landscape Architects* (May 1960), p. 5. He is also noted as a contributor to a discussion on landscape policy at the ILA Edinburgh Conference 6–12 September 1960, following this with a letter that resolutions were rarely acted upon; *Journal of the Institute of Landscape Architects* (November 1960), p. 27–28. He also participated in a discussion on the Institute's policy on education following publication of *The Report on the Recruitment, Training and Employment of Landscape Architects*; *Journal of the Institute of Landscape Architects* (May 1961), p. 14.
43 Miscellany, *Journal of the Institute of Landscape Architects* (August 1960), p. 2. Susan Jellicoe was chair of the Committee.
44 David Thirkettle, 'Chelsea Flower Show',

Journal of the Institute of Landscape Architects (May 1959), pp. 12–13. This garden appears to be based on Brookes's 1956 design for a roof garden at Chesham Street SW1.

45 A small North London garden. Exhibit for the Design Section of the Chelsea Flower Show. Undated but probably 1960 or 1961.

46 Correspondence, *Journal of the Institute of Landscape Architects* (February 1960), p. 16. Brookes reiterated these ideas in a letter following the Chelsea Flower Show 1961; *Journal of the Institute of Landscape Architects* (August 1961), pp. 21–22.

47 A competition was held for professional and student members of the ILA. The judges were Peter Youngman, Miss J.F. Adburgham and Peter Shepheard; *Journal of the Institute of Landscape Architects* (February 1962), p. 2, (May 1962), p. 3.

48 He was co-opted to the Public Relations Committee to assist in the preparation of a script for a proposed film on landscape architecture and later suggested the ILA should take part in the Congress of the International Union of Architecture in the summer of 1961. Notes from Council Minutes, *Journal of the Institute of Landscape Architects* (February 1961), p. 2.

49 The set pieces were designs for the restoration of a coal mining area and Letchworth Garden City. The examiners were Sheila Heywood, Herbert Tayler and David Green. Their general report is included in *Journal of the Institute of Landscape Architects* (August 1960), p. 19. Reports in the Institute's journal indicate that the majority of examinees failed the set piece each year and that steps were being taken to address this. See, for example, Peter Youngman, 'Final Examination Set Piece 1962: Criticism', *Journal of the Institute of Landscape Architects* (August 1962), p. 4; and Correspondence (August 1965), p.16, in which Brian Clouston commented that 'there are failings and deficiencies in the examination system'. Brookes did not retake the examination and has remained ineligible for membership at associate level.

50 John Brookes, 'A new link with our public', *Landscape Design* no. 234 (October 1994), p. 29.

51 Diana Rowntree, 'Buildings for Architects, *The Guardian* (29 June 1961).

52 Brookes's column ran from October 1961 to January 1964, when he left *Architectural Design* to practise garden design full-time.

53 John Brookes, 'Landscape Design', *Architectural Design* (February 1962), p. 63.

54 John Brookes, 'Landscape Design', *Architectural Design* (May 1962), p. 217.

55 John Brookes, 'Landscape Design', *Architectural Design* (June 1962).

56 John Brookes, 'Landscape Design', *Architectural Design* (July 1962).

57 'House at Leatherhead, Surrey', *Architectural Design* (March, 1962), pp. 135–6. The house and grounds featured in a number of other magazines including *Home* (February 1962) and Brookes included the plan and photographs of the

courtyard in *Room Outside*, p. 35.

58 In addition to Golden Grove, Michael Manser commissioned Brookes to design two further gardens for himself and wife José (Dorking, Surrey, 1972, and Bosham, West Sussex, 2005). In total, between 1961 and 1991, Brookes designed the gardens or landscapes around 15 buildings designed by Manser. With thanks to Michael and José Manser for this information provided in an interview with the author, 16 August 2006.

59 For an explanation see John Brookes, 'Choosing and Using a Grid' in *John Brookes' Garden Design Book. The complete practical guide to planning, styling and planting any garden* (London: Dorling Kindersley, 1991), pp. 56–63 'Choosing and Using a Grid' and, more recently, *Garden Masterclass* (London: Dorling Kindersley, 2002), pp. 80–89.

60 'Exhibition Garden 1962. Chelsea Flower Show', *Architectural Design* (July 1962), p. 343. See also 'Competition Garden, Chelsea Flower Show', *Journal of the Institute of Landscape Architects* (August 1962), pp. 6–7. The competition was not repeated the following year: the decision to revert to an exhibition of drawn designs was again criticized in 1963 as too technical for the general public. See, for example, the letter from Hal Moggridge in Correspondence, *Journal of the Institute of Landscape Architects* (August 1963), p. 23. The competition was next held for the 1965 Chelsea Flower Show.

61 'Concrete Means the End of Terrace Gardens', *Garden News* (15 May 1962). The garden was sponsored by the Cement and Concrete Association (CCA), the Universal Asbestos Manufacturing Company and the Horticultural Trades Association and built by the landscaper, Gavin Jones. The prize was £100. Brookes later contributed a chapter on 'Some garden design principles' to a CCA publication, illustrated with photographs of his own garden in Oxfordshire. See Nicolette Franck, *Concrete in garden-making* (London: Cement and Concrete Association, 1972.

62 Brochure for the ILA Garden Design Competition for the Chelsea Flower Show 1962.

63 'Concrete Means the End of Terrace Gardens', *op. cit.*

64 *Evening News* (March 1927), *op. cit.*

65 'Fiddlers Copse, Plaistow, Sussex', *Journal of the Institute of Landscape Architects* (May 1964), pp. 8–11.

66 'A small garden in SW10', *House and Garden* (June 1965), pp. 72–3.

67 John Brookes in conversation with the author, 25 August 2004.

68 *Ibid.* See also 'Designer Profile. An Eclectic Style', *Garden Design Journal* (Autumn 1998), pp. 8–11 for an overview of Shanley's work.

69 See 'Courtyard design for Penguin Books Ltd', *Journal of the Institute of Landscape Architects* (February 1966), pp. 12–13. In the 1980s Brookes was asked to upgrade the canteen courtyard and other areas on the garden.

70 Susan and Geoffrey Jellicoe, *op. cit.*, pp. 34–36. The Gimpel garden was also included (pp. 23–4).

71 In his review of plantswoman Margery Fish's book on ground cover plants, Brookes also proposed, possibly with students in mind, that some form of 'classified system…. would have made the book more valuable'. *Journal of the Institute of Landscape Architects* (May 1965), p. 17.

72 Notes from Council Minutes, *Journal of the Institute of Landscape Architects* (August 1965), p. 20; Correspondence, *Journal of the Institute of Landscape Architects* (May 1969), p. 38.

73 Miscellany, *Journal of the Institute of Landscape Architects* (August 1966), p. 25. The Journal Committee thanked Brookes 'not only for the many hours he has devoted to the Journal but for the cheerful willingness with which he has invariably responded immediately to all calls for help'. Brookes resigned his responsibility due to 'pressures of work', his place being taken by Hal Moggridge. He remained on the Committee.

74 Book Reviews, *Journal of the Institute of Landscape Architects* (August 1968), p. 34.

75 Brookes was reviewing Isamu Noguchi, *A Sculptor's World* (London: Thames and Hudson, 1968). *Journal of the Institute of Landscape Architects* (November 1968), p. 34.

76 With thanks to David Papworth and Beverley Hilton for information supplied in interviews with the author on 4 and 14 July 2005 respectively. Brookes also recalls working with Robert Harling on *House and Garden* in the 1960s.

77 'A garden from scratch', *House Beautiful* (November 1967), pp. 81–6. The series continued until August 1968. Information on planting was provided by the Sussex nursery of J. Cheal & Son. The story of the garden is also told in John Brookes, *Garden Design and Layout* (London: The Queen Anne Press in association with The Gardening Centre Ltd., Syon Park, 1970), pp. 12–19.

78 Although the drawings exist they are undated and contain no details of the locations of the gardens.

79 Peter Coates, 'British designers in the garden', *House and Garden* (March 1966), pp. 63–77.

80 The garden was featured (without attribution) as a good example of 'intricate patterning of brick and tile' in *Good Housekeeping* (July 1966), p. 23.

81 A garden at St George's Hill, Weybridge, and a London studio garden by Brookes were included in 'Five small private gardens', *Journal of the Institute of Landscape Architects* (February 1969), p. 11–18. The other gardens were by Geoffrey Smith and Anthony du Gard Pasley. A garden designed by Brookes near Hampstead Heath (1968) featured in *Journal of the Institute of Landscape Architects* (August 1976), p. 12–19. The other gardens were by John Darbourne, Gordon Patterson and Philip Hicks.

82 Nan Fairbrother (1913–17) was a writer and journalist on landscape and land use. She wrote her first book *An English Year* (1954) about raising her sons in the country while her husband served with the Royal Air Force. This was followed by *Men and*

Gardens (London: Hogarth Press, 1956], *The Cheerful Day* (London: Hogarth Press, 1960] and *The House in the Country* (London: Hogarth Press, 1965]. Her time as John Brookes's assistant focused her writing on landscape and garden design, and she later produced *New Lives, New Landscapes* (London: Architectural Press, 1970) and *The Nature of Landscape Design* (London: Architectural Press, 1974).

83 Brookes (1969), *op. cit.*, p. 21.

84 The book was reviewed by Geoffrey Smith in *Journal of the Institute of Landscape Architects* (August 1969), p. 35. Smith commented that it was written with 'infectious enthusiasm' and 'will encourage the novice to exercise his own talents, and provide him with a sensible approach to design and good standards of construction' and could 'influence public attitudes in a progressive way'.

85 John Brookes, 'Other People's Gardens', *Good Housekeeping* 97/4 (April 1970), pp. 109–110; 97/5 (May 1970), pp. 89–90; 98/1 (July 1970), pp. 103–4; 99/6 (June 1971), pp. 143–4.

86 *Living in the Garden* and *Garden Design and Layout* (London: The Queen Anne Press in association with The Gardening Centre Ltd., Syon Park, 1970); and *Gardens for Small Spaces* (London: Pan Books Ltd, 1970).

87 *Garden Design and Layout*, p. 80.

88 Anthony Huxley (ed.), *The Financial Times Book of Garden Design* (Newton Abbot, London, Vancouver: David & Charles, 1975). Foreword by the Earl of Drogheda, p. 7.

89 Information from *Financial Times Garden* leaflet. Courtesy John Brookes.

90 With thanks to Mrs Lort-Phillips for this information in interview with the author, 18 July 2006.

91 With thanks to David Ransom for spending time discussing his involvement with gardens designed by John Brookes on Jersey and for helping to locate the gardens, 16 July 2006.

92 With thanks to Jacqueline Duncan for information given during an interview with the author, 17 October 2006. The Inchbald Garden Design School is now at 32 Eccleston Square, London SW1.

93 Finding the travelling too time-consuming in the days before a motorway to the south-west, Brookes returned to live in London, buying a flat in Shepherds Bush.

94 Inchbald School of Garden promotional literature designed for the Chelsea Flower Show 1976 (Jekyll Garden). The ten-week course was designed for 'both junior and mature students in horticulture: to those already engaged in the nursery and garden trades: and to all those interested in having a basic training in garden design as owners, architects or planners'. It was run three times a year (January to March, May to July and October to December) and cost £450 'inclusive of VAT, insurance, drawing materials, instruments and outside visits'.

95 James Rose, 'Freedom in the Garden', *Pencil Points* (February 1938), reproduced in Marc Treib (ed.), *Modern Landscape Architecture: A critical review* (Cambridge, Massachusetts, and London: MIT Press, 1998), p. 71. First edition 1993.

96 Roberto Burle Marx speaking in the BBC Omnibus 25 documentary *The Gardens of Roberto Burle Marx* 1992.

97 Kathryn Gustafson (b.1951) gained a degree in fashion design from the Fashion Institute of Technology, New York, in 1972, but after several years in the fashion industry she retrained in landscape architecture at Versailles, Paris. Much of her subsequent work has been in collaboration with engineers, architects and artists. For an evaluation of Gustafson's work see Jane Amidon, *Moving Horizons. The Landscape Architecture of Kathryn Gustafson and Partners* (Basel, Berlin, Boston: Birkhauser, 2005).

98 Sylvia Crowe and Mary Mitchell, *The Pattern of Landscape* (Chichester: Packard Publishing Ltd, 1988), p. 110.

99 John Brookes, *Improve Your Lot* (London: Heinemann, 1977), p. 70.

100 Sir Edwin Landseer Lutyens (1869–1944) was the leading Edwardian architect, whose design rationale was that 'anything built by man should harmonize with nature and be built of local materials'. He collaborated with the plantswoman Gertrude Jekyll to create a house and garden style that became known as the Surrey style, creating approximately 100 gardens between 1898 and 1928. See Jane Brown, *Gardens of a Golden Afternoon. The Story of a Partnership: Edwin Lutyens and Gertrude Jekyll* (London: Penguin Books, 1994) and Christopher Hussey, *The Life of Sir Edwin Lutyens* (London: Country Life, 1953).

101 Betty Massingham, *Gertrude Jekyll* (Princes Risborough: Shire Publications, 1975). This was based on her earlier book *Miss Jekyll. Portrait of a Great Gardener* (London: Country Life Ltd, 1966). Other occasional lecturers at the Inchbald included Anthony du Gard Pasley, Miller Gaunt (formerly superintendent of Regents Park), Nancy-Mary Goodall (horticultural writer), Susan Jellicoe, Frank Knight (formerly Director of RHS Wisley), Allen Paterson (Director of the Chelsea Physic Garden) and Frances Perry (gardening editor of the *Observer*).

102 John Brookes in conversation with the author, 25 August 2004.

103 Graham Stuart Thomas, *The Old Shrub Roses* (London: Phoenix House, 1963).

104 John Brookes in conversation with the author, 14 May 2002.

105 John Brookes, *The Small Garden* (Greenford, Middlesex: Aura Books, 1979), p. 182.

106 *Ibid.*, *The Small Garden*, p. 184.

107 See Brenda Colvin and Jaqueline Tyrwhitt, *op. cit.*

108 Preben Jakobsen, 'Shrubs and Groundcover' in Brian Clouston (ed.), *Landscape Design with Plants* (London: Heinemann, 1977), p. 41. Jakobsen (b.1934) worked for nurseries in Denmark, France and Great Britain before completing a Diploma in Horticulture at the Royal Botanic Gardens, Kew, and studying landscape architecture at the Royal Academy of Fine Arts in Copenhagen under Professor C. Th. Sørensen.

109 Although Brookes had always emphasized the importance of providing a framework of different types of plants, these five categories are first formally expressed in 1991. See 'Designing with Plants' Chapter 4, *John Brookes' Garden Design Book. The Complete Practical Guide to Planning, Styling and Planting any Garden* (London, New York, Stuttgart: Dorling Kindersley, 1991).

110 The contract between Brookes and the Chamber of Commerce Industries and Mines was initially for a 12-month period from 1 October 1978 as principal lecturer in interior design and decoration at an annual salary of £1,583.33. Contract of Employment dated 1 October 1978. Courtesy John Brookes.

111 John Brookes in conversation with the author, 17 September 2004.

112 In the late 1970s Hutt published a number of books on Islamic history and architecture including two volumes on Iran (with Leonard Harrow) and one on North Africa, and contributed to a number of others. See *North Africa* (London: Scorpion Publications, 1977), *Iran* Vol.1 (London: Scorpion Publications, 1977) and *Iran* Vol. 2 (London: Scorpion Publications, 1978).

113 He completed the book while in Iran but, due to the political climate, was unable to interest a British publisher until the mid-1980s. See John Brookes, *Gardens of Paradise. The History and Design of the Great Islamic Gardens* (London: Weidenfeld and Nicolson, 1987).

114 Brookes (1987), *op. cit.*, p. 19.

115 Joyce Robinson, *Denmans Garden 1946–1996. Celebrating the First Fifty Years of its Planning and Planting* (1985), pp. 35–6. These chapters were included in *Glorious Disarray: Creation of a Garden* (London: Michael Joseph, 1990).

116 John Brookes in conversation with the author, 17 September 2004.

117 *Garden Design with John Brookes* 1984 course brochure. Courtesy of Michael Brookes. The cost for the four-week course (non-residential, but with lunch provided and cooked by Brookes) was £500 plus VAT. One-week courses were £125 plus vat and weekend courses £30 per day plus VAT.

118 The name was changed in March 1982 to the Society of Landscape and Garden Designers, and in May 1990 to the Society of Garden Designers. See 'Reason to Celebrate', *Garden Design Journal* (February 2006), pp. 30–33 for a brief history.

119 The Institute of Landscape Architects became the Landscape Institute in 1978. The name change followed the decision to broaden the membership to include those whose professional work involved landscape management and landscape sciences. Brookes remained a member until 1994.

120 John Brookes, *A Place in the Country* (London: Thames and Hudson, 1984), inside front cover.

121 Carson, *op. cit.*, inside front cover.

122 Brookes (1984), *op. cit.*, p. 7.

123 *Ibid.*, p. 8.

124 With thanks to Richard Adams, Managing Director of Samarès Manor Ltd for providing information on the garden and its development.

125 John Brookes in conversation with the author, 17 September 2004.

126 John Brookes in conversation with the author, 25 August 2004.

127 Jens Jensen, *Siftings* (Baltimore and London: John Hopkins University Press, 1939). See also Robert E. Grese, *Jens Jensen. Maker of Natural Parks and Gardens* (Baltimore and London: John Hopkins University Press, 1992).

128 In addition to *A Place in the Country*, during the 1980s Brookes wrote a further seven books, the majority for Dorling Kindersley.

129 John Brookes, *John Brookes' Garden Design Book. The complete practical guide to planning, styling and planting any garden* (London: Dorling Kindersley, 1991). Brookes was principal lecturer at the Kew Garden Design School, Royal Botanic Gardens, 1990–96.

130 Brookes (1991), *op. cit.*, p. 40.

131 *Ibid.* p. 100. The selection and use of plants are considered in Chapter 4. 'Designing with plants', pp. 99–141.

132 *Ibid.* p. 114. Brookes considered the emphasis on plantsmanship over design principles a failing of the professional gardening fraternity. Published in association with the Royal Botanic Gardens, Kew, however, Brookes saw the book as going 'some way towards healing the breach between the horticulturist and the garden designer' (p. 7).

133 John Brookes, *Planting the Country Way. A Hands-on Approach* (London: BBC Books, 1994). The preface is by Miriam Rothschild.

134 William Robinson, *The Wild Garden* (London: John Murray, 1870). Robinson caught the public's imagination with the idea of the wild garden – 'the placing of perfectly hardy exotic plants under conditions where they will thrive without further care' (1881 preface). Its message on the enhancement of landscapes by the use of carefree hardy plants was revolutionary at a time when the High Victorian garden still dominated the horticultural world. Robinson's subtitle to the fourth edition (1894) was *The naturalisation and natural grouping of hardy exotic Plants with a chapter on the garden of British wild flowers*.

135 Miriam Rothschild's (b. 1908) garden at Ashton, Northamptonshire, is a good example of wild flower and grassland planting.

136 Brookes (1994), *op. cit.*, p. 175.

137 Dorling Kindersley, with publishing houses in London, New York and Stuttgart, was key to the promotion of Brookes's work outside England, publishing his most popular books in United States co-editions and foreign language editions. *John Brookes' Garden Design Book* was published in a briefer American edition as *John Brookes Garden Design Workbook. A practical step-by-step* (1994).

138 The conference was organized by *Landscape Australia*, the Journal of the Australian Landscape Architects Society on March 10–12 1994. Other speakers included Marc Treib, James Hitchmough, Topher Delaney and Pamela Burton. See also John Brookes, 'Gardens for tomorrow', *Vitis* (Summer 1994), p.13.

139 John Brookes, 'In search of an Australian way', *Landscape Australia* 88/4 (November 1995), pp. 292–93.

140 John Brookes, *Garden Masterclass* (London: Dorling Kindersley, 2002), p. 6.

141 See Anthony Archer-Wills, *The Water Gardener. A complete guide to designing, constructing and planting water features* (London: Frances Lincoln, 1993) with foreword by John Brookes.

142 Society Page, *Garden Design Journal* (Summer 1998), p. 4.

143 Duncan Heather is principal of the Oxford College of Garden Design and runs an international design practice from Henley-on-Thames, Oxfordshire.

144 Andrew Duff is director of part-time courses in garden design at the Inchbald School. He lectures and designs worldwide and is a regular contributor to the gardening press.

145 Peter Gillespie in discussion with author, 12 January 2007.

146 John Brookes, 'The Art of Distinction', *Garden Design Journal* 20 (December 2002/January 2003), p. 28. See also Opinion, (2003). As a veteran passenger, however, Brookes admits that plane travel does have advantages, as, viewed from the air, the land patterns detailed on a topographical survey (level, field boundaries, river courses, the shoreline) come 'alive'.

147 *Ibid.*, p. 30.

The Gardens: Case studies

Penguin Books Courtyard

1 For a history of Penguin Books see Phil Baines, *Penguin by Design: A Cover Story 1935–2005* (London: Penguin Books Ltd, 2005) and Jeremy Lewis, *The Life and Times of Allen Lane* (London: Penguin Books Ltd, 2006).

2 With thanks to John Spence and Charles Rathburn for providing information on this.

3 John Brookes, *Room Outside. A New Approach to Garden Design* (London: Thames & Hudson, 1969), p. 41.

4 See Susanne Deicher, *Piet Mondrian 1872–1944. Structures in Space* (Koln: Benedikt Taschen, 1995) for an appraisal of Mondrian's work.

5 John Brookes in conversation with the author, 5 November 2006.

6 'Courtyard design for Penguin Books Ltd', *Journal of the Institute of Landscape Architects* (February 1966), p. 12.

7 *Ibid.*

8 *Ibid.*

9 John Brookes, *Report on Courtyard Gardens* (1988). A Report prepared for Penguin Books Ltd.With thanks to Nigel Eastment at Penguin Books (1999) for allowing access to both the garden and Brookes's report.

10 *Ibid.*

Bryanston Square

1 Information on Bryanston Square is taken from *The London Inventory of History Green Spaces*, which includes details on the history of over 2000 parks, gardens and other green spaces in Greater London. For further information see

www.londongardenstrust.org. See also Bridget Cherry and Nikolaus Pevsner, *The Buildings of England. London 3: North West* (London: Penguin Books Ltd, 2001), p. 634. first published 1991.
2 A number of the houses in Bryanston Square are listed grade II by English Heritage as architecturally important in a national context. These are: on the east side, nos. 1a and 1 to 21; on the north side nos. 25, 25a and 26; on the west side nos. 27, 27a, 28 to 32 and 44 to 48; and on the south side nos. 49 and 50.
3 The St James's Square Act 1726 was the catalyst for many garden squares to apply for, and be granted, their own Acts and thus take control of the design, maintenance and use of their communal space. For a history of London garden squares see Todd Longstaffe-Gowan, *The London Town Garden* (New Haven and London: Yale University Press, 2001), Chapter 8.
4 Charles Knight (ed.), *London*, Vol. 6 (London: Charles Knight & Co., 1844).
5 John Brookes, *Bryanston Square W1*. A report on the completed works dated 5 June 1967. (Private collection.)
6 *Ibid.*

Fitzroy Square
1 Fitzroy Square is the only London square by Robert Adam, whose drawings for the façades of the east side of the square can be seen at the Sir John Soane's Museum, 13 Lincoln's Inn Fields, London WC2. Numbers 1, 1A, 2–8 and 33–40 Fitzroy Square are English Heritage listed buildings.
2 Minutes of meetings. Fitzroy Square 1815. Entry for 24 April 1815. With thanks to Neil Phoenix, Chair, Fitzroy Frontagers, for allowing access to the Minute Book. See also Todd Longstaffe-Gowan, *op. cit.*, pp. 203–5.
3 *Ibid.*
4 *Ibid.* Thanks to Robert Bargery, Secretary of the Georgian Group, for scanning the plan contained in the Minutes.
5 Charles Knight (ed.), *London*, Vol. 6 (1844).

Denmans
1 For a detailed history of Robinson's creation of the garden see Joyce Robinson, *Denmans Garden 1946–1996. Celebrating the First Fifty Years of its Planning and Planting* (1996), pp. 35–6. First edition published in 1985 as *Denmans Gardens. The Planning and Planting 1946–1985 and Looking Forward*. Information from early versions is also included in *Glorious Disarray: Creation of a Garden* (London: Michael Joseph, 1990).
2 Robinson (1996), *op. cit.*, p. 4.
3 Farrs of Chichester bought Westergate House for use as a furniture depository, selling in 1960 to Oldbys of Bognor Regis, who used it as a wholesale electrical warehouse. Since 1992 the building with an additional wing has been a residential care home, run by Barchester Healthcare. With thanks to Ann Swarbrick for providing this information.
4 Robinson (1996), *op. cit.*, p. 4.
5 *Ibid.*, *op. cit.*, p. 10.
6 *Ibid.*, *op. cit.*, p. 18.
7 *Ibid.*, *op. cit.*, p. 33. Mrs Robinson was familiar with the works of her namesake, William Robinson, whose publications encouraged this 'natural' style of planting. See William Robinson, *The Wild Garden* (London: John Murray, 1870) and *The English Flower Garden* (London: John Murray, 1883).
8 *Ibid.*, *op. cit.*, p. 34.
9 *Ibid.*, *op. cit.*, p. 37–38.
10 From 1980 Brookes had a 50-year lease on Clock House and a licence to use the garden for his design students. In 1980 he contributed 25 per cent towards the expenses of the garden, rising by 25 per cent each year until he had sole responsibility for the costs by the end of 1984, when Mrs Robinson retired. On her death in 1996 the Brookes and Neve business partnership bought the property. With thanks to Michael Neve for providing this information and discussing the development of Denmans Ltd and John Brookes Ltd, 27 November 2006.
11 Since 1970 plants were propagated for use in the garden and for sale to garden visitors.
12 Robinson (1985), *op. cit.* p. 12.
13 John Brookes, *Planting the Country Way. A Hands-on Approach* (London: BBC Books, 1994), pp. 143–44.
14 John Brookes in conversation with the author, 13 November 2006.
15 *Denmans Garden* promotional leaflet 2006.
16 The Garden Café was Les Routiers Café of the Year 2005 for London and the South East.
17 John Brookes in conversation with the author, 13 November 2006.

Samarès Manor
1 With thanks to Richard Adams for spending time discussing the development of the gardens at Samarès Manor and for providing plans and slides, 18 July 2006.
2 See Vincent Obbard, *Samarès Manor. A Personal Guide* (1997) for further details.
3 The Seigneural Rights Abolition (Jersey) Law 1966 abolished most of these ancient rights and the title now has historic value only.
4 Obbard, *op. cit.*, p. 10. *The French Gardiner: instructing how to cultivate all sorts of fruit-trees, and herbs for the garden* was originally written in French by Nicholas de Bonnefons, but translated into English by John Evelyn. The 1669 edition also contained an annex entitled *The English Vineyard* written by Evelyn based on material supplied by the gardener John Rose. With thanks to Sally Fleming (Samarès Manor Ltd) for providing details of the Evelyn letter (Diary iii 189, 227/8), mentioned in C. Langton, 'The Seigneurs of Samarès', *Annual Bulletin of the Société Jersiaise* (1931) Vol. 1, p. 402.
5 The canal is shown on the *Map of Jersey* 1694 and on an engraving of a map presented to James II in 1685, now in the morning room at Samarès Manor.
6 Edward White (1873–1952) was the son-in-law of Henry Ernest Milner who, with his father Edward, ran a celebrated 19th-century landscape architecture practice. White eventually took over the practice, which continued into the 20th-century as Milner White and Partners.
7 John Brookes in conversation with the author, 5 November 2006.
8 Vincent Obbard was a collector of historic agricultural equipment and this was to be included in the visitor displays.
9 London's International Exhibition of 1862 featured a Japanese Court and the Exposition Universelle in Paris in 1867, the Vienna Exposition of 1873 and the Centennial Exposition in Philadelphia in 1876 all included displays of Japanese objects and prints showing Japanese gardens.
10 One of the most important books was Josiah Conder, *Landscape Gardening in Japan* (Yokohama: Kelly and Walsh, 1893).
11 *Country Life* 139 (1971), pp. 732–34
12 Lawrence Weever, *Country Life* (27 February, 1915), p. 277.
13 See Amanda Herries, *Japanese Gardens in Britain* (Princes Risborough: Shire Publications Ltd, 2001) for an overview of the subject.

La Napoule
1 With thanks to Barbara Said for spending time in discussion, 1 July 2006.
2 La Napoule Art Foundation was set up as a not-for-profit organization in 1951 by Marie, Henry Clews's wife. Its mission statement is 'to promote the arts, the creative process, and the work of Henry Clews as a means of fostering global understanding and world peace'.
3 Christopher S. Clews, 'From the President', *La Napoule Foundation Annual Report 2005–2006*, p. 2.
4 See Marie Clews, *Once Upon a Time at La Napoule: The Memoirs of Marie Clews* (Beverley, Massachusetts: Memoirs Unlimited, 1998).
5 'Castle of Weird Images Becomes a Museum', *Life* (15 October 1951), pp. 119–122.
6 From a poem by Henry Clews engraved on his tomb.

The English Walled Garden
1 See www.chicagobotanic.org for information on the gardens and other facilities.
2 With thanks to Kris Jarantowski, Deputy Director, Chicago Botanic Garden, for spending time discussing this project, 15 August 2003.
3 John Brookes, 'An English Walled Garden in Chicago', *Vitis* (Winter 1991), p. 9.
4 *Ibid.*
5 *Ibid.*
6 *Ibid.*, p. 11.
7 *Ibid.*

Englewood Place
1 See www.albany.org for further information on the city.
2 Olmsted, Vaux & Co., New York City, *Report on the Proposed City Park* 1868. The designs were developed by the engineering firm of Bogart, Culyer & Co., who had previously worked with Olmsted & Vaux on Central Park in New York City. For a brief history of Washington Park see Diana S. Waite (ed.), *Albany Architecture. A Guide to the City* (Albany: Mount Ida Press, 1993).
3 With thanks to the owners of Englewood Place for the opportunity to visit and discuss the garden with them, 10 August 2003.
4 John Brookes, *Garden Masterclass* (London: Dorling Kindersley, 2002), p. 89.
5 *Ibid.*

Barakura English Garden
1 For further information see E. Yamada, 'Barakura English Garden', *Curtis's Botanical Magazine* 16/2 (May 1999), pp.115–19 and Jane Pettigrew, 'Taking Tea in Japan's English Garden', *Tea and Coffee Trade Journal* (20 October 2000).
2 John Brookes in conversation with the author, 5 November 2006.
3 John Brookes, 'The Road to Barakura', *Garden Design Journal* (Autumn 1995), pp. 11–13.
4 Pettigrew, *op. cit.*

Ecclesden Manor
1 T. Hudson, A. Baggs, C. Currie, C. Elrington, S. Keeling and A. Rowland (eds.), *A History of the County of Sussex: Volume 6 Part 1 – Bramber Rape (Southern Part)* (London: Institute of Historical Research, 1980).
2 The land was first held by the Abbey of Feschamp and then by the Abbey of Syon.
3 D.G.C. Elwes, *A History of the Castles, Mansions and Manors of Western Sussex* (London: 1876) suggests that the house was erected 'about the middle of the 17th century', but Skeet, *History of Angmering*, suggests 1634. See also Leslie Baker, *Old Angmering* (1980) and R.W. Standing, *Ecclesden Manor*, www.eastpreston.inthepast.org.uk.
4 Ian Nairn and Nikolaus Pevsner, *The Buildings of England. Sussex* (New Haven and London: Yale University Press, 2003), p. 83. First published by Penguin Books, 1965.
5 With thanks to Mr and Mrs Holland for the opportunity to visit and discuss the garden with them, 2 August 2004.
6 For an overview of historic houses and gardens see John Farrant, *Sussex Depicted, Views and Descriptions 1600–1800* (Lewes: Sussex Record Society, 2001).
7 The Sussex Gardens Trust maintains a database of parks and gardens of historic interest in Sussex. See www.sussexgardenstrust.org.uk.
8 See John Brookes, *A Place in the Country* (London: Thames and Hudson, 1984), Chapter 13 'Some Thoughts on Garden Restoration', pp. 196–204.
9 John Brookes, *John Brookes Garden Design Course* (London: Mitchell Beazley Publishers Limited, 2007), p. 162.
10 John Brookes in conversation with the author, 5 November 2006.
11 The windmill was originally part of the Ecclesden Manor estate, but is now in separate ownership.

College Garden
1 The quote is purported to be from a charter of King Offa of Mercia (785). For further information see Ben Weinreb and Christopher Hibbert (eds.), *The London Encyclopaedia* (London: Macmillan, 1993),

pp. 971–75.
2 John Brookes in conversation with the author, 13 November 2006.
3 John Harvey, 'The Infirmarer's Garden', *Garden History* 20/2 (Autumn 1992), p. 97.
4 *Ibid.*, p. 98. See also Barbara Harvey, 'Daily Life in Westminster Abbey' in *Living and Dying in England 1100–1540: The Monastic Experience* (Oxford: Clarendon Press, 1993).
5 John Brookes in conversation with the author, 1 January 2007.

Springhill Grove
1 John Brookes, 'In search of an Australian way', *Landscape Australia* 88/4 (November 1995), pp. 292.
2 *The New Garden. How to design, build and plant your garden with nature in mind* (London: Dorling Kindersley, 1998), p. 149.

The Old Rectory
1 With thanks to the owners of The Old Rectory for the opportunity to visit and discuss the garden with them, 2 June 2003.
2 Archaeological excavation has uncovered Roman urns and coins and it is known that a villa was built at Lickford to the north. See Samuel Winbolt, *A Roman villa at Lickfold, Wiggonholt*, (Lewes: Sussex Archaeological Collections).
3 After the Norman Conquest, the church was administered by the Abbey at Fécamp in Normandy. The font is late Norman and most of the windows are in the Perpendicular style (1360–1485).
4 Samuel Lewis, 'Wiggenhall–Wigton', *A Topographical Dictionary of England* (1848), pp. 571–75. Robert Curzon, 14th Baron Zouche (1810–73) was heir to Parham Park and one of the best-known Victorian travellers and writers. See Ian Fraser, *The Heir of Parham, Robert Curzon 14th Baron Zouche, 1810–73* (Harleston: Paradigm, 1986).
5 Ian Nairn and Nikolaus Pevsner, *The Buildings of England. Sussex* (New Haven and London: Yale University Press, 1965), p. 378.
6 John Brookes in conversation with the author, 13 November 2006.
7 John Brookes, *Garden Masterclass* (London: Dorling Kindersley, 2002), p. 315.
8 *Ibid.*, p. 82.
9 *Ibid.*, p. 315.
10 John Brookes in conversation with the author, 13 November 2006.

The Saltings
1 See also Ian Nairn and Nikolaus Pevsner, *The Buildings of England. Sussex* (New Haven and London: Yale University Press, 1965), pp. 110–13.
2 See Ann Williams (ed.), *The Sussex Domesday* (London: Alecto Historical Editions, 1990); and Michael Swanton, *The Anglo-Saxon Chronicles* (London: Phoenix, 2000).
3 Nairn and Pevsner, *op. cit.*, p. 110.
4 With thanks to the owners of The Saltings for the opportunity to visit the garden, 9 August 2004.
5 John Brookes, *Garden Masterclass* (London: Dorling Kindersley, 2002), p. 164.
6 *Ibid.*, p. 168.

7 John Brookes in discussion with the author, 4 January 2007.

Casa De Campo En Oleiros
1 John Brookes in conversation with the author, 13 November 2006.
2 John Brookes, *Garden Masterclass* (London: Dorling Kindersley, 2002), p. 250.
3 *Ibid.*, p. 141.

A New England Estate
1 The concept of the English Landscape Garden developed from the early 18th century as a reaction against the rigid formal geometry of the French garden inspired by the designer, Andre le Nôtre. It was popularized by the landscape gardener Lancelot 'Capability' Brown (1716–83), who was renowned for removing boundary walls and hedges, creating vast expanses of water and rolling green parkland and incorporating the 'borrowed landscape' of the surrounding countryside into his large-scale garden designs.
2 With thanks to the owner for allowing access to the estate, to Gwendolyn van Paasschen for arranging the visit and the estate manager for information on site, 11 August 2003.
3 John Brookes in conversation with the author, 13 November 2006.
4 Adam Levine, 'View Master', *Garden Design* (November/December 2002), pp. 28–34.
5 Humphry Repton (1752–1818) began his career as an 'improver' of grounds to the landed gentry in the style of Lancelot 'Capability Brown', where the grass came right up to the house. He later developed his own individual style in which there was a separation between the garden nearest the house and nature beyond. He began to use terraces, balustrades and urns around the house, and ornamental shrubberies, flower beds and specialist flower gardens became an integral part of his work.
6 Humphry Repton, *Red Book for Woburn* (1805), Woburn Abbey. For an evaluation of Repton's work see Stephen Daniels, *Humphry Repton. Landscape Gardening and the Geography of Georgian England* (New Haven and London: Yale University Press, 1999).
7 *John Brookes Garden Design Course* (London: Mitchell Beazley Publishers Limited, 2007), p. 127.
8 In *Mansfield Park* Jane Austen used a conversation between Mr Rushworth and Miss Bertram as the vehicle to express her views on 'improvement' and, in particular, Repton's work at her cousin Thomas Leigh's property, Stoneleigh Abbey, for which he completed a Red Book in 1809. See Jane Austen, *Mansfield Park* (London: Penguin Books, 1996), Chapter VI, pp. 45–53. First edition 1814.

Zespol Palace Park
1 Information from Patrick Taylor (ed.), *The Oxford Companion to the Garden* (Oxford: Oxford University Press, 2006), p. 389.
2 In 2002, the Centre for the Preservation of Historic Landscape was absorbed by the National Centre for the Study and Documentation of Monuments, which made

an inventory of historic gardens in Poland and was charged with their conservation.
3 *John Brookes' Garden Design Book. The complete practical guide to planning, styling and planting any garden* (London: Dorling Kindersley, 1991).
4 Information from a report on the history of the site by Longin Majdecki. With thanks to the owners for allowing sight of the report and to Aleksandra Kalisz for translation.
5 *John Brookes Garden Design Course* (London: Mitchell Beazley Publishers Limited, 2007), p. 138.
6 *Ibid.*, p. 144.
7 The author thanks the owners of Zespol Palace Park, Mr and Mrs Roman Karkosik, for the time spent in discussing their garden, 19 August 2006.

San Isidro
1 Information and quotations from www.barzicasares.com.ar: 'una de las escuelas de diseño más prestigiosa de Europe', 'una fluida y fructifera relación'.
2 The Epicentro-John Brookes School of Garden Design, Santiago.
3 See www.pampa-infinita.ar for further details. Brookes continues to be active in the teaching at the school and has also involved other well-known garden designers, such as Andrew Duff (director of garden design courses at the Inchbald School, London) and Jill Billington (also author of a number of garden books).
4 Brookes provided the design for the garden, which was constructed and planted by the owners.
5 John Brookes in conversation with the author, 13 November 2006.
6 Roberto Burle Marx (1909–94) was a Brazilian artist and plantsman, who worked on over 2,000 projects ranging from private gardens to public parks. His modernist-inspired designs used unusual sculptural shapes and colour and demonstrated his skill in juxtapositioning the contrasting forms and textures of hard landscaping and native planting.
7 John Brookes in conversation with the author, 7 January 2007. Luis Barragon (1902–88) was a modernist-inspired architect, whose work used stark geometric forms often combined with colourful Mexican vernacular features. In his landscape design he frequently used crisp, horizontal walls and water features.

Appendices

LIST OF PUBLICATIONS BY JOHN BROOKES

Room Outside. A New Approach to Garden Design (London: Thames & Hudson, 1969)

Living in the Garden (London: The Queen Anne Press in association with The Gardening Centre Ltd., Syon Park, 1970)

Garden Design and Layout (London: The Queen Anne Press in association with The Gardening Centre Ltd., Syon Park, 1970)

Gardens for Small Spaces (London: Pan Books Ltd., 1970)

'Outdoors', Beverley Hilton and Maria Kroll (eds.) *Terence Conran. The House Book* (London: Mitchell Beazley Publishers Limited, 1974), pp. 363–89

'Design' in Anthony Huxley (ed.), *The Financial Times Book of Garden Design* (Newton Abbot, London, Vancouver: David & Charles, 1975)

Improve Your Lot (London: Heinemann, 1977)

The Small Garden (London: Marshall Cavendish, 1977)

The Garden Book. The complete guide to creating your ideal garden (London: Dorling Kindersley, 1984)

A Place in the Country (London: Thames and Hudson, 1984)

The Garden Book (London: Dorling Kindersley, 1984)

The Indoor Garden Book (London: Guild Publishing, 1986)

Gardens of Paradise (London: Weidenfeld and Nicolson, 1987)

The Country Garden (London: Dorling Kindersley, 1987)

The Gardener's Index of Plants and Flowers with Kenneth Beckett. (London: Dorling Kindersley, 1987).

The New Small Garden Book (London: Dorling Kindersley, 1987)

The Pocket Encyclopaedia of House Plants (London: Dorling Kindersley, 1989)

John Brookes' Garden Design Book. The complete practical guide to planning, styling and planting any garden (London: Dorling Kindersley, 1991)

Garden Planning (London: Dorling Kindersley, 1992). Contributing editor

Planting the Country Way. A Hands-on Approach (London: BBC Books, 1994)

John Brookes Garden Design Workbook. A practical step-by-step (New York: Dorling Kindersley, 1994)

Home and Garden Style. Creating a unified look inside and out with Eluned Price (London: Ward Lock, 1996)

Planning a Small Garden (London: Dorling Kindersley, 1996). Contributing editor

The New Garden. How to design, build and plant your garden with nature in mind (London: Dorling Kindersley, 1998). Published simultaneously in an American co-edition as John Brookes' Natural Landscapes. How to design, build and plant your garden with nature in mind (New York: Dorling Kindersley, 1998)

Garden Masterclass (London: Dorling Kindersley, 2002)

Small Garden (London: Dorling Kindersley, 2006). A revised version of The New Small Garden

John Brookes Garden Design Course (London: Mitchell Beazley Publishers Limited, 2007)

Room Outside. A New Approach to Garden Design (Woodbridge: Garden Art Press, 2007). A revised version of the 1969 publication

LIST OF AWARDS TO JOHN BROOKES

1975: Civic Trust Heritage Year Awards for (a) the conversion of Castle Mill, Dorking, Surrey, England, with Michael Manser (architect) and (b) the conversion of Bisham Grange, West Sussex, England, with Stanley P. Merer (architect)

1987: BPI Garden Writers Award in recognition of excellence in horticultural journalism and contributions to making our world more beautiful through the use of flowers and plants

1988: Prix Saint-Fiacre de l'Association des Journalistes de l'Horticulture for Le Grand Livre des Jardins, Plantes et Jardin d'Interieur

1992: Garden Writers Association of America Quill and Travel Awards Program in recognition of excellence in garden writing and communications

1992: MacMillan Publishing Award of Excellence for John Brookes' Garden Design Book

1998: Horticultural Society of Chicago's Hutchinson Prize for horticulture for the English Walled Garden at the Chicago Botanic Garden, USA

2002: Garden Writers Guild 'Enthusiasts' Book of the Year for Garden Masterclass

2003: Sussex Heritage Trust Landscape Award for Ecclesden Manor, Angmering, West Sussex, England

2004: American Association of Professional Landscape Designers Award of Distinction for a unique and exceptional contribution to the profession of landscape design

2004: MBE for services to horticulture in the UK and overseas

2006: Honorary doctorate from the University of Essex for services to the horticultural industry and specifically garden design.

LIST OF SHOW GARDENS BY JOHN BROOKES

1962: Chelsea Flower Show Courtyard Garden (Institute of Landscape Architect)

1971: Chelsea Flower Show Town Garden (Financial Times)

1972: Chelsea Flower Show Suburban Garden (Financial Times)

1973: Chelsea Flower Show Country Garden (Financial Times)

1975: Chelsea Flower Show Potager Garden (Inchbald School of Garden Design)

1976: Chelsea Flower Show Jekyll Garden (Inchbald School of Garden Design)

1977: Chelsea Flower Show Exotic Garden (Inchbald School of Garden Design)

1995: San Francisco Landscape Garden Show (Garden Design)

1997: Tokyo International Forum, Japan (Barakura English Garden)

1998: Gardeners' World Live, Birmingham (permanent outdoor exhibition)

2000: Flora Osaka Flower Show, Japan (British Council)

2000: Exhibition stand for the Chelsea Flower Show (Dorling Kindersley)

Appendices

PICTURE CREDITS

Cover and Prelims

John Brookes: p. 2, pp. 4–5

Peter Gillespie: p. 7

Barbara Simms: Title page

Gracie Ullman: Cover

John Brookes: Garden and Landscape Designer

John Brookes: p. 9: Figures 1–3; pp. 10–11: Figures 4–7; p. 15: Figures 14–15; pp. 17–37: Figures 18–57; pp. 38–39: Figures 60–63; p. 40: Figure 65; p. 43: Figures 69–70; p. 45: Figure 73

Dell & Wainwright/RIBA Library Photographs Collection: p. 13: Figure 10 *Gardens in the Modern Landscape*, 1950 edn., p.98 (Willi Soukoup sculpture);

Jill Hedges: p. 42: Figure 67 William Robinson, *The Wild Garden*

Andrew Lawson/Ashton Wold, Peterborough: p. 42: Figure 68 Ashton Wold Garden, Wisteria

Milwaukee Art Museum, Gift of Mrs Harry Lynde Bradley, M1977.140: p. 16: Figure 17 *Green, Red, Blue*, Mark Rothko, 1955

Jerome O'Hea: p. 38: Figure 58

RIBA Library Photographs Collection: p. 12: Figure 8 *Garden in Hampstead*, London, by Brenda Colvin (fig. 90, page 68); p. 12: Figure 9 *Garden in Lansbury*, London, by G.A. Jellicoe (fig. 95, page 69); p.13: Figure 11 *Modern Gardens* (fig. 135, p.83) (Halland, the terrace); p. 14: Figure 12 *Modern Gardens* p.46 fig 44 (Sonoma redwood slatted deck); p. 14: Figure 13 Roof garden of Resurgeros Insurance Building in Rio de Janeiro

Barbara Simms: p. 38: Figure 59; pp. 40–41: Figures 64, 66; p. 44: Figures 71–72; p. 47: Figure 76

Solomon R., Guggenheim Museum, New York, 55.1419: p. 16: Figure 16 *Composition*, Willem de Kooning, 1955

Gracie Ullman: p. 46: Figure 74

Case Studies

John Brookes: pp. 50–57: Figures 1.1, 1.2, 1.4–1.10; pp. 58–64: Figures 2.1, 2.3–2.8; pp. 66–71: Figures 3.1, 3.4–3.6, 3.8; pp. 73–81: Figures 4.2, 4.5–4.11, 4.13–4.17, 4.19; pp. 85–91: Figures 5.5, 5.9, 5.11; pp. 92–97: Figures 6.1–6.5, 6.7, 6.8; pp. 100–106: Figures 7.2–7.6, 7.9, 7.11–7.13; pp. 108–113: Figures 8.2, 8.4–8.9; pp. 114–121: Figures 9.2–9.9; pp. 124–127: Figures 10.3, 10.5, 10.7; pp. 129–135: Figures 11.3–11.10; pp. 136–141: Figures 12.1, 12.3, 12.9; pp. 143–147: Figures 13.2–13.4, 13.6–13.8; pp. 150–157: Figures 14.1, 14.3, 14.4, 14.6, 14.9; pp. 158–165: Figures 15.1–15.6; pp. 171–172: Figures 16.5, 16.6; pp. 174–183: Figures 17.1, 17.3–17.5, 17.9, 17.12; pp. 184–190: Figures 18.1–18.6

Dallas Museum of Art, Foundation for the Arts Collection, gift of Mrs. James H. Clark: p. 52: Figure 1.3 *Composition with large Blue Plane, Red, Black, Yellow and Gray*, Piet Mondrian, 1921

Fitzroy Frontagers: p. 68: Figure 3.3

Garden World Images/M. Bolton: p. 139: Figure 12.5 *Buddleija davidii* 'Empire Blue';

Garden World Images/Botanic Images Inc.: p. 141: Figure 12.8 *Phormium tenax* (New Zealand flax)

Guildhall Library, City of London: p. 67: Figure 3.2 View of Fitzroy Square's east side, James Peller Malcolm, 1807

Photolibrary Group Ltd: p. 139: Figure 12.4 *Cortaderia argentia* (now known as *Cortaderia selloana*); p. 141: Figure 12.6 *Kniphofia* 'Fiery Fred'; p. 141: Figure 12.7 *Hemerocallis fulva* hybrids

Portman Estate: p. 60: Figure 2.2

Samarès Manor Ltd: p. 84: Figures 5.3–5.4

Barbara Simms: p. 71: Figure 3.7; pp. 72–73: Figure 4.1; p. 78: Figure 4.12; p. 81: Figure 4.18; pp. 82–83: Figures 5.1–5.2; pp. 85–87: Figures 5.6–5.8; p. 89: Figure 5.10; p. 91: Figure 5.12; pp. 98–99: Figure 7.1; p. 103: Figures 7.7–7.8; p. 105: Figure 7.10; p. 107: Figure 7.14; p. 110: Figures 8.3–8.4; p. 113: Figure 8.10; p. 115: Figure 9.1; pp. 122–127: Figures 10.1–10.2, 10.4, 10.6, 10.8, 10.9; p. 128: Figures 11.1, 11.2; pp. 142–143: Figure 13.1; p. 146: Figure 13.5; pp. 148–149: Figures 13.9–13.10; p. 151: Figure 14.2; pp. 154–157: Figures 14.5, 14.7, 14.8; pp. 168–170: Figures 16.2–16.4; p. 173: Figure 16.7; pp. 174–175: Figure 17.2; pp. 178–180: Figures 17.6–17.8; pp.182–183: Figures 17.10–17.11

Oliver Strewe/Photographer's Choice/Getty Images: p. 137: Figure 12.1 Hunter Valley

Ann Swarbrick: p. 74: Figures 4.3–4.4

Time & Life Pictures/Getty Images: p. 96: Figure 6.6 Mrs Henry Clews, 1951

Colin Wing: p. 65: Figure 2.9

AUTHOR'S ACKNOWLEDGEMENTS

This book would not have been possible without the enthusiasm, support and commitment of John Brookes, who has been not only a rich source of information, but also an entertaining collaborator on this evaluation of his place in the history of garden design. Over the five years of the project he has contributed generously with his time for interviews and discussions, in allowing free access to his drawings and picture archive, and in reading numerous drafts and proofs. To him is extended warm and special thanks. Mention must also be made of those of Brookes's family, friends, colleagues and clients, who have willingly contributed their reminiscences, personal archives and photographs, and permissions to visit and photograph their gardens. Unfortunately, not all the information collected could be included in the book, but it has, nonetheless, provided the necessary context to Brookes's work.

Thanks are particularly given for their time and encouragement to (in alphabetical order) Richard Adams, Mr and Mrs Aiden, Mr and Mrs Andrew, Dr Lesley Bailey, Robert Bargery, Richard Bowden, Michael Brookes, Mr G. Brown, Annabel Downs, Mrs Drescher, Andrew Duff, Anthony du Gard Pasley, Jacqueline Duncan, Nigel Eastment, Mr and Mrs Fleck, Sally Fleming, Peter Gillespie, Mr and Mrs Goldspink, Anne and Angus Hewitt, Beverley Hilton, Peter and Sue Holland, Dr Izzatt, Kris Jarantowski, Aleksandra Kalisz, Mr and Mrs Roman Karkosik, Peter and Diane King, David Lamb, Kate Lander, Violet Lort-Phillips, Dr and Mrs Lutte, Michael and José Manser, Claudia Murphy, Michael Neve, Mr and Mrs Jerome O'Hea, Mr and Mrs Thomas Older, David Papworth, Neil Phoenix, David Ransom, Charles Rathburn, Mr and Mrs Reeves, Mr and Mrs Robertson, Sally Rowlands, Glenys Rowe, Barbara Said, John Spence, Ian Stoutzker, Ann Swarbrick, Gwendolyn van Paasschen, Mark and Liz Warom, Michael and Caroline Wates, Mr and Mrs Watney, Mr and Mrs Wilde, Liz Williams and Mr and Mrs Norman Young.

Sincere apologies are given for any omissions in the list of contributors and also for any errors in the text, which are the sole responsibility of the author.

Index

*Page numbers in italics refer
to captions and illustrations*